YORK AND LANCASTER

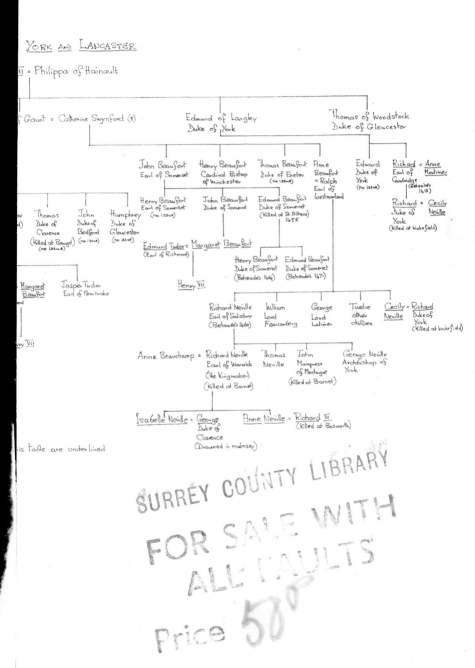

III = Philippa of Hainault

f Gaunt = Catherine Swynford (3)   Edmund of Langley   Thomas of Woodstock
                                      Duke of York   Duke of Gloucester

John Beaufort   Henry Beaufort   Thomas Beaufort   Anne   Edward   Richard = Anne
Earl of Somerset Cardinal Bishop   Duke of Exeter   Beaufort   Duke of   Earl of   Mortimer
                  of Winchester   (no issue)   = Ralph   York   Cambridge (Beheaded
                                                          Earl of   (no issue)   (Beheaded 1415)
Henry Beaufort   John Beaufort   Edmund Beaufort   Westmorland   1415)
Earl of Somerset Duke of Somerset   Duke of Somerset   Richard = Cecily
(no issue)   (Killed at St. Albans)   Duke of   Neville
                                        1455   York
ev   Thomas   John   Humphrey   (Killed at Wakefield)
d)   Duke of   Duke of   Duke of   Edmund Tudor = Margaret Beaufort
      Clarence   Bedford   Gloucester (Earl of Richmond)
      (Killed at (no issue) (no issue)   Henry Beaufort Edmund Beaufort
      Baugé)   Duke of Somerset Duke of Somerset
      (no issue)   Henry VII (Beheaded 1464) (Beheaded 1471)

  Margaret   Jasper Tudor
  Beaufort   Earl of Pembroke
nd   Richard Neville   William   George   Twelve   Cecily = Richard
                                    Earl of Salisbury Lord   Lord   other   Neville Duke of
ry VII   (Beheaded 1460)   Fauconberg Latimer   children   York
                                                                                             (Killed at Wakefield)

              Anne Beauchamp = Richard Neville   Thomas   John   George Neville
                               Earl of Warwick   Neville   Marquess   Archbishop of
                               (The Kingmaker)   of Montague York
                               (Killed at Barnet)   (Killed at Barnet)

              Isabelle Neville = George   Anne Neville = Richard III
                                 Duke of   (Killed at Bosworth)
                                 Clarence
                                 (Drowned in malmsey)

is table are underlined

The Ardent Queen

Margaret of Anjou and the Lancastrian Heritage

JOCK HASWELL

PETER DAVIES : LONDON

Peter Davies Ltd
15 Queen Street, Mayfair, London W1X 8BE
LONDON   MELBOURNE   TORONTO
JOHANNESBURG   AUCKLAND

Printed and bound in Great Britain by
Morrison & Gibb Ltd,
London and Edinburgh

Contents

Acknowledgements 11

Introduction 15

1 Childhood (1429–1443) 23

2 Negotiations (1443–1444) 34

3 From France to England (1444–1445) 42

4 Queen's College (1445–1448) 57

5 Suffolk, Cade and Somerset (1449–1452) 75

6 Birth of an Heir (1451–1455) 93

7 The Rout of Ludford (1455–1459) 110

8 Wakefield (1459–1460) 125

9 Towton (1460–1461) 140

10 Invasion (1461–1463) 153

11 Exile (1463–1470) 169

12 Tewkesbury (1470–1475) 188

Epilogue 211

Bibliography 217

Index 219

Illustrations

Plates (Between pages 144 and 145)
1. Margaret of Anjou
2a. Isabelle de Lorraine
   b. René d'Anjou
   c. Yolande d'Aragon
   d. Louis d'Anjou
3a. Henry VI
   b. Edward IV
   c. Charles VII of France
   d. Louis XI of France
4a. The marriage of Henry VI and Margaret of Anjou
   b. Philip the Good and his son, Charles the Bold
   c. Edward Prince of Wales

Maps   *Page*
   I.   France   25
   II. England and Wales   82
   III. The Campaign of Tewkesbury   200

Endpapers
Front: The Houses of York and Lancaster
Back: The House of Valois

For my wife Annette

Acknowledgements

Any attempt to write a definitive biography of Margaret of Anjou would be so full of surmise and speculation as to be little more than a personal opinion. Contemporary sources such as Philippe de Commines and Monstrelet mention her only cursorily, and her own letters contain no information on the great events in her life. I have therefore tried to write only the story of her; a task undertaken because I felt that in common with her enemy Richard of Gloucester (Richard III) and the unfortunate James II of England, she has been the victim of a great deal of misrepresentation. Richard certainly did not murder her son Edward in the way Shakespeare describes, any more than she ordered the beheading of Richard Duke of York after the battle of Wakefield – she happened to be in Scotland at the time.

Because there are several different accounts and dates of her birth, marriage and death, I spent some time in France, in the areas of Angers, Saumur, Pont à Mousson, Saint Mihiel and Nancy, where I was given a great deal of help by the curators of local museums and directors of public libraries and archives.

There is little doubt that Margaret was born at Pont à Mousson, although all traces of the Château Keure disappeared when a barracks was built on the site. She was certainly not married (by proxy) in the cathedral at Nancy, as stated by some authorities – it is an eighteenth-century building – and the Director of the Musée Lorain assured me that the ceremony must have been held in the chapel of the ducal palace. This chapel, shown on old prints, no longer exists. Many writers have given details of her death, the longest account being that of Bodin, the historian of Saumur, who recorded the inscription said to have been put up over the gateway of the Château de Dampierre where, so he says, she died. Unfortunately, according to present day historians in Saumur, Bodin was apt to add 'authentic details' from his imagination, and there never was a 'château' at Dampierre, even though the second volume of Mrs Hooker's biography of Margaret contains an engraving of it. There was, apparently, a little *maison forte* on the high ground above the Loire, but Margaret undoubtedly spent the last years of her life at Souzay and actually died in the little *manoir de Morains*, both of which belonged to François de la Vignolles, an old friend of the family.

One of my problems in expressing gratitude is that I do not know the names of all the people who helped me – the curator in Angers, for example, who locked the door of his museum so that we could talk undisturbed; the charming châtelaine of the Château de Brézé who spoke of Pierre de Brézé as if he had been staying there for the previous weekend; the gendarme in Nancy who insisted on acting as my guide, and all sorts of people who seemed to be really interested in *l'heroine de la Guerre des Deux Roses*.

In England I have been over much of the ground where the battles were fought. One can still see why pontoons were needed on the slow sliding Aire at Ferrybridge, though there are two great bridges across it now. Lord Dacre sleeps on the northern side of Saxton Church within sight of the ridge where the Lancastrians camped on the night before Towton. The battlefield, marked by an obelisk, is just as it was, although it is doubtful whether anyone could now drown in the Cock Becke, even in spate. The Lead Church, close to the mass graves, is reputed to be badly haunted. The bridge at Tadcaster has been rebuilt. Sandal Castle stands in ruins on its hill overlooking the open ground where Richard Duke of York died in battle, the great walls of Pontefract still dominate the town and the huge fortresses of Ludlow and Middleham are magnificent in decay.

The enormous mound of Pleshey Castle rises from its surrounding moat, a fascinating example of 'motte and bailey', though it seems a tragedy that what must have been the oldest brick bridge in Europe – across the moat – has been so carefully 'restored'. It is still easy to trace the military movements before the final battle of Tewkesbury, and the battle itself. A signboard marks Bloody Meadow, where cattle graze, and there is still a ferry at the Lower Lode. The house, Gupshill Manor, where Margaret is said to have spent the night before the battle, still stands (dated 1438 it is now an inn and a restaurant) and across the road is the site of the Lancastrian camp. Perhaps it was at

Gupshill that Somerset told Margaret of his tactical plan for the battle.

Margaret's only child lies in the centre of the choir of Tewkesbury Abbey, a brass plate marks his grave, and in a vault near the high altar, in glass cases, are the bones said to be of 'false, fleeting, perjured Clarence' and his wife Isabella, Warwick the Kingmaker's daughter.

Among many people who have been generous with their time and knowledge I must thank Miss Sarah Wimbush of the National Portrait Gallery, Mr Tompsett of the Folkestone Public Library – an unfailing source of information – Mr Potts and Miss Seaman of the Ministry of Defence Central Library, Mrs Grace of the Sir John Moore Library at Shorncliffe, Mr Freeman, Sacristan of Tewkesbury Abbey, Mr Ailben the curator at Pleshey, and Mr Davies of The Camera Shop in Hythe.

I am also extremely grateful to my neighbour Brigadier Laurie Cholmeley for making good all my deficiencies in the French language. In writing out translations and taking infinite trouble to find relevant material, his help was invaluable. Finally, without the administrative and other support of my wife I would not be able to write at all.

J. H.

Lyminge 1975

Introduction

> Know thou this – that men
> Are as the time is; to be tender minded
> Does not become a sword.
> *(King Lear, V, iii)*

The character and reputation of Margaret of Anjou – she has been called the 'she-wolf of Anjou' – have suffered much at the hands of contemporary chroniclers and early historians, for two reasons. First, she was a Frenchwoman, and ever since the days of Edward the Confessor, when arrogant Normans made themselves so unpopular in London and Dover, the English and the French have looked upon one another as enemies. Even Philippe de Commines, writing in the middle of the fifteenth century, refers to 'the natural animosity of the English against the French which has existed in all ages'.

Secondly, she was not, in the end, on the winning side, and one only has to recall the historical treatment of Richard III by the Tudors, and of James II by the Whigs, losers on the same scale, to realize that the general attitude to Margaret may not be justified. Even now, nearly five hundred years after her death, she is regarded by many as the queen whose hands are red with the blood of her political enemies, vindictive to the point of savagery, consumed and finally destroyed by the fierce flame of her own ambition; the woman who, for her own ends, kept the Wars of the Roses going, and thus can be held largely responsible for the destruction of the English nobility. This is an over-simplification although it contains one or two seedlings of truth. It also has a bias which does not take into account her background, her character and her aim.

Throughout the time when she was Queen of England, Margaret's purpose was to maintain upon the throne what she and the vast majority of the people of England considered to be the rightful dynasty, the House of Lancaster. She was resolved that her husband, the anointed king, would remain king until he died and then be succeeded by his heir, her son Edward Prince of Wales. Her alleged vindictiveness, much of it unproved, was in keeping with the times in which she lived, when men's actions were governed mainly by the law of the jungle, where the strong prey upon the weak, and the law set forth in the twenty-first chapter of the Book of Exodus – 'Thou shalt give life for life, eye for eye, tooth for tooth . . .' prevailed.

Life was cheap. The rate of infant mortality was, by modern standards, horrifying. Plague, a term which covered a wide variety of diseases, reduced the average expectation of life to thirty-five years, and everyone knew what the Psalmist meant when he wrote of 'the pestilence that walketh in darkness' and 'the sickness that destroyeth in the noonday'.

In any contest, particularly one for power and influence at court, the loser was likely to lose everything, his life, property and estates, and his wretched family became dependent on the charity of relations. The ordinary man could protect himself from the lawlessness, greed or violence of his neighbours only by associating himself with someone who was strong. Thus it became the custom for people to attach themselves, in one way or another, to a local potentate who might be anyone from the lord of the manor to a royal duke, and to let it be known where their allegiance lay. Since the king had no standing army with which to support his authority and there was no sort of police force for the protection of the individual, the nobility tended to collect round them a flock of retainers pledged to support them in return for a measure of security against other powerful nobles and even against the king's law.

This form of personal service has been called 'bastard feudalism', and perhaps the worst aspect of it was that it led to the breaking down of the normal processes of justice. Great men were able to intimidate juries or manipulate matters in favour of litigants they supported. In other ways bastard feudalism was no bad thing. It gave a certain amount of stability to society. The local lord dealt with local disputes himself, kept the peace and exercised a wide measure of control over his adherents. When it suited him, he upheld the king's Justices on Assize. As a form of local government it played a valuable part in national administration. Yet, from the point of view of the king's central government, there was one major snag. The system could operate successfully on a national basis only when the central government was strong and the king could control his lords.

The king did not expect all his lords to be loyal and obedient. There were always turbulent spirits among the great families who questioned the principle of authority based simply on an oath of fealty, but while the balance of loyalty outweighed that of disloyalty he could command enough force, in the form of feudal levies and the troops of private armies belonging to his nobles, to crush any opposition or at least discourage any rebel.

Personality and self-confidence were vital factors in the mystique of kingship. Henry IV and Henry V were warrior kings, men of powerful personality who never had the least doubt about their right to wear the crown or their ability to control the nobles. All Margaret's problems, and indeed all the problems of the unfortunate people of England during the time she wore a crown, arose from the inability of her husband, Henry VI of Lancaster, to control anyone. She herself had enough personality and resolution to make up for his shortcomings, but England was a man's world.

Although Margaret was the driving force behind the Lancastrian cause she could keep that cause alive only by persuading the supporters of the House of Lancaster that it was to their advantage to remain loyal. She could exercise power only in her husband's name or through the noblemen who were on her side. This must have been very frustrating. She was a natural leader because she was the granddaughter of Yolande of Aragon and the daughter of Isabelle of Lorraine, two formidable women who had been leaders all their lives.

The history of France is liberally sprinkled with the names of dominant women; to a far greater extent than that of England. But then France, far more than England, has always inclined towards a matriarchal society in which the voice of Madame, perhaps because it is often penetrating and interminable, has been the voice of authority. This may well be because in the age of feudal chivalry the nobility and gentry frequently went off to war, leaving all responsibility for administering their estates in the hands of their wives. These women were the nominated 'Lieutenant Generals' of their husbands' domains and their functions covered everything from administering justice to, as in the case of Yolande of Aragon at the battle of Baugé,* leading the local military contingent in active operations.

Margaret's grandmother was perhaps exceptional, but she had exceptional responsibilities. Her husband, Louis II of Anjou, inherited from his father the titles of King of Naples, Sicily and Jerusalem, Duke of Anjou, Calabria, Touraine and Pouille, Grand Peer of France, Prince of Capua, Count of Provence, Maine, Forcalquier and Piemonte, Lord of Montpellier and Governor of Languedoc and Guienne. In terms of material wealth these titles were of little value, and Louis, who married Yolande on 2 November 1399, spent most of the rest of his life in Italy, trying to establish his claim to Naples by force of arms. He was unsuccessful. From 1404 until he came home to die at the age of forty, in 1417, Yolande his 'Queen' managed all his affairs in France, but he saw her often enough for her to bear him five children.

René, the third child and second son, who was to be the father of Margaret of Anjou, was born in one of the circular gate-towers of the huge castle of Angers on 6 January 1408. At the age of nine he was committed to the care of his great-uncle Louis the Cardinal Duke of Bar. The Cardinal nominated René as his heir, and though he arranged for the boy to be instructed in all the martial arts, he had no intention of bringing him up to be a mindless soldier, like so many of his contemporaries. The brothers Hubert and Jehan Van Eyck were persuaded to set up a school of painting at Bar le Duc and René was their first pupil. Their teaching had a profound effect on him; all his life he took great delight in illustrating his *Livres des Heures*, drawing and painting portraits of his family and depicting scenes on his travels and great events such as the tournament at Saumur. He grew up to be one of the best educated men of his age, a soldier, a poet, a musician and an artist of considerable merit. His skill and interest in the arts led him to become a great patron of troubadours, the wandering historians of those days, who filled his head, and the

---

* Fought on 21 March 1421 near Saumur on the river Loire. An English force led by Thomas, Duke of Clarence, and brother of Henry V, was defeated by a mixed army of Armagnacs, Scots and Angevins led by John Stuart, Earl of Buchan, later Constable of France. The Angevins were commanded by Yolande who, mounted on a grey charger, wore armour of steel plate and silver mail.

heads of his children, with songs and tales of chivalry and 'courtly love', romance and the deeds of past heroes.

In 1419 René was created Marquis of Pont à Mousson by his great-uncle the Cardinal, and in the following year his mother Yolande achieved a great diplomatic success in uniting the houses of Anjou and Lorraine by arranging the marriage of René, aged twelve, to Isabelle, daughter and heir of Charles II of Lorraine, aged nine.

France at this time was ruled by that unhappy schizophrenic Charles VI and divided between the factions of Burgundy and Armagnac;* a situation exploited to the full by Henry V of England. Reviving Edward III's claim to the French throne, Henry allied himself to the Burgundians, invaded France, captured Harfleur after considerable difficulty and then set out across what he called 'this good land of France, which is all our own', towards Calais. By any standards the risk he took is hard to justify. Charles VI, lucid for the moment, assembled an immense feudal host from which the Burgundians stood aloof, and made preparations to destroy the invaders. Succumbing once more to insanity, he had to be left behind at Rouen, and on 21 October 1415 his army, led by the Constable of France, was slaughtered at Agincourt.

In 1419 Henry V entered Rouen and all Normandy came under the English flag. In July he crossed the Seine and took Pontoise. The French began to realize what was happening but the feud between the Burgundians and Armagnacs continued with sanguinary vigour. Henry V, extracting every ounce of advantage from the confusion of personal feuds, broken promises and despair, signed, in May 1420, the Treaty of Troyes. Since the French king was mad, and his wife, Isabeau of Bavaria, a notorious nymphomaniac, had very little political authority, the widowed Queen Yolande of Aragon played a considerable part in the negotiations for the treaty. But though she was perhaps the most

---

* In 1407 Louis Duke of Orleans was murdered in Paris by the agents of John the Fearless, Duke of Burgundy. Louis's heir, Charles, had married a daughter of the Count of Armagnac and therefore had the support of the House of Armagnac. The murder of Louis split France into rival factions; the red scarf and white cross of the Armagnacs against the green hood and red cross of Burgundy. The Armagnacs upheld the royal House of Valois, the Burgundians allied themselves with the English.

powerful woman in France she was no match for the astute
Henry. The treaty gave him the regency of France, recognition
as the heir to the French throne – to succeed when Charles VI
died – and the Princess Catherine of France in marriage.

Catherine was young and very beautiful. The bald, depressing
wooden effigy of her in the museum in the Undercroft of Westminster Abbey, made from a death mask, is no real indication of
what she must have looked like, and no doubt she had inherited
some of the physical appeal so strong in her mother. Henry and
Catherine were married in the same year that René of Anjou
married Isabelle of Lorraine, and at Windsor Castle on 6 December
1421 Catherine gave birth to the child who was to be Henry VI
of England and the husband of René and Isabelle's child Margaret.

On the first of May in the following year, 1422, Charles VI of
France and Henry V of England rode together into Paris to
symbolize the 'perpetual peace' heralded by the Treaty of Troyes.
Henry was only thirty-five. Charles was fifty-three. France lay
under the heel of the conqueror.

To all outward appearances Henry was a lean, fit young man,
hardened by campaigning and likely to live for years, but during
the prolonged siege of Meaux, all through the previous winter
among the marshes of the river Marne, he had contracted
dysentery. Only four months after his triumphant entry into Paris,
in the early hours of the morning of 31 August, he died in the
royal chamber of the great keep in the castle of Vincennes. He
can have had no conception of the legacy he had bequeathed to
his only son, a baby now nine months old, nor can he have realized
how impossibly difficult he had made everything for the future
wife of that infant.

Barely two months later, on 21 October, Charles VI came to
the end of his tormented life. At Saint-Denis, fulfilling the terms
of the Treaty of Troyes, the Herald of France proclaimed
Catherine's baby as Henry VI, by the grace of God, King of
France and of England; a title not abandoned by the kings of
England until the Peace of Paris in 1763.

Henry V's brother John Duke of Bedford, became Regent of
France and ruled most of the northern part of the country from
Paris. The Dauphin the disinherited Charles VII, fled with his
young wife Marie to Bourges, where they lived in poverty, and
it was here, in the Archbishop's palace, that their first child, Louis

(later Louis XI), was born on 3 July 1423. Queen Marie was Yolande of Aragon's second child and therefore the elder sister of René d'Anjou.

The Dauphin's mother, Isabeau of Bavaria, had always disliked him, and purely out of spite had given him to understand that she could not remember who his father was. He was haunted by the thought of illegitimacy, and largely for this reason made no attempt to rally the Armagnacs, of whom he was the nominal leader, either to resist Bedford or to claim his own inheritance. For seven years after the death of his father he was still known as the Dauphin, or referred to contemptuously as the 'little king of Bourges', yet there was no disguising the physiognomy, the long nose and thick lips, of the Valois. The combination of a mad father and a notorious mother had destroyed his self-confidence.

By the middle of 1424 Bedford's troops dominated northern France, and on 17 August their hold was made even more secure by their overwhelming victory at Verneuil over a force of Armagnacs and Scots, commanded by the Earl of Buchan, Constable of France. This battle, second only to Agincourt as the most decisive in the fifteenth-century phase of the Hundred Years' War, put an end to Scotland's attempts to provide England's enemies with effective military aid, and it also marked the lowest point in the fortunes of France.

Torn by civil war and with much of her land held by her traditional enemies, France desperately needed a leader and a strong monarchy to unite her against the English, but Charles the Dauphin cowered in his castle and Marie sold most of her jewels to buy food, candles and faggots. Then, just at the time when it seemed that the English and the Burgundians would establish joint rule over the whole of France, a new and extraordinary figure appeared on the political scene; and Marie's brother René was one of the first nobles to hear about her because Domrémy was only about thirty-five miles away from his château at Pont à Mousson. Naturally, in so religious and superstitious an age, the story of the visions seen and voices heard by the girl Jeanne of the peasant family of d'Arc had come to his ears.

Jeanne went off to see the Dauphin at Chinon, the great castle that crowns the ridge above the town beside the sleepy Vienne, and René's mother Yolande, in her castle at Angers forty-five miles from Chinon, heard of her arrival and went over to see the girl for herself. Satisfied that Jeanne's mission was entirely genuine, she and her daughter Marie then began to work on Charles the Dauphin, whose apathy and reluctance to allow Jeanne to do anything seem to have stemmed mainly from hopelessness.

There is a splendid story that Yolande, losing patience with Charles's inertia and excuses, had herself buckled into the armour she had worn at Baugé and then strode, or possibly clanked, into his quarters demanding to know why the King of France skulked in his castle while his enemies wasted his lands. Since he apparently had no honour and no shame, she personally, inspired by this remarkable peasant girl, was prepared to lead his armies in the field.

Under the pressure exerted by his mother-in-law and his wife, Charles bestirred himself and Jeanne was allowed to play her part in the relief of the besieged city of Orleans. This happened in May 1429, two months after the birth of Margaret of Anjou.

1 Childhood (1429-1443)

Margaret, the fourth surviving child of René d'Anjou and Isabelle of Lorraine, was born at the Château Keure in Pont à Mousson on 23 March 1429. She came into the world just at the moment when the fortunes of France were balanced on the edge of a sword, and the sword was in the hand of Jeanne d'Arc.

Much has been written about this patron saint of France yet it is difficult to get any clear idea of contemporary opinion. Outside Lorraine and the actual area of operations against the English, few people seem to have heard of her. She is hardly mentioned by the English chroniclers. She certainly did not lead the French army, which was commanded by men like the Duke of Alençon and the famous Bastard of Orleans, Jean Dunois. Bedford did not bother to circulate any information on her trial and martyrdom in the territories under his control, and therefore it can be assumed she had very little effect on the morale of the occupation forces, but any attempt to denigrate her can be countered by her achievements.

At a time of fearful crisis she gave France a leader. Not herself, for she was only what many people believe to have been an instrument in the hand of God. Her faith was serene and unshakable, her devotion to her 'gentle King' was fanatical and she was perhaps the greatest patriot in the history of France. Her objectives were clear-cut; to give the Dauphin faith in his birthright, to destroy the aura of invincibility surrounding the English ever since Verneuil, and to have the Dauphin properly crowned and consecrated in the cathedral at Rheims. She attained them all and thereby changed the whole course of the war; removing for ever any idea lurking in the minds of the English or Burgundians of an Anglo-French state. In pursuing her primary aim of French unity she placed the symbol of it, the crowned king, under the protection of the people, and in making the people responsible for the monarchy she joined them all in a common purpose – one that was too abstract for most people to grasp at the time. Nevertheless, Jeanne d'Arc, carrying her white oriflamme into Orleans, marked the beginning of the end for the English in France. In due course, realization of this by the English themselves did nothing to help Margaret when she came to England. They distrusted any woman, particularly a Frenchwoman, who obviously possessed the qualities of a leader.

Six weeks before Margaret was born, her father inherited the title of Duke of Bar when his great-uncle died, and in the spring of 1429 René declared his allegiance to the Armagnac cause by leading an armed force to join the Armagnac army in the relief of Orleans. In July René stood in the throng of nobles round the dais in the centre of the cathedral at Rheims to acclaim his brother-in-law as Charles VII of France.

The Duke of Lorraine, René's father-in-law, died on 25 January 1431, and the title now came to René, through Isabelle, under the terms of Duke Charles's will. After more than a century of separation the dukedoms of Bar and Lorraine were united under one ruler, and the young duke seemed to be on the threshold of a great career. He was close to the king, he was acknowledged to be a brave and experienced soldier, the revenues of his estates would enable him to live in unwonted magnificence, he was happily married and possessed a growing family of sons and daughters. The world lay open to him, but unfortunately Philip of Burgundy decided to exact retribution for René's support of Charles VII and the Armagnacs.

Soon after the new Duke and Duchess of Lorraine had moved to the ducal palace in Nancy, a rival claimant to the dukedom, Antoine Count of Vaudémont, eldest nephew of René's father-in-law, came forward to assert that under the Salic Law the title could not pass through a woman and he was the nearest male heir. Vaudémont had the support of the immensely powerful Duke of Burgundy. Knowing he would have to fight for his title, René mustered his army and on 2 July 1431 a battle was fought on the plain of Bulgnéville, eleven miles south-east of Neufchâteau.

René cannot have been a particularly good soldier because Vaudémont was able to surprise him with a sudden artillery attack – not at all an easy thing to do with the cumbersome cannon of those days – and in less than an hour René's force had suffered 3,000 casualties and had been virtually destroyed. Half-blinded

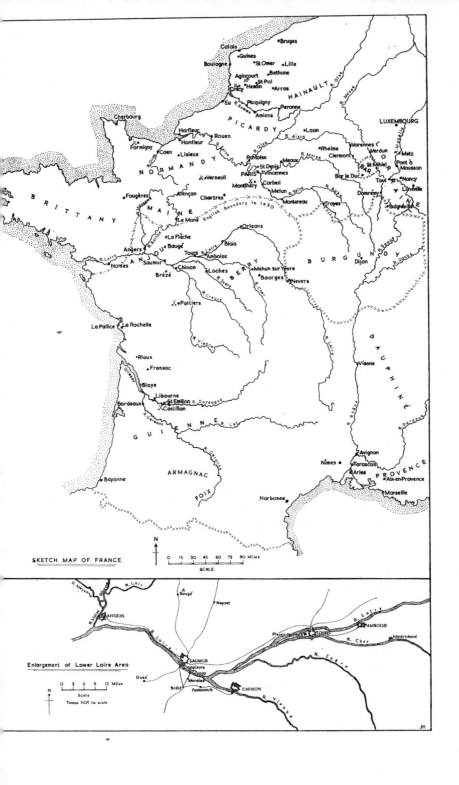

SKETCH MAP OF FRANCE

English boundary in 1430

0 15 30 45 60 75 90 Miles
SCALE

N

Enlargement of Lower Loire Area

0 3 6 9 12 Miles
Scale
Towns NOT to scale

N

JH

by blood from an arrow wound on the left side of his forehead, which scarred him for life, René is said to have fought like a lion until compelled to surrender to Marshal de Toulongeon, Philip of Burgundy's army commander. For the next three years he was a prisoner-of-war, and his wife Isabelle had to govern his lands, negotiate for his release and bring up their family by herself.

Like most minor engagements in this type of dispute, the battle of Bulgnéville did not in effect decide anything. In any case, Isabelle of Lorraine was a fighter, just as determined as her mother-in-law, Yolande.

'Within the body of a woman,' wrote the chronicler Etienne Pasquier, 'the Duchess carries the heart of a man.' Very much the same thing was said, years later, of her daughter Margaret.

When she heard that her husband had been captured, Isabelle arranged for her mother, the Dowager Duchess Margaret of Lorraine, to look after her four small children, John of Calabria, the eldest, Louis, Yolande and Margaret, in Nancy, while she with considerable success raised another army. She then warned Antoine de Vaudémont to keep well away from Nancy and to regard her as his implacable enemy until he released her husband. Considerably impressed, Vaudémont agreed to a three months' truce. Isabelle then decided to make a direct appeal to Charles VII on behalf of her husband, and in the hope that her two 'fatherless' daughters would help to arouse the king's sympathy, she took Margaret and Yolande, who was three, with her on the long journey to find the French court, known to be down in the province of Dauphiné in the south.

Thus it was that at the age of two, Margaret was taken from the nursery in the palace at Nancy and entered for the first time the strange world of diplomacy, faction and intrigue in which so much of her life was to be spent.

No doubt Charles VII, who at heart seems to have been a kindly man, said all the right things about his nieces, but since Philip of Burgundy had military resources far greater than anything directly under the control of the crown, there was little he could do to help Isabelle. Nevertheless, her visit to his court at Vienne in Dauphiné had a profound effect on him, not because of her children but of another girl, older and much more appealing in quite a different way.

Isabelle had taken with her a girl named Agnes Sorel who had been brought up and educated in her household in Nancy, and, so the story goes, Charles fell immediately and deeply in love with her. Subsequently he openly acknowledged her as his mistress and thereby created a precedent in the French monarchy. From all accounts her character matched her physical beauty, and it is a strange fact that she and Marie of Anjou, the queen, became close friends whose combined influence on Charles was one of the reasons why his reign was so successful. Agnes bore the king four daughters. She died young, in suspicious circumstances, and Charles was certain she had been poisoned by his son, the Dauphin Louis. She lies now in the Royal Lodgings of the forbidding castle of Loches, and the epitaph inscribed below the marble effigy on her tomb bears witness to her 'pitiful loving kindness to the poor and the religious'.

Isabelle returned to Lorraine without Agnes, who had become a Maid of Honour to Queen Marie, and without achieving anything. In the meantime René himself, from prison, had begun negotiations on his own behalf. In March 1432 he was released on parole to enable him to put into effect an agreement which involved ceding the castles of Clermont en Argonne, Châtille, Bourmont and Charmes to the Duke of Burgundy, and paying a ransom of 20,000 gold crowns. Furthermore, the Lorraine dispute was to be settled by the formal betrothal of his daughter Yolande to Ferri, heir to Antoine de Vaudémont.

These terms seemed unduly harsh to his mother-in-law, the Dowager Duchess Margaret, and in 1434 she appealed to her brother-in-law, the Emperor Sigismund, to intervene and persuade Philip of Burgundy to moderate his demands. Everything went wrong. Philip, infuriated by what he regarded as Sigismund's unwarranted interference, broke off negotiations and, because René's ransom had not been paid, ordered him to return to captivity; this time bringing his two sons as hostages with him. The code of chivalry left René no choice.

Since, according to the custom of the age, her elder sister Yolande had already gone off to live with the de Vaudémont family, Margaret, now aged five, was left alone with her mother, but Isabelle was fully occupied with running René's estates and fighting her lone battle against Philip of Burgundy. Financially, things were becoming extremely difficult. In addition to René's ransom of 20,000 gold crowns, now, according to Philip, to be regarded only as a down payment on a far larger sum that would be stipulated later, there was another debt of 18,000 florins claimed by Marshal de Toulongeon as a personal ransom for René who had originally surrendered to him. There was a further obligation to pay the Burgundian troops garrisoning the castles René had handed over, and his resources could not possibly satisfy all these demands. Isabelle's court became more and more impoverished.

Her mother died on 27 August 1434, and the loss of the Dowager Duchess's influence in Lorraine added to her daughter's problems. In all this upheaval Margaret was sent off to live with her grandmother Yolande of Aragon at Saumur. Yolande's family nurse, Tiphaine la Magine, who had brought up all Yolande's five children, was no doubt delighted when one of the next generation was put in her charge, and Margaret probably spent far more time with Tiphaine than with her grandmother.

Yolande can have had little time to spare for her granddaughter. For some years she had been acting as regent for her eldest son, Louis III of Anjou, who was away in Italy, trying to establish his claim to the throne of Naples by force of arms. During his absence Yolande had been governing the Duchy of Anjou with wisdom and skill, and in her determination to keep the English out of her lands she had even led troops into battle at Baugé. She was an extremely able woman, deeply concerned with the well-being of the people she ruled and resolved that the effort needed to support military operations would not disrupt the social, economic or even educational activities of her subjects. She was a great patron of the University of Angers.

Margaret came directly under the influence of this exceptional woman from the time she was five years old until the age of thirteen. She lived in a disciplined household where men of all ranks obeyed her grandmother's orders without question, and during these years she absorbed, from the troubadours, from the works of Boccaccio and from the tournaments held in the district round about, all sorts of ideas about chivalry, feudalism and hereditary rights just at the time when they were all becoming out of date.

When Margaret first went to Saumur she was only the younger daughter of a second son whose attempts to uphold his claim to Lorraine had so far been disastrous. Though still Duke of Bar and Marquis of Pont à Mousson, René had but little standing among the nobility. His debts and prospects reduced his status even more. This was all changed quite suddenly when his elder brother Louis died of 'fever' at Cosenza, the capital of Calabria, on 15 November 1434. Louis had been married for less than a year and his wife Marguerite, daughter of the Duke of Savoy, had no children.

The news was brought to René in his cell in the castle of Braçon by the Baron de Montelar, a gentleman of Provence, and René had the dubious satisfaction of knowing that he was now the 'King' of Sicily, Jerusalem and Naples. Margaret became a princess, and her grandmother insisted that she be taught to conduct herself as such on formal occasions and to have a proper understanding of all that 'royalty' implied.

René was now also the Duke of Anjou and the Count of Provence. Less than three months later, on 2 February 1435, Queen Joanna II of Naples died and René's affairs became even more complicated by the news that she had appointed him as her heir; heir in fact to a throne which for the past fifty years had been in dispute with the House of Aragon. Since Naples and Sicily were politically one kingdom, the captive René was now King of the Two Sicilies, Jerusalem and Hungary, but in name only. Both his father and his elder brother had failed to establish their authority in Naples, René was in no position to assert himself, and the field was left clear for the rival claimant to the throne, Alfonso of Aragon. Somewhat unexpectedly the Duke of Milan, Filippo Maria Visconti, intervened on René's behalf, apparently because, through the recently widowed Marguerite of Savoy, he was distantly related to him by marriage. He marched against Alfonso, defeated him in battle and took him prisoner.

When news of this reached Isabelle she realized that the House of Anjou must stake its formal claim to Naples, and since René's acquisition of all the new titles had not made the slightest difference to his imprisonment, she would have to do it herself. Leaving her elder son John Duke of Calabria behind to represent René's interests in Lorraine, and with Anjou and Provence secure under the firm hand of her mother-in-law Yolande, she went herself to Naples, taking her second son Louis, the new Marquis of Pont à Mousson, with her.

Neither Alfonso nor Isabelle had any resources of their own with which to wage war and they were both compelled to exploit the feuds, factions, jealousies and ambitions in the jungle of

Italian politics. For the next two and a half years Isabelle fought a long and sometimes desperate campaign alone. Then, on 25 November 1436, Philip the Good of Burgundy released René, again on parole. Anjou provided the ransom money and the long quarrel with Philip was ended when René's elder son, John of Calabria, married Philip's niece, Marie of Bourbon, at Angers in April 1437. The bridegroom was twelve years old.

After a very brief stay in Anjou with his mother and daughter Margaret, René set out to join Isabelle in Naples; arriving there on 9 May 1438. He was welcomed with great enthusiasm but his fortunes did not prosper. Perhaps five years of imprisonment had blunted his perception but he was unable to cope with all the treachery and double-dealing on which the Italians thrived. In 1441 Alfonso invested Naples with such determination that René sent Isabelle and Louis back to Provence. It was an unwise move. The Neapolitans at once assumed he had little hope of defending his kingdom and began to withdraw their support. On the night of 3 June 1442 a small party of Aragonese gained access to the city through the same aqueduct used by Belisarius, the great Byzantine general in the reign of Justinian, when he captured the city nine centuries before. The gates were opened, enemy columns stormed in, and René was lucky to escape with his life. A Genoese galley carried him back to France. Worn out, far more by the intrigues of the Italians than by the activities of the enemy from Aragon, disillusioned and penniless, he had achieved nothing.

René had learned a great many lessons in a hard school, and he profited from them. Though he never abandoned the title of king he made no further attempts to fight for a crown. He had come to realize that war solves no problems and he gave up all hope of ever becoming one of the great martial heroes of France. He had made the great mistake of reaching out for the unattainable and neglecting the inherited possessions which no one disputed. He made up his mind that in future he would govern his territories of Anjou and Provence with wisdom and in peace.

Throughout the period of the unfortunate Italian adventure Margaret had been living with her grandmother at Saumur and occasionally in the huge fortress of Angers, twenty-eight miles away to the north-west. For Margaret the year 1440 had been made memorable by the royal visit of her uncle and aunt,

Charles VII and Queen Marie, for Yolande revived all the splendours of the Angevin court for the occasion. But Yolande was now beginning to feel her age, she was sixty, and this was the last public function in which she took part. In the following year she decided to settle down at Saumur, the magnificent castle made virtually impregnable by the notorious Fulk Nerra, Count of Anjou, in the tenth century, and it was either in the castle itself or in a house in the Faubourg des Ponts, which she used as a retreat, that she died peacefully on 14 December 1442.

She was buried in her husband's tomb in front of the high altar in the cathedral of Angers, and her youngest son, Charles Duke of Maine, paid the costs of her funeral.

René and Isabelle were in Marseilles when they heard of Yolande's death. Anjou was now without a regent, it was obvious that Margaret could not live by herself at Saumur, and they came hurrying back. Isabelle must have been surprised by the changes in the daughter she had not seen for eight years. Margaret was now thirteen and, like most children of noble families at that time, precocious. From all accounts she was attractive, vivacious, intelligent and very like her grandmother Yolande who in her youth had been a noted beauty. With her striking looks, long reddish-gold hair, not tall but slim and graceful figure, and quick mind she was now one of René's most valuable assets. She was aware of her own value as a princess in a world in which marriage was the seal of treaties and alliances, and she also knew that a wedding seldom had anything to do with love. Any pleasure in the marriage bed was subordinate to the need for heirs, but whereas a man could take a mistress to compensate for an ugly or unlovable wife, the wife who took a lover could be strangled, smothered or otherwise disposed of for the crime of adultery.

The tranquillity of Margaret's happy childhood at Saumur had several times been broken by alarms and skirmishes involving the traditional English enemy, and though from an early age she must have known she would have no choice in her own marriage, it is unlikely that any thoughts of the English, except as adversaries, entered her mind.

Her father and mother established their court at Angers. They at once set to work to develop the resources of Anjou and repair the damage done by years of war. The victories of Charles VII in the south and the failure of the King's Council in London to maintain the English forces in the north had compelled Bedford to concentrate his troops in reasonably defensible areas such as Rouen and Caen. Though still holding fast to the fortresses of Maine, the English withdrew from Anjou, and René was able to reorganize the administration, encourage commerce, rebuild roads and bridges and turn the city of Angers into a centre of culture and learning.

Nevertheless, despite all his interests in Anjou, he did not neglect his responsibilities as Count of Provence, and he frequently visited his castle of Tarascon on the east bank of the Rhône, some fourteen miles east of Nîmes. It was here, in January 1443, that he received an important delegation from Philip of Burgundy who wished to arrange for a marriage between his nephew Charles Count of Nevers and René's daughter Margaret. This was not the first time that a marriage for her had been discussed. Some years previously there had been talk of the Count of Charolais, Duke Philip's son and heir who subsequently succeeded his father as Charles the Bold of Burgundy, and there had also been preliminary negotiations concerning a son of the Luxembourg House of St Pol, but for various reasons these had come to nothing.

René and Isabelle accepted the delegation's proposals and René even undertook to provide his daughter with a stipulated dowry of 50,000 *livres*, though he cannot have had the faintest idea where the money was to come from. His finances had never recovered from all the trouble in Lorraine and the Italian disaster. Nevertheless a marriage contract containing all sorts of complicated clauses was signed at Tarascon on 4 February 1443. In one of these it was stated that Margaret's children would inherit Sicily, Provence and Bar to the exclusion of any children of the marriage between Margaret's elder sister Yolande and Ferri de Vaudémont. There was also a reservation to the effect that if Yolande should marry again, any male child of the second marriage would take precedence over Margaret's children in the inheritance of Bar. This was René's involved way of indicating to Antoine de Vaudémont that the wounds received at Bulgnéville were by no means healed.

Furious, Antoine and his son Ferri appealed to Charles VII. Charles laid the whole matter before Parliament, and since in those days few things except possibly a cavalry charge happened at all quickly, Margaret's marriage to the middle-aged Count of

Nevers was postponed indefinitely. It was eventually abandoned, for two reasons. Charles VII would not agree to the 'revenge clause' his brother-in-law had put into the contract, and secondly, a far more attractive offer was made for the hand of the Princess Margaret.

2 Negotiations (1443-1444)

It is not certain who first suggested that Margaret should marry Henry VI, King of England. One source says it was the Duke of Orleans, still a prisoner-of-war in England after being taken at Agincourt; another that it was René's brother Charles, and another that it was Isabella of Portugal, Duchess of Burgundy. It is equally possible that the idea may have come from an Englishman, Cardinal Beaufort, Bishop of Winchester, Henry's great-uncle.

It is said that he met Margaret for the first time at Chinon in 1442. She was visiting her aunt and he had gone there on one of his missions to try to arrange a lasting peace between the English and the French. The beautiful and quick-witted young Margaret created quite a sensation in court circles and the Cardinal was impressed by her obvious strength of character. He felt she would be the perfect counter-balance for the irresolution and other weaknesses of his great-nephew. He foresaw that through her he would have much greater control over Henry, and accordingly, so the story goes, when he returned to England he extolled the virtues and charm of this lovely French princess to such an extent that Henry, now twenty-one could hardly wait to see her.

Prévost d'Exiles, in his *History of Margaret of Anjou*, says that in 1443 Henry sent an Angevin prisoner-of-war, a man named Guy de Champchevrier, who was in the custody of Sir John Fastolf, on a secret mission to the court of Anjou to obtain a portrait of Margaret. He wanted the truth, 'her face unpainted and her hair in coils', and he also wanted details of 'her height, her form, the colour of her skin, her hair, her eyes and what size of hand she hath'. Champchevrier managed to get a portrait, but in the meantime Sir John Fastolf, who had not been told anything, reported the 'escape' of his prisoner to the equally uninformed uncle of the king, Humphrey Duke of Gloucester. At Fastolf's request the duke wrote to Charles VII asking him to send

Champchevrier back to England because his ransom had not been paid. Arrested in France, Champchevrier was brought before Charles at Vincennes where he produced a safe-conduct signed by Henry and explained why he had come over from England. Apparently Charles was much amused, ordered the immediate release of the prisoner and wished him success.

There was nothing new in the idea that the young King of England should marry a French girl. Both sides were weary of the long war which, with comparatively brief intermissions, had been going on for nearly 200 years, and it seemed that such a union might offer the best hope for a permanent peace. The circumstances of the previous royal marriage, between Henry V and Princess Catherine of France, had been very different. Henry's motive then had been to strengthen his position as the conqueror and future King of France. Jeanne d'Arc had changed all that, and now the English, aware of a new determination in their enemies, saw that unless hostilities ended soon they might be driven out of France altogether.

The progress Charles VII was making in uniting his country and driving the English out of it imposed an ever-increasing financial burden on England, and fiercely resented taxation mounted proportionately. Yet, even so, the great victories over the French, and the centuries-long occupation of large areas of France, had created a sense of superiority and established deep in the minds of Englishmen a conviction that France should, by right of conquest, be their dominion. There was no question whatsoever of arranging peace at any price. To the people of England the marriage of their king to a Frenchwoman was acceptable only if the girl had an adequate dowry and if there were material benefits to be gained from it. Thus Cardinal Beaufort was fishing in dangerous waters when he proposed that Henry VI should marry Margaret of Anjou.

Her father had impoverished himself by waging profitless war and was finding it difficult enough to support his family. Any dowry could therefore take the form only of some mythical claim to territory over which René had never been able to establish his jurisdiction. From the English point of view it would have been far more satisfactory if Charles VII had offered one of his own daughters as a wife for Henry – he had plenty, in his total of sixteen children – but Charles had very definite ideas about royal hostages. His niece was quite near enough to the throne to justify the title of Princess, and her father called himself a king even though he had never been, nor ever would be, crowned. Furthermore, Charles could see in this marriage certain political advantages which may not have been apparent at first to the King's Council at Westminster.

René's younger brother Charles was the titular Count of Maine, a territory in which the English held Le Mans and so many other towns that they were able to maintain a firm grip over the whole county. If Henry was as eager to marry Margaret as rumour said he was, and if he was as prodigal with English possessions in France as he was with his own property, it might well be possible to come to some arrangement over the future of Maine.

At this moment Henry's future, and the future of England, really lay in the hands of the immensely rich and powerful Cardinal Beaufort, who had succeeded in removing virtually all authority from Humphrey Duke of Gloucester in a struggle that had begun with the death of Henry V. Until Henry VI officially came of age in 1437 England had been governed by a Council of Regency, and Gloucester, thwarted in his attempt to be nominated Regent, had had to be content with the vague title of Protector. By this time, in the year 1442, he had been excluded from the presence of the king and his opposition to Margaret as a bride for his nephew counted for very little. Thus, even before Margaret came to England, there was a dangerous rift in the nobility; one faction, led by the Duke of Gloucester, being in direct opposition to the court party of the Cardinal Bishop Beaufort. Therefore it cannot be said that Margaret, when she came to England, created the factions that already existed.

The Cardinal Bishop, a far-sighted man of outstanding diplomatic and financial ability, could see clearly enough what was happening in France, and he knew that as time went on and the military situation, from the English point of view, became worse, it would become increasingly difficult to reach a peaceful settlement. He had in fact been negotiating for peace ever since the death of the Duke of Bedford in 1436, and each year the terms that Charles VII wished to impose became harder. The main obstacle was always the same; the conditions laid down by Henry V for the Treaty of Troyes which established the English claim to the throne of France. If that claim could have been dropped it might have been possible to solve all the other problems. The French insisted that any lands held by the English in France should be the fief of the French crown, and this in effect meant that the King of England must pay homage to the King of France for lands which the English had occupied for hundreds of years.

To the victors of Agincourt and Verneuil this was out of the question, and Cardinal Beaufort well understood how explosive the whole situation was. Any English politician who agreed to the French terms laid himself open to a charge of high treason; and this was one of the enormous disadvantages of a royal minority. While Henry VI was still a child, those who managed his affairs dared not, if they valued their lives, tamper with the 'birthright' bequeathed by his conquering father.

Cardinal Beaufort also saw that any English presence at all, in France, depended on the Anglo-Burgundian alliance which prevented Charles from uniting his country and mustering all its resources against England. It was thus of paramount importance to keep this alliance going, but in 1435 the Duke of Burgundy came to the conclusion that his opposition to the authority of the French crown brought him no real advantages, largely because during the minority of Henry VI the English grew steadily weaker instead of exploiting the military and political gains of Henry V. Matters came to a head at the peace conference held at Arras in July 1435, attended by Beaufort although the Archbishop of York headed the English delegation. At this meeting the English might have been able to make a satisfactory, perhaps even a lasting, settlement if they had been able to give up their claim to the French throne, but as it was, they were only able to arrange a truce, and Burgundy abandoned his alliance with them.

This aroused anger and consternation in England and widened the split between the two factions at court. On the one hand the powerful Beaufort clan formed the 'peace party' which took the realistic view that if England was to salvage anything from the ruins of her French possessions there must be a permanent settlement and no mere postponement of the real issues by a series of truces. Opposing this was the party of Humphrey Duke of Gloucester, supported by Richard Duke of York who had, for a time, succeeded Bedford as Governor-General of France.

Gloucester, impulsive and irresponsible, fancied himself to be a warrior in the same mould as his brother, Henry V, heartily endorsing his opinion, as expressed by Shakespeare, that 'I thought upon one pair of English legs did march three Frenchmen'. Gloucester was a man who sought popularity, and war against the French was always popular – until the time came to pay for it. He therefore wanted to continue the fighting in France and, because his party was in the minority, he and his supporters were for ever on the watch to make political capital out of any attempt by his adversaries to sacrifice any of England's interests in the cause of peace.

Thus when William de la Pole, Earl of Suffolk, a prominent member of the peace party, was told by the King's Council early in 1444 that he was to lead an embassy to France and negotiate the terms of a marriage contract between Henry VI and Margaret of Anjou, he at once protested, for good reasons.

He had spent seventeen years fighting in France. Captured at the battle of Jargeau on the Loire in 1429 he had been the prisoner of Jean Dunois, the Bastard of Orleans, with whom he had formed a close friendship, and he had many friends among the French nobility. He knew Margaret had no dowry. He also knew that far from making concessions of any sort, Charles VII would drive a hard bargain which, almost certainly, would involve the handing over of some of the English possessions in France. Naturally enough he wanted no part of any arrangement which Gloucester and his faction could subsequently use against him, and he was well aware how slim were the chances that anything would really be achieved by such a marriage. Charles VII had no cause to be generous. He believed, with good reason, that the end of all English occupation was in sight and that the reduction of all the English garrisons would be comparatively easy, since they had been long neglected and were much below strength because of the divided court in England.

Against his better judgement, Suffolk allowed himself to be persuaded to accept the task. Nevertheless he took the precaution of making a formal petition to the effect that if his mission was not successful 'no charge be laid upon him that he might not therefore run into any danger or heaviness'. In a document signed at Westminster on 25 February 1444, Henry wrote of his 'great desire for peace, the matrimony of our person and the quiet and tranquillity of our faithful English subjects' and then made a declaration exonerating the ambassador and his heirs for ever and ever from any consequences resulting from the discharge of his embassy. It seemed effective enough at the time.

The delegation consisted of Dr Adam Moleyns, Keeper of the King's Privy Seal and Dean of Salisbury, Sir Robert Roos, Sir Thomas Hoo, Richard Andrews, the King's secretary, and John Wenlock. Suffolk, as its leader, was authorized to negotiate a peace or, failing that, a truce with Charles VII. The French king nominated Charles, Duke of Orleans, Jean Dunois, Louis of Bourbon, Bertram de Beauvau and Pierre de Brézé to represent him, and the Spanish, Danish and Hungarian Ambassadors were asked to act as mediators between the two delegations.

This is the first mention of Pierre de Brézé who was to play so large a part in Margaret's life. It is reasonable to assume that he had known Margaret from early childhood, no doubt when she came to Saumur to live with her grandmother, for he was the Grand Seneschal of the court of Anjou, and the château of the de Brézé family is only some six miles away to the south.* He was the son of Pierre de Brézé and his wife Clemence Carbonnel and inherited the titles of Lord of Varennes and Count of Maulevrier.

The English delegation landed at Harfleur on 13 March 1444, and a month later met the Duke of Orleans and his party at Blois. Both delegations remained there for some weeks and it was not until 16 April that they arrived at the French court at Tours, thirty-six miles down the Loire to the west. On the following day the Englishmen, accompanied by Margaret's father, her uncle Charles of Anjou, and her brother John Duke of Calabria, were presented to Charles VII, and the negotiations which were to decide Margaret's fate began in an atmosphere of goodwill and good intentions.

Suffolk soon learned what the French wanted. In return for Margaret the English were to surrender the province of Maine. This was far too thorny a problem for Suffolk to handle himself, and he succeeded only in arranging a two-year truce. Even this

---

* The de Brézé family still live in the beautiful château surrounded by its deep moat and lying amongst great vineyards enclosed by a high wall; unfortunately there are no family records of Pierre largely because his daughter lived in the château from the time of Margaret's marriage and he, subsequently appointed Seneschal of Normandy, was seldom there.

took a long time to negotiate because the meetings of the delegations were frequently interrupted by lavish fêtes and entertainments. According to Mrs Hooker, Margaret's Victorian biographer, 'great sums were expended and there was much display in apparel'.

In the first week of May, about six weeks after her fourteenth birthday, Margaret came to Tours with her mother, from Angers, and stayed with her parents at the abbey of Beaumont-le-Tours. All three took part in the festivities and Suffolk met Margaret for the first time. He, like Cardinal Beaufort, was impressed by her beauty, vivacity and intelligence, and having talked with her he felt confident she would be the wife Henry needed, and might do much to restore the authority of the English crown.

Despite her youth, Margaret does not seem to have been particularly excited or flattered by the prospect of becoming England's queen. She was being required to marry the traditional enemy of her family and her country. She had no idea what her future husband looked like and she may have realized, from the abundant evidence of the deterioration of the English cause in France, that he was not a particularly effective monarch. She knew she was little more than a clause in a truce, and if that truce did not grow into a permanent treaty she would be confronted with the difficult choice between loyalty to her husband and loyalty to her father and her uncle, Charles VII. But, for the moment she was not offered any choice. Charles VII had persuaded her father to sacrifice her in the interests of diplomacy, and there was nothing she could do about it.

On 22 May 1444 two agreements were signed. One dealt with a truce between the Kings of France, England, Sicily and Castile which was to last for twenty-two months, and the other was the marriage treaty between Henry VI of England and Margaret of Anjou. The latter had been somewhat delayed by the problem of a dowry. René had no money to give to his daughter and Charles VII was not prepared to lend or give money to anyone. There was no question of making his niece any grant of lands in France, yet to have provided nothing at all would have been an insult to the English delegation. Purely as a face-saving expedient it was agreed that René would endow his daughter with the islands of Minorca and Majorca, which he claimed to have inherited from his mother Yolande though he had no control over them whatsoever.

A possible explanation for Suffolk's acceptance of this imaginary dowry is that he may well have felt that by elevating this penniless French princess to one of the great thrones of Europe he would earn her gratitude, and thereby further his own interests. He certainly gained her trust, affection and unswerving support. It is not unlikely that the English delegation as a whole felt that by providing their weak and uninspiring king with a wife who would undoubtedly dominate him, their influence at court would be vastly increased; and in those days influence was synonymous with wealth.

Thus it seems that the whole business of Margaret's marriage was carried through by small-minded men motivated more by the prospect of personal gain than by any real hope of peace. They must have realized, early on in the negotiations, that Charles VII would not have traded his niece to the enemy without being determined to exact substantial concessions in return. Margaret's future had been decided, but nothing had yet been arranged about the future of Maine. This was the potential detonator.

Suffolk himself can have had no illusions about the probable repercussions in England if any more territory in France was lost, either by military action or political bargaining, and it is clear from his insistence upon a signed document freeing him from any blame over the negotiations that he knew how dangerous the situation was. Yet, perhaps like many who scale the heights of power, he could not believe that anything would happen to him. He was mistaken.

3   From France to England (1444-1445)

On 24 May 1444, two days after the signing of the marriage treaty, an elaborate betrothal ceremony was held in the church of St Martin at Tours. Processions headed by the two kings, Charles and René, the two queens, Marie and Isabelle, and the Earl of Suffolk, converged on the sanctuary, and Margaret, escorted by the Dauphin Louis and the Duke of Orleans, was brought to King Charles who, taking her by the hand, led her up to the papal legate, Peter di Monti, the Bishop of Brescia. Because Henry and Margaret were related in the fourth degree (their great-grand-fathers, Charles V of France and Louis I of Anjou, had both been sons of John II (the Good) of France) he had to grant a pro-visional dispensation to the marriage. Suffolk, as Henry VI's proxy, and then Margaret, made their promises, and the con-gregation in slow and stately procession marched to the abbey of St Julian. Here, at a magnificent banquet, Margaret was treated with all the honour and respect due to a Queen of England, equal in status to her aunt Marie.

The feasting was followed by unusual entertainments which delighted and amused the onlookers. Two men-at-arms jousted on camels and two giants appeared, carrying trees in their hands. It is possible that legend has embellished the contemporary account of the giants; they may merely have been large Scottish allies demonstrating the tossing of the caber. The celebrations ended with a ball which, according to one report, went on until 'an untimely hour'.

The Lord of Vendôme, accompanied by the Archbishop of Rheims and a small deputation, carried copies of the marriage contract across the Channel for Henry to sign, and subsequently returned home laden, as Holinshed says, 'with presents and every mark of distinction'.

There seems to have been a genuine feeling on both sides of the Channel that something had been achieved and that the truce and the treaty signed at Tours really would end the war. The clergy and local parliament of Anjou defrayed all René's expenses incurred by the celebration of the betrothal, and granted him money to pay for the wedding. The air was full of optimism. Suffolk's journey from Tours to Harfleur took a month because of the fêtes and rejoicing in every town on the way, and Londoners turned out to give him a tremendous welcome when he arrived in the city on 27 June. As a mark of his great satisfaction, Henry made him a marquis.

Henry was now eager to meet his bride and consummate the marriage but the formal welcome for a queen, followed by a royal wedding and then a coronation could not be arranged overnight. Moreover, there was the awkward question of cost. The war in France had emptied Henry's Treasury and the great barons were certainly not prepared to provide funds for a royal function which many of them, with justification, regarded as another move in the cold war between the factions of Beaufort and Gloucester. Suffolk, addressing the King's Council, said that Margaret 'ought to be considered as the certain pledge of peace', and on that basis Parliament voted the money which the Privy Council estimated would be needed to bring the bride over from France and place her on the throne beside Henry.

In any case, Henry was as unworldly about money and possessions as he was about most things. When Cardinal Beaufort died in 1447 and left him what was then the very large sum of £2,000, Henry told the astonished executors that he did not want the legacy. 'He was a very dear uncle to me,' he said, 'and most liberal in his lifetime. The Lord reward him. Do ye with his goods as ye are bound; we will receive none of them.' He was later persuaded to take the money for the colleges he had founded at Eton and Cambridge.

There was much to be done to prepare for Margaret's coming, and the list of essential repairs and renovations for the royal palaces at Eltham, Shene and Westminster is a long one. A great many horses would be needed for the royal progress through the southern counties to London after Margaret had landed; scaffolding would have to be erected in Westminster Abbey to support the seating for large numbers of guests and spectators at the coronation, and there was the all-important question of a suitable wedding ring. Henry found an inexpensive answer to this. Years before, on 2 December 1431 at the age of nine, Henry had been taken to Paris by his great-uncle Beaufort, his uncles Bedford and Gloucester, his tutor the Earl of Warwick, the young Duke of York and a party of warriors and bishops, to be crowned as King of France in the cathedral of Notre Dame. It had all been rather muddled and disappointing. The French, naturally enough, had stayed away; the state banquet had been shoddy and inadequate and a brawl had developed when the hall was invaded by the mob, but the Cardinal Bishop Beaufort had marked the occasion with a gift which Henry now described as 'a ring of gold garnished with a fair ruby, sometime given to us by our bel oncle the Cardinal of England, with the which we were sacred in the day of our Coronation at Paris'. This would do admirably for Margaret. It was given to the jeweller Matthew Philip 'to break and thereof to make another ring for the Queen's wedding ring'.

In August 1444 two members of Suffolk's original embassy, Sir Robert Roos and Sir Thomas Hoo, were sent back to France carrying personal letters from Henry to Margaret and her uncle the king. In them Henry said how glad he was that the negotiations at Tours had been such a success and how much he hoped the truce would be extended into a lasting peace. He also said he was longing to meet Margaret.

It must have taken the couriers a long time to reach Charles, for it was not until the end of October that he replied, from Lunéville in Lorraine, but it was an encouraging letter. He agreed to Henry's request that ambassadors be sent to England to negotiate a permanent peace and went on to say that although his brother-in-law René would need plenty of notice of the date when Margaret was to be collected, so that he could make proper preparations, 'we consent to hand over and cause to be escorted our fair niece at such day and hour as shall suit your good pleasure and wish'.

By this time Henry's preparations were well advanced and so, on the strength of this letter, a large entourage of noblemen, ladies, knights and squires, set off at the beginning of November to bring Queen Margaret to England. Their destination was Nancy, René's ducal capital of Lorraine, but Suffolk, leading the escort party, found his mission was to be long delayed by civil war in that duchy caused, initially, by René's debts to the citizens of Metz. They, hoping to recover some of the money owed to them, had attacked and captured the baggage train of his wife Isabelle who, soon after Margaret's betrothal ceremony at Tours, was making a pilgrimage to the monastery of St Antoine, high on the hill overlooking Pont à Mousson.

To René this was a heaven-sent excuse to fight his creditors instead of paying them, and Charles VII, glad of an opportunity to employ the troops of his regular army, agreed to help him. From late autumn, all through the winter, the city was besieged by a force of 30,000 men, and by the end of February the people of Metz had reached the stage where they were forced to pay dearly for relief. All the stolen baggage was returned, René's debts were written off and Charles received the sum of 200,000 golden crowns – which paid for the maintenance of his army.

While this siege was going on there was nothing Suffolk could do but wait, and by the time Margaret arrived from Angers, early in February 1445, Suffolk and his party had been in Nancy for a month. Finally, on 3 March the siege of Metz came to a conclusion satisfactory to Charles and René, and thereafter very little time was wasted. A few days later – the exact date is not known – the wedding of Margaret to Henry, by proxy, took place in the chapel of St George which was part of the ducal palace.

The bride, taken to the altar by her father and her uncle the king, wore a robe of white satin embroidered with gold and silver marguerites – the marguerite had been adopted as the symbol of the festivities which lasted a week. Prominent among the ladies-in-waiting surrounding Queen Marie and Queen Isabelle was the lovely Agnes Sorel who, during the great tourney arranged by René as part of the celebrations, appeared in a suit of silver armour encrusted with jewels and, as Jacques Levron says, the onlookers applauded '*cette radieuse apparition*'.

One cannot help feeling sorry for Margaret on her wedding day. The man beside her at the altar was not her husband but an old man – in her eyes at least, for Suffolk was in his fifties – merely doing his duty, and she was not even allowed to have the ceremony to herself. It was a double wedding, for her sister Yolande married Ferri de Vaudémont, and afterwards the exquisite Agnes effortlessly stole the limelight.

From René's point of view it was all eminently satisfactory and there was much to be celebrated. He was able to feel noble and patriotic over the gift of his daughter to the enemy in the cause of peace; the marriage of his elder daughter Yolande would end the civil war against the de Vaudémonts which had been tearing the heart out of Lorraine; and, for once in his life, he had completed a really rewarding military campaign which had removed a great burden of debt. By sacrificing Margaret he had placed his brother-in-law under an obligation – since Charles had refused to let Henry VI have one of his daughters – and there was good reason to suppose that as Queen of England Margaret would be of great political and financial value to him.

His arrangements for the festivities worked extremely smoothly and the jousting, held in the great Place de la Carrière, the arena in Nancy, was a great success. He won a personal contest against Charles VII, who hated fighting, and at the end of it all Ferri de Vaudémont was declared the champion and received his prize from Margaret, Queen of England, his new sister-in-law.

Nevertheless, the day of reckoning had to come. Neither René nor his wife Isabelle, nor indeed Margaret herself, had appreciated the true significance of the wedding and all the celebrations, but on 10 March, when the time came for Suffolk and his wife – appointed Mistress of the Robes to the new queen – to begin the long journey to England, the truth began to sink in. Margaret must now leave the country of her birth, perhaps for ever, and cross the dangerous seas to meet the man she had never seen, to live with him, and be the queen of a people about whom she knew virtually nothing except that they were, by long tradition, the enemies of France.

Her uncle, at the head of a glittering cortège, rode with her through the streets of Nancy and then along the road through the forest of Haye as far as Toul, ten miles to the west. They parted in tears, and it may well be that Charles, secretive and crafty like most of the Valois, had last-minute misgivings about the future in store for his niece. He must have known she was not really a pledge for any lasting peace since he was certain that the expulsion of the English from France – one of his basic aims – could only be achieved by force of arms. He went some way towards expressing this when he said to her, 'I am doing little for you, my daughter, in placing you on one of the greatest thrones in Europe, since there are none worthy of possessing you.' They did not see each other again.

Her father and mother went with her as far as Bar le Duc and she wept miserably when the time came to say goodbye to them, although in her life hitherto she had seen so little of either that there cannot have been very much intimacy in the relationship between parents and daughter. She was understandably apprehensive. At the age of fifteen she was being carried away from her family and all the surroundings of a reasonably happy childhood and, encompassed by a retinue of foreigners, albeit deferential and charming, taken to a country whose people did not even speak her language. The Earl of Shrewsbury, who was in this retinue, showed considerable understanding of her problems when he gave her a beautifully illuminated little volume of French romances (now in the British Museum) so that, as he told her, 'after she had learned English she might not forget her mother tongue'.

Although she had to bid farewell to her parents at Bar le Duc, her brother John and the Duke of Alençon went on with her to Paris, through Saint-Denis, the little town to the north of the capital whose abbey is the burial place of the great men and women of France. The cortège travelled comparatively swiftly, with Margaret riding for most of the way in a horse litter. It was a far more comfortable means of transport than the usual solid-wheeled, unsprung waggon although it swayed, perhaps sometimes rather sickenly, to every movement of the two horses carrying it. Throughout the journey, everywhere she passed, she was treated with the pomp and circumstance due to a queen of England, and for the first time she must have felt the isolation and loneliness of high station. The nobles and their ladies who escorted her knew very well how much depended on gaining and holding the goodwill of this young woman and, not yet knowing her, they were very careful in their behaviour.

Her escort, headed by the Marquis and Marchioness of Suffolk – she was a granddaughter of Chaucer and a first cousin of Cardinal Beaufort – included the Earl and Countess of Shrewsbury, James Butler, Earl of Wiltshire, Lords Clifford and Greystocks and Lady Emma de Scales. It was a large party, for in addition to a strong military guard there were seventeen knights, two esquire-carvers, sixty-five squires, twenty grooms, 174 other men servants of various kinds and a number of serving maids and dressers. The members of the nobility, both male and female, each received a salary of four shillings and sixpence a day for their services; the knights had only two shillings and sixpence. Each nobleman was accompanied by three scutifers or squires, and two valets. The scutifers were given one shilling and sixpence a day, and the valets sixpence. These were the 'war rates of pay' for 'proceeding from the County of Suffolk to parts of France to bring over the Lady Margaret, into the presence of King Henry of England in the Twenty-Third Year of the said King'. The total cost to Henry amounted in the end to £5,573 17s 5d; an enormous sum. It is not possible to give an accurate modern valuation of mediaeval money, but some indication can be gained from the wages of craftsmen and cost of food in 1450. The daily rate of masons was 6¼ pence, that of carpenters 5¼ pence, and thatchers and tilers received 5 pence. Beef was four shillings and one penny per hundredweight, 120 eggs cost 5¾ pence and butter was a halfpenny a pound.

Charles Duke of Orleans was waiting in Paris to greet Margaret when she arrived, and he led a great procession to Notre Dame where a Te Deum was sung. At length, on 18 March 1445, about a fortnight after the proxy wedding in Nancy, Margaret, escorted by Charles of Orleans, reached Pontoise, the border town of the English territories, where Richard Duke of York and twenty-two lords, knights and squires welcomed her. That evening she gave a farewell supper for her brother and the Dukes of Orleans and Alençon and saw them ride away, leaving her among the English. By this time, after all the wedding festivities, the long, uncomfortable journey, meeting so many strangers and hearing so many loyal addresses, she must have been exhausted, but there was to be no pause. On the following day she travelled to Mantes and was carried from there in a specially prepared barge down the Seine to Rouen.

Here she was given a tremendous reception. Preceded by a battalion of 600 archers and a procession of knights and nobles she entered the city on the day before Palm Sunday, riding in a sumptuously decorated litter. Suffolk, as Henry's personal representative, rode immediately in front of her. The Duke of York and Lord Talbot rode on either side, and the Marchioness of Suffolk, the Countess of Shrewsbury and Lady de Scales, also mounted, followed the litter. All through Easter Week Margaret was unable to rest, for there were many feasts, celebrations and long religious services. Another of her problems was money. While in Rouen she had to provide fifteen garments and fifteen pairs of shoes – one garment and one pair of shoes for each year of her age – to the poor, and her father had given her very little for the expenses of her journey. She must have been considerably embarrassed by having to pawn some of her silver wedding presents to the Marchioness of Suffolk to obtain money for gifts to boatmen and sailors who were to take her down the river and across the Channel.

On 31 March, in a boat belonging to a man named Collin Freon, she went to Harfleur where two vessels, the *Cokke John* of Cherbourg and the *Mary of Hampton* lay at anchor, but the weather, as it so often is in March, was too rough to attempt any crossing. Not until Friday, 9 April, was it possible for her to embark. The Duke of York, Governor of Normandy, took his leave and subsequently wrote a polite note to her uncle, Charles VII, telling him he had escorted Margaret from Pontoise to the place where '*elle fut montee sur mer*' to go to the king in England.

Accompanied by Suffolk and his wife and a few attendants, Margaret went aboard the *Cokke John* and was again disconcerted by being asked to produce five pounds four shillings and tenpence for the pilot's fee, thirteen pounds six shillings and eightpence for new hawsers, and nine pounds seven shillings for alterations to the vessel's superstructure for the royal voyage. (Henry reimbursed her.) The rest of her suite travelled in the *Mary of Hampton*.

From all accounts it was a most unpleasant crossing, and Margaret was dreadfully sick, but the strong south-east wind blew the little rounded, broad-beamed cogs swiftly across the Channel and they reached Porchester Castle in the afternoon of the same day (9 April). By this time, like many a seasick traveller before and since, Margaret was past all caring whether she lived or died, and Suffolk carried her ashore, wading through the surf with the young queen in his arms. It was then discovered that she was not merely seasick, and the Proceedings of the Privy Council record that she was 'sick of the labour and indisposition of the sea, by the occasion of which the pokkes been broken out upon her'. To the joyful sound of church bells and through cheering crowds gathered to greet her, Margaret was taken to a convent on the outskirts of Southampton. Named 'God's House' and founded by

Peter de Rupibus in the reign of King John, it was more of a hospital than a religious house, and Margaret appears to have been in good hands.

The 'pokkes' turned out to be chicken pox and not the far more dreaded smallpox, but she was ill for several days and the formal wedding to Henry VI had to be postponed. On 10 April Suffolk gave instructions for the queen's doctor, Master Francisco, to be given the sum of three pounds three shillings and two pence for various 'aromatic confections particularly and specially purchased by him and privately made into medicine for the preservation of the health of the Queen, as well by sea as by land', so she had probably been feeling unwell before she sailed.

Lying on her hospital bed she now had time to think about the past and the future, and many of her thoughts may perhaps have been on the husband she was soon to see. Any descriptions given to her by the ladies of her escort in the journey across France – and it is hard to believe she did not ever ask about him – might not have been much help because, to the people of his time, Henry VI must have been very difficult to understand.

His tutor during his childhood had been Richard Beauchamp, Earl of Warwick, described by the Emperor Sigismund as the 'father of courtesy'. Using an adroit combination of discretion, diplomacy and severity – Warwick did not hesitate to apply corporal punishment when he deemed it was necessary – he taught the boy king lessons of kindliness, thoughtfulness and Christianity which were never forgotten, and helped Henry to endure the troubles of his reign with extraordinary fortitude. He never tried to take revenge for the injuries and humiliation he suffered, and instead merely thanked God for punishing his sins in this world so that he would be able to have an easier life in the next.

Much has been written in support of a theory that Henry VI was either an imbecile or, if not actually mad, certainly mentally retarded. This supposition is usually based on the undoubted lunacy of his grandfather, Charles VI of France. In Henry's veins the blood of the unstable, sickly Valois was mingled with that of the House of Plantagenet, going back to the great Henry II and his wife Eleanor of Aquitaine. It could have been a potent mixture, for though the Valois kings were not physically strong they were, on the whole, able, tenacious and far-sighted, but Henry did not apparently inherit any of their, or his father's, resoluteness and fixity of purpose. In any age, if a ruler is to be successful he must be dominant and to a certain extent ruthless. He must be self-confident. Henry was a charming, kindly, modest man, and because he lacked so many of the attributes of a leader it was, and is, easy enough to say he must have been weak in the head, and that he inherited this weakness through his mother, Catherine of France. Yet when his widowed mother married again, choosing the Welshman Owen Tudor mainly because he was one of the most handsome men in England (or Wales), there was no sign of any hereditary mental weakness in either of her two sons, Edmund and Jasper Tudor. And when Edmund married Margaret Beaufort there was no weakness in the son born to them. This child, Henry, later Earl of Richmond, became Henry VII, founder of the Tudor dynasty, and no one has ever suggested there was madness in the Tudors.

It is true enough that Henry VI had several nervous break-downs, one being a prolonged period of acute depression, but there is no evidence of any hereditary madness although, even before his birth at Windsor on 6 December 1421, some people were ready to believe that the insanity of Charles VI would be apparent in his grandson. Nevertheless, Charles's own son, Charles VII, was perfectly normal and turned out to be one of the great kings of France.

The real trouble was that Henry VI did not fit into the age in which he had been born. All would have been well if he could have become a peaceful monk, contentedly copying and illuminating religious works in some great monastic foundation like Bury St Edmunds, his favourite place of retreat, but, as the heir to Henry V, he had no choice. There are many stories which throw light on the nature of this gentle, good man to whom Margaret was now married – by proxy.

Henry's biographer, Blacman, emphasizes that he was without guile, 'with none did he deal craftily, or ever would say an untrue word to any' – so uncharacteristic of the Valois. Much of his time was spent in prayer and meditation, 'so that often he would let his royal cap drop to the ground even from his horse's back, unless it were quickly caught by his servants'. He could have been merely absent-minded. In his dress he was, in the opinion of his courtiers, positively eccentric, wearing dowdy round-toed shoes and boots, a long gown with a rolled hood and a full coat reaching below his knees, 'rejecting expressly all curious fashion of clothing'.

On one occasion, 'At Christmastide a certain great lord brought before him a dance or show of young ladies with bared bosoms who were to dance in that guise before the king'. Henry was deeply shocked, and angered by what he regarded as an insult. Turning his back he walked swiftly to his chamber saying, 'Fie, Fie, for shame! Forsooth, ye be to blame!' Once, when riding down to London from St Albans he saw displayed on a stake above Cripplegate part of the horrible remains of some wretched man who had been hanged, drawn and quartered, and, not recognizing what he was looking at, asked what it was. He was told that a man had paid the penalty for treason, for being 'false to the King's majesty'. He was horrified. 'Take it away,' he said. 'I will not have any Christian so cruelly handled for my sake.' On being told that one of his servants had been robbed he sent him money and advised him to take more care in looking after his possessions, but not to prosecute the thief.

Yet Henry was no coward. During the riots in 1450 he put on armour and, following the example of Richard II during the Peasants' Revolt, showed no fear as he rode through streets where a chance arrow could so easily have killed him, but he would not fight against his fellow men. In the bloody battles of the civil war he merely stayed where he was until either his side won or he was captured. He never had the slightest doubts about his right to the throne and it seemed almost incredible to him that anyone could dispute it. Since he would not fight he could not rule. He enjoyed and had some success in the role of peacemaker. What he could not see was that the very weakness of his rule was leading to anarchy, and the political vacuum created by his ineffectiveness must, sooner or later, be filled. In these circumstances there could be no peace. No surface differences could be resolved until the power struggle in his own court had been fought and won.

The wealth and power of the great nobles, with their private armies of retainers, raised problems of command and control which Henry could not solve. He had no army with which to enforce obedience and the rule of law, and England was not ready for a man who tried to rule with wisdom, courtesy and reason. Yet his mode of life, his piety and his charm won him the respect and love of the great majority of his people. He possessed unlimited moral courage and he was probably a very lovable but absolutely infuriating man.

It is not therefore surprising that in an age when physical power was the decisive factor in politics and when at any time the anointed king had to be prepared to take up the sword in defence of his right to wear the crown, those of Henry's courtiers who remembered the iron grip of his father must have felt that perhaps their misgivings about the union of the Houses of Lancaster and Valois were justified. Cardinal Beaufort certainly had his doubts about the ability of his great-nephew to hold on to his throne, and he may well have felt that in Margaret of Anjou lay the only hope for the future of the Lancastrian dynasty.

The women of the House of Anjou were natural leaders and born fighters. They were faithful and loyal, single-minded and resolute. There was therefore some reason to hope that the fusion of Anjou with Lancaster would produce a stable administration which, supported by the respect felt by most people for hereditary kingship, would unite the factions, control the more troublesome nobility, and establish law and order in a country greatly unsettled by the losses of territory in France.

It was all rather too much to expect of a girl who was just sixteen.

Being able to rest and to be properly looked after by her doctor and the nuns of the hospital, Margaret began to recover, and Henry, understandably in view of all he had heard about her, badly wanted to see his bride even though she was not considered to be well enough for a formal meeting. He went to some trouble to satisfy his curiosity. He arranged for Suffolk to take him to the queen dressed as a squire, so that he could hand her a letter 'from the King'. Henry knelt before her, gave her the letter, and remained on his knees while she read it; he watching her and she too engrossed to pay any attention to the 'squire'. When Henry had gone, Suffolk asked Margaret what she thought of the squire, and she said she had not noticed him. 'Most serene Queen,' said Suffolk, 'the person dressed as a squire was the most serene King of England.' Margaret was very distressed at not having known who he was because 'she had kept him on his knees'.

Henry seems to have realized from seeing her that Margaret was not yet well enough for the marriage ceremony, for on 16 April he wrote to John Stafford, Lord Chancellor and Archbishop of Canterbury, telling him he would not be able to return to Windsor in time for the celebration of the feast of St George, 'because the Queen is not yet free of the results of the sea-sickness by occasion of which the pox being broken out upon her'.

At length, on Thursday, 22 April 1445, Henry and Margaret were married by William Ayscough, Bishop of Salisbury, in the abbey of St Mary and St John the Evangelist at Titchfield.* The Bishop's address and blessing centred on the theme in the 128th Psalm about wives being fruitful vines upon the walls of the house and children like olive branches round about the table.

Among Margaret's wedding presents was a lion, there is no record of who gave it to her, but she received it graciously enough and Henry arranged for it to be handed over at once to Robert Mansfield, the keeper of the Royal Menagerie in the Tower of London.

The king and queen appear to have spent the first few days of their married life at the abbey, for some time later, to acknowledge the abbot's hospitality, Henry granted certain privileges to the foundation, in connection with tax relief and local fines. In any case there must have been some delay in their departure from Titchfield because Henry discovered that Margaret's wardrobe had been so scantily furnished by her father that 'her clothing was in no way suitable to her rank'. He told one of his servants, a valet named John Pole, to ride swiftly to London and bring back a certain Margaret Chamberlayne, a 'tire-maker' (dress-maker). Mistress Chamberlayne did what was required of her and was paid twenty shillings for her labours. The royal progress to London could then begin. It went on all through May, wandering in a leisurely way through Hampshire, Sussex and Surrey, and was a great success.

All the nobility and gentry on the route vied with each other in seeking to impress the young queen with their influence, import-ance and the number of their retainers, and no doubt many of them were genuinely glad to see her because she represented peace with France and the end of the long war. To Margaret, coming to live in a strange land, the welcome must have been reassuring.

* The abbey, founded in 1232 by Peter des Roches, Bishop of Winchester, for Premonstratensian canons, is now an imposing ruin, much altered since the time of Margaret's wedding, lying only a few yards to the north of the A.27, just to the west of Fareham in Hampshire.

Her husband was obviously popular, the landowners she met seemed loyal enough, the value of her personal goodwill was made clear to her, and she could see that henceforth her life would be much more interesting and exciting than it had ever been in Saumur or Angers.

She and Henry reached Eltham Palace in the last week in May, stayed there for a day or so and then, on Friday, 28 May, rode up to Blackheath where, on the open plain above the river, a large number of dignitaries waited to escort her to lodgings prepared for her in the bishop's palace by St Paul's. In front of the Lord Mayor, aldermen and representatives of the City Guilds was Humphrey Duke of Gloucester, at the head of five hundred of his retainers all splendidly arrayed in his livery and badge. He invited Margaret to refresh herself at his palace named Placentia, at Greenwich. Everyone wore a marguerite or daisy in their caps and bonnets, and, as the poet* subsequently wrote:

> Of either sex, who doth not now delight
> To wear the daisy for Queen Marguerite?

Gloucester, presented with a *fait accompli*, was anxious to impress upon Margaret that there had been nothing personal in his previous opposition to her marriage. No doubt like many others he felt that in future the way to the king might lead through this attractive young Frenchwoman.

A large and inquisitive crowd had come out from London to see the queen, and the people lined the route and followed behind the procession which moved slowly through Southwark and across London Bridge, past a series of pageants and allegorical tableaux, believed to have been designed by the poet Lydgate. The cheering, waving crowds, the stately procession, the magnificent liveries of the retainers, the blue and red and gold of the gowns of the civic worthies, and the whole atmosphere of jubilation may have been some compensation to Margaret for the loss of her family and homeland. She could at least see that a great deal of time, effort and money had been spent on making her feel welcome.

Her entry into London must have been a great day in her life, and it was followed immediately by others, just as impressive.

* Michael Drayton (1563–1631).

On Saturday morning the procession formed up again, but this time it was headed by forty-six new Knights of the Bath, created by Henry to celebrate Margaret's arrival in the capital, and she was escorted to a thanksgiving service in St Paul's. Followed in the procession by her ladies she rode in a horse litter lined and hung with white cloth of gold, the horses were draped with white damask and Margaret herself was dressed in white. Her golden auburn hair hung about her shoulders, held off her face by a crown of gold; round her neck was a golden collar studded with rubies, sapphires and pearls, and a great pendant 'Jewel of St George'. Both were presents from Henry. They had been specially made by the Goldsmiths and Silversmiths Company at a cost of £4,000, which he could ill afford. Indeed he had been compelled to summon Parliament a few months previously, on 23 February 1445, and persuade the Commons to vote more money for Suffolk's delegation, the wedding, the welcome and jewellery for his bride.

At the service in St Paul's, John Stafford the Archbishop of Canterbury preached on the text 'Justice and Peace have kissed each other' and pointed out the benefits bound to accrue from this union of the English crown with – though somewhat remotely – that of France. Afterwards the procession went through the city, where there were more pageants dealing with 'many devices and stories with angels and other heavenly things, with song and melody', and came at length to Westminster, where the parties who formed it took their leave and went their separate ways.

On the next day, 30 May, the first Sunday after Trinity, with majestic ceremony Margaret was crowned by the Archbishop of Canterbury in Westminster Abbey. The Parliament that had assembled in February was still in session and the presence of the Commons in all their finery added considerably to the occasion. The coronation was followed by three days of feasting and jousting and processions in which the delegations sent to represent King René and James II, King of Scotland, took part. Margaret was radiant throughout and aroused much admiration. Baudier says she was a princess who, to the beauties of her body added all the perfections of the mind, but no doubt all those who met her and came to see her were equally impressed by her stamina.

Then it was all over, and despite all the optimistic rejoining there were several hard facts to be faced.

4 Queen's College (1445-1448)

Margaret and Henry had been married on the strength of a truce, not of any permanent peace, and it was the underlying thought of permanent peace which had prompted all the rejoicing at Margaret's arrival, at her wedding and at her coronation. It was thus of vital importance for Henry and the court party to convert the truce into a proper settlement without delay.

But Charles VII was not in any hurry. He was in a strong position. Confident of ultimate victory, he had no intention of ending the war except on his own terms which, since his aim was to expel the English from France, inevitably included the surrender of territory.

On the other hand, no peace delegation from England dared risk accusation of treason by giving up any French soil. There was bound to be trouble, but in view of Charles VII's obvious intentions, the options were perfectly straightforward – fight or surrender. There must be either a concerted effort to check the French erosion of English territory or it must be accepted that lands which could not be properly defended could not be held.

Cardinal Beaufort may have hoped Margaret would instil some sense of leadership into her husband, but it was unrealistic to expect her to fight for any policy directed against the interests of her uncle and her father. Furthermore, she had problems of her own. She had arrived in a court presided over by the easy-tempered, frail-bodied Henry, in which violent and turbulent factions, split in many directions by personal feuds, wrestled for control of the king. She was quick to see that the crown was not a power, it was only a form of authority tolerated by the powerful nobles provided it did not interfere with their interests. The sovereign was dependent on the will of the majority. If called upon to defend himself he had to rely on the private armies of those who were prepared to support him against his enemies.

In the long delay before her proxy wedding at Nancy, and during the journey to London, Margaret had formed close friendships with the Suffolks, Lord and Lady Talbot and others in her escort. These were people she came to know and like and depend on without understanding, or caring, about political affiliations or cross-currents. She could not, at her age, have been aware that they had supported the marriage for their own ends, that there were underlying motives which had nothing whatsoever to do with her happiness or peace with France, or indeed the security of the House of Lancaster. She became closely identified with the Beauforts and the court party, who gave lavish rewards to all who had been involved in arranging the marriage and made large payments to her foreign suite. The opposition noted all this down against her.

She had been brought up to believe she owed her husband obedience and respect. It did not take her long to discover that he was too humble and reasonable a man ever to have borne the burden of the crown in such an age, or even to have taken on so dynamic a wife. All he asked for was the love and loyalty of his consort, his servants and his people. He had little interest in politics or in government, largely because it had been the consistent policy of his Council during his minority, and his ministers when he came of age, to isolate him from state affairs, shelter him from the outside world and, so far as possible, keep him in ignorance of their decisions.

Margaret was by nature partisan. She was also clever, proud, courageous and enterprising, but in her determination she was inflexible; her loyalty was blinding as well as binding. Relentless in the pursuit of her aims she had no idea how to conciliate, or how to come to terms with those who opposed her. She was indeed the strong queen that England needed, but because of her nature and her nationality she was apt to arouse resistance and resentment where she should have sought co-operation and affection. Before she came to England her father, who knew, through his brother-in-law, what was going on in the English court, advised her to lie low at first and cultivate friendships with the people closest to Henry. Then, when the time was ripe, she and her husband should assume the royal power and govern without ministers who came exclusively from the nobility; like Charles VII, most of whose administrators and members of his

Council were of the *bourgeoisie*. It was a system that was working extremely well in France because it divided the nobility against each other and, by denying real authority to all of them, made it possible to exercise reasonably effective control.

Henry did not feel strongly about his father's conquests. Ever since Philip of Burgundy had upset him by refusing to address him as King of France he had rather lost interest in a country full of Frenchmen, and if his uncle Charles VII wanted to rule them, there was really no moral justification for standing in his way. It was all far too tangled in his mind to be sorted into a firm policy line, and even if he had been able to make a decision between fighting and surrendering he lacked the power to impose his will on his ministers.

Margaret, naturally, inclined towards surrender. She had told her uncle before she said goodbye to him at Toul that his interests and those of France would always be close to her heart, but from her point of view the whole question of territory was a very sensitive subject. She had brought no dowry to Henry, she did not even have a trousseau. She must have known about the French demand for Maine, since in the eyes of the French negotiators of her marriage contract she was being exchanged for it. In effect, as Suffolk knew well enough, permanent peace with France depended on the handing back of Maine and not the handing over of Margaret.

Margaret's position was not made any easier by the need for Henry and his Parliament to provide for the maintenance of her household with funds and resources which should have been supplied by her father. As it was, soon after her coronation, Parliament conferred upon her the sum of £4,666 13s 4d in money, and to this was added an income of £2,000 a year from land. Among various properties scattered over nearly a dozen counties she was given the large farm of Gunthorp in Nottinghamshire, the castle and estate of Pleshey and the manors of Dunmow and Walden (Saffron Walden) in Essex, the castle and town of Hertford and several buildings in London.

When the euphoria surrounding Margaret's coronation died away, people began to ask questions about the peace with France that she was said to signify, because nothing seemed to be happening. Early in June Suffolk spoke in Parliament about certain approaches made to him in France but he was careful to insist that no details had been discussed. He was able to report that he had arranged for a French delegation to come to England, and at the same time had advised the Duke of York to reinforce the frontier garrisons of Maine and Normandy, look to their defences and ensure they were properly supplied against attack or siege. He made it clear that any peace negotiations in London would be conducted from a position of strength and in a spirit of determination. This seemed to deal effectively with all the current rumours that Maine was about to be given up. The relief was considerable and Suffolk was publicly congratulated by the Speaker in the Commons and the Duke of Gloucester in the Lords. For the moment, he rode high on a wave of popularity.

On Saturday, 3 July, the French delegation arrived at Dover, rode to Canterbury and stayed there over the weekend. It consisted of the Counts of Vendôme and Laval, the great chronicler and Archbishop of Rheims Juvenal des Ursins, Charles VII's secretary Etienne Chevalier, Bertrand de Beauvau and Guillaume Cousinot. On Monday this party was joined by King René's secretary and representatives from the Duke of Alençon and King of Castile. They all moved on to Rochester where they remained, for no apparent reason, until 13 July. On the following day, Wednesday, they entered London and crowds gathered to watch them ride through the streets. Spending the night in lodgings in the City they went next day by water to Westminster where they were greeted ceremoniously by Henry and Margaret. Henry, in a long robe of red cloth of gold, sat on a stool of red tapestry surrounded by a golden arras embroidered with the lilies of France. In view of his claim to the French throne this might have been a little tactless. Grouped round the king and queen were the Archbishops of Canterbury and York, the Dukes of Gloucester and Buckingham, and the Earl of Warwick, Richard Neville. He had inherited his title through his wife Anne Beauchamp, and was the son-in-law of Henry's old tutor who had died in 1439.

All came to nothing. Both sides talked at length of their great desire for peace, but Maine was the obstacle. After two weeks of fruitless discussion it was agreed to extend the truce, arranged at Tours, to give time for further talks, and there were suggestions of a meeting at the highest level so that Henry VI and Charles VII could resolve their differences in peace and goodwill. It was perhaps a pity that the old Cardinal Bishop Beaufort had by this time retired from active politics and took no part in the negotiations.

The French embassy returned to France, and hard behind them went Adam Moleyns, the Bishop of Chichester, instructed by Henry to arrange for the truce to be extended.

Charles VII's terms for peace were nothing short of the surrender of Maine, and there is reason to believe that round about the time of the Tours agreement Henry did undertake, though not in writing, to do this before 1 October 1445. In that month two members of the delegation that had come to London in July – Guillaume Cousinot and King René's secretary Jean Havart – returned to England to see Henry, bringing with them letters written by Charles and René to Henry, Margaret and Suffolk. These letters made it clear that the giving up of Maine was really the only acceptable basis for permanent peace. Several weeks later, writing from the palace of Shene on 17 December, Margaret told her uncle that she would do all she could to persuade her husband, but it is possible that Henry's concern was really the time factor and not the surrender itself – which he had agreed to in principle. He wrote to Charles on 22 December, this time making a definite promise that the key fortress of Le Mans and all that the English held in Maine would be handed over to the rightful owners, King René and his brother Charles of Anjou, Count of Maine, within four months, that is to say, before the end of April 1446. In his letter he said he had reached this decision on the assurances by the French ambassadors that it was the most satisfactory way to ensure peace and because he wanted to please Margaret who several times had asked him to do it. Charles agreed to extend the truce for another fourteen months, until April 1447.

Since the County of Maine was not surrendered by the promised date it seems likely that in writing to the King of France Henry acted on the spur of the moment, without consulting his ministers and against Suffolk's declared policy. He may have been influenced by Margaret; he probably was, but no one will ever know what they said privately to one another. On several occasions Suffolk had stated in public that English forces in France would be kept up to strength and there was no question of trying to buy peace with English possessions. Apparently he now made Henry change his mind, and the negotiations dragged on for months without making any progress. Yet the problem was not one which could be volleyed to and fro between the courts of England, France and Anjou indefinitely, and Margaret, as her father and uncle must have foreseen before she was married, found herself in an extremely awkward position. She and her uncle exchanged personal, friendly letters; he saying he hoped to see her at the proposed meeting between him and Henry, and she replying she hoped so too, and was doing her best to bring about peace and a happy understanding between her husband and her relations.

It would be wrong to imagine that during the first years of her marriage Margaret had any real influence or say in the conduct of affairs of state. She had no political experience, she was extremely young, and though she inherited all the virile qualities and abilities of her mother and grandmother she was never a strategist, though she developed into a competent short-term tactician. Her close friends at court, particularly Suffolk and his wife, may well have discussed possible French reactions to a proposed course of action, asking her, reasonably enough, what the French point of view might be, but it is most unlikely – nor is there any contemporary evidence – that she formulated policies herself. Paradoxically, her real weakness lay in the strength of her partisanship. She was incapable of acting as a mediator, and since there is good reason to believe she genuinely loved her husband, all the wrangling over territory in her own country must have been very upsetting.

Moreover, in addition to her youth, her inexperience and her ignorance of English affairs at this stage, there was another reason, perhaps the strongest of all, why she had so little influence. No one paid much attention to Henry and so there was no reason why anyone should pay much attention to her. He sought refuge from public affairs in prayer and meditation. He evaded an issue whenever possible, and his ministers found it as difficult to make an impression on him as it is to leave a footprint in the shifting sands. As his consort, Margaret could do very little without his permission, and his reluctance to use his royal authority left her with virtually none.

In the vexed question of handing over Maine to her father's brother, Charles of Anjou, she probably did her best. 'In this matter,' she wrote to her father, 'we will do your pleasure as much as lies in our power, as we have always done already,' and no doubt she was not sparing in her pleas to Henry. But the time factor kept cropping up. Her husband and his ministers have been accused of weakness, hesitancy and dilatoriness but it seems possible that they deliberately dragged out the negotiations, playing desperately for time in the hope of some change in the feelings of Englishmen about France. Suffolk and Shrewsbury, who had soldiered in France for years, had no illusions about what was happening there, and about what could happen in England if provinces which the English regarded as their own were given back, ostensibly so that a feeble English king could have a pretty French wife. The resulting explosion might shatter the whole structure of English society; as indeed it did.

There is no doubt that Margaret wanted peace, and a lasting peace, between England and France, for to her the surrender of Maine was the solution to many problems. It would restore to the House of Anjou the land and revenues to which it had a legitimate right, and above all it would remove the source of conflict, perhaps even open war, between her husband and her father. It must therefore have been particularly frustrating that, as the months passed and the couriers flitted back and forth across the Channel, nothing ever seemed to be agreed. Even after Henry, by letter patent, had undertaken to surrender Le Mans and Maine to King René, and actually commissioned Matthew Gough and Foulkes Eytone to take them over from the Marquis of Dorset and deliver them to Charles VII, there was more trouble. Only three days before the time limit, Henry wrote to Dorset, giving him a direct order to surrender Maine. Dorset ignored it, for fear of becoming a scapegoat. The deadline went by, yet negotiations continued, and finally, on 15 March 1448, the surrender was made and the truce extended to 1 April 1450.

Meanwhile, the whole business of handing over territory in France had been slowly coming to a head in England, where the Duke of Gloucester had been making a sustained attack on the king's ministers in general and Suffolk in particular. In this personal assault Gloucester used to advantage the special relationship between Suffolk and Margaret, and the intensely strong public feeling against voluntarily giving anything back to the French. Margaret was regarded with deep suspicion as a thoroughly undesirable French influence on Henry and his administration; no less than an agent for Charles VII, working on his behalf in the English court.

This was unjustified. Even if Margaret could influence Henry – and most wives can affect their husbands' decisions – she had virtually no influence at all over his administration because his ministers, following the precedent set by Cardinal Beaufort during his minority, were not in the habit of discussing policy or politics with the king. Margaret was certainly not an agent of Charles VII. Their uncle-niece relationship had never been particularly close. She was very conscious of being the Queen of England, and by nature she was too strong-willed and independent to carry out instructions unless it suited her to do so. Her desire for peace and for reconciliation of the differences between England and France did not extend to placing the interests of her uncle or her father before her own.

But the spotlight was focused on Suffolk, for it was he who had brought Margaret over to England. It is ironical, in the light of subsequent events, that Suffolk looked back on the negotiations for her marriage as the supreme achievement of his diplomatic career.

Richard Duke of York joined Gloucester in his campaign, and their objective was to pull down the men round the king and establish themselves in their place. At this stage it was not the crown they wanted, but direct control of it. Cardinal Beaufort, trusting neither, had seen to it that for years both had been excluded from the King's Council. Both now took advantage of Beaufort's absence, Henry's ineffectiveness, the growing unrest in the country at the surrender of Maine, and the rapidly worsening financial situation brought about by the lack of stable government. Both did their best to make Suffolk's task as chief minister as difficult as possible, and to prevent any peace with France, the only hope of restoring stability.

For most of her life Margaret had been in touch with treachery and intrigue, but she did not regard her lack of experience in dealing with either as any handicap – it seldom is to anyone of spirit. Because she had formed so close a friendship with Suffolk's wife, Margaret associated herself completely with his cause and his defence. Her prestige in court circles was growing. She was openly admired for her beauty and intellect, and she was too young to recognize flattery for what it was or to tread with caution the path leading to the centre of affairs. Her courage was equalled by her impetuosity. She wanted a principal role, and in taking it she involved the crown in the sordid struggle for power from which, if it was to survive, it had to remain aloof.

Had Suffolk been strong and honest, and genuinely determined to rescue the country from the depths into which it had fallen since the death of Henry V, all might have been well, and Margaret's championing of him could have brought credit upon her. But he was like nearly all the rest of the nobility; inordinately greedy for money and power. As the man who had provided the wife adored by the king he enjoyed a privileged position with Henry, and he took full advantage of it to seize vacant sinecures, add to his already large estates and manipulate trading regulations to his personal advantage.

All his failings were exploited by Gloucester who, by the end of 1446, had succeeded in arousing strong feelings against him as a politician and as a man. Deciding that the best form of defence is attack, Suffolk took action. Perhaps if he had thought of consulting the 'rich old Cardinal' he might, as a result, have moved more warily, but Beaufort was now on his deathbed and far removed from party politics.

Suffolk may really have felt Gloucester was about to stage a coup, and therefore drastic steps had to be taken, for his plans were well-laid. He persuaded Henry to summon Parliament in February 1447 so that Gloucester, somewhat belatedly charged with malpractices during his protectorate when Henry was still a minor, could be arraigned before it. Since the people of London were devoted to 'the good Duke Humphrey' and would probably have risen in great strength to support him, Suffolk arranged for Parliament to meet at Bury St Edmunds on 10 February, amongst his own dependants. He also took the precaution of telling the knights of the shire to come armed. He called out his own private army of several thousand men and all the roads leading to Bury St Edmunds were guarded by his patrols.

The winters of the mid-fifteenth century seem to have been particularly severe – in 1435 the ice right across the Thames for most of its length was so thick for so long that the ferry-boatmen became destitute – and the month of February in 1447 was colder than usual in East Anglia. Among Suffolk's troops 'many died of cold and waking' and he soon disbanded them, not because of the cold, or of the expense in maintaining them, but because he heard that Gloucester, coming up from his strong castle at Devizes, was bringing an escort of only about eighty men.

Although Parliament assembled as arranged, on 10 February, Gloucester did not arrive until the morning of Saturday, 18 February. He was met, just outside the town, by Sir John Stourton and Sir Thomas Stanley, officers of the King's Household, and escorted to a house called St Saluatores near the North Gate. That afternoon a small delegation which included Buckingham, Salisbury and Dorset, called upon him, read out the charges against him and told him the king had given orders that he should remain as a prisoner in his lodgings until a proper inquiry into the charges was made.

Gloucester was taken completely by surprise. That evening many of his officers and servants were also arrested and sent off to various prisons.

Five days later, on Thursday, 23 February, the 'good Duke Humphrey' was found dead in his bed. All the circumstances pointed to political assassination, and Shakespeare's version of the incident leaves us in no doubt who the murderers were, but the real probability is that Gloucester died of a heart attack, brought on by a long, exhausting journey in bitter weather, followed immediately by the shock of arrest. There are at least four contemporary reports of his death; one by Richard Fox, a monk of St Albans who simply says, 'on Thursday next following after the arresting of the said Duke of Gloucester, he died soon upon three of the bell at afternoon, at his own lodging ... on whose soul God have mercy, amen.' Others were written by men who were his friends and ardent supporters; Hardyng, William of Worcester and Abbot Whethamstead of St Albans. William, writing of the meeting of Parliament at Bury St Edmunds, merely adds, 'there died Humphrey, the good Duke of Gloucester, the lover of virtue and State', and the Abbot writes that 'after being placed in strict confinement, he sank from sorrow'.

There is no hint of murder from any of them. Yet a story began to circulate, and like all such stories it lost nothing in the telling. At first the death was a mystery, then it was suspicious, then suggestions were made, of suffocation between two feather mattresses and of the hideous method used to kill Edward II in

Berkeley Castle; means which would leave no mark on the body. Gradually opinion became almost equally divided, and by the time the Tudor historians had set their quill pens to the story all doubt had vanished: Suffolk was the murderer, ably assisted by Margaret, acting the role of Lady Macbeth, and even old Cardinal Beaufort, dying far away at Winchester, was brought into it.

From Suffolk's point of view the duke's death was most unfortunate. Although for the moment it had removed the leader of all the attacks against him, he knew it would not be long before someone just as antagonistic and possibly more formidable took the duke's place, and it was more than likely that the next thorn in his side would be Richard Duke of York, the heir to the throne if Henry and Margaret had no child. There was a real danger that Gloucester would be made into a political martyr, and Suffolk did all he could to avoid giving any hint of relief, gratification or maliciousness. All the arrested servants were released with the king's pardon, the duke's household was given every help in making whatever funeral arrangements they felt were suitable, the body lay in state for twenty-four hours in the abbey of Bury St Edmunds, and was then carried with dignity and ceremony to burial at St Albans.

Unfortunately Suffolk's greed got the better of him over the disposal of Gloucester's estates. The duke had no legitimate children and his wife Eleanor had no claim on his possessions because six years previously, in July 1441, she had been found guilty of sorcery and sentenced to imprisonment for the rest of her life. Suffolk seized everything, gave Margaret the castle and estates of Devizes, kept a large proportion of the rest for himself and divided the remainder among his own family. Margaret's enemies accused her of unseemly haste in taking possession of Devizes. This was all used subsequently as evidence that she was Suffolk's fellow conspirator in the murder of the duke, and her association with Suffolk did her nothing but harm.

Shakespeare makes out they were lovers – particularly in Act III, Scene 2 of the *Second Part of King Henry VI,* when they have to part – but this is quite untrue; not just because Suffolk was more than thirty years older than Margaret, though age need have no bearing on an intimate relationship, but because Margaret was far more fond of Suffolk's wife than of him. Margaret loved her husband. There is no evidence that she was ever unfaithful to him, and certainly she had need of an emotion as powerful and binding as love to remain, as she did, his indomitable prop and stay, right to the end.

Even before all the unpleasantness of Gloucester's death at Bury St Edmunds, Suffolk was well established as an object of envy, hatred and malice, and at the zenith of his power he held the offices of Chamberlain of England, Warden of the Cinque Ports, Constable of Dover Castle, Captain of Calais, Chief Steward of the Duchy of Lancaster, Chief Justice of Chester, Flint and North Wales, Steward of the Chiltern Hundreds and Steward and Surveyor of all the mines in England and Wales – and these were only the most lucrative of his many offices. Finally, in 1448 he was elevated to a dukedom. In the days when the holding of public office carried no obligation to serve the public, and was regarded merely as a means of enriching oneself, the enemies of such a man as Suffolk were bound to be legion, and their dislike of him was based on jealousy; the least charitable of emotions. The envious nobles joined with the Commons in attacking him for gathering so much wealth to himself at a time when the financial state of the country was deteriorating every year, and though the weight of this attack decreased immediately after Gloucester's death, it was doubled when, as Suffolk had feared, Richard Duke of York stepped into Gloucester's place.

York's motives were personal. He was quite certain that Suffolk had persuaded Henry to give the post of Captain-General of France and Guienne to the Duke of Somerset instead of to him in 1443, and although York seemed to be friendly enough to Suffolk's delegation when Margaret passed through Rouen two years later, there was hatred smouldering under the surface. It flared up in 1445 when Suffolk, indirectly, accused York of peculation. York's reaction to this was to come home and charge Bishop Moleyns with bribing troops in France to say they were being cheated out of their pay. Moleyns succeeded in proving this to be untrue but the charges and countercharges created consider-able tension which Suffolk sought to relieve by arranging for York to be posted to Ireland as the King's Lieutenant. The date of this posting was 29 September 1447, but nearly two years passed before York chose to take up the appointment. The delay proved fatal to Suffolk.

In associating herself with Suffolk and his government, Margaret began to play an increasingly active part in affairs and in the details of administration, beginning with her own estates. There is little evidence of her being able to exert much influence, but it appears from her correspondence that she tried hard. Like her mother and grandmother, she was interested in people and felt responsible towards those who worked for her. To her servants and dependants she became known as a good and trusted friend, and to those she disliked she was a relentless enemy. Her upbringing, her education and the influence, such as it was, of her scholarly and artistic father, endowed her with a feeling for romance and of sympathy for the unfortunate. She wanted the stories she read or heard to have a happy ending, and wherever she thought this could be achieved by her own influence or efforts she was prepared to take considerable trouble. Unfortunately, this applied only to those who were dependent on her or over whom she could exert some authority. She had very little charity to spare for any nobles who opposed her.

Her private letters, of which there are at least seventy-five still in existence, show her to have been an enthusiastic match-maker, tireless in her interference in other people's private affairs, and quite unscrupulous in her efforts to divert the course of justice should it run against anyone whose cause she supported. They cover the first ten years of her married life, from soon after her arrival in England in 1445 until 1455, the year of the first battle of the civil war.

Like most women, in her interest in the love affairs of others she was incurably romantic, inquisitive and hopeful. She seldom missed an opportunity to question young women about their loves and longings. Margaret Paston writes of one of the queen's visits to Norwich when a cousin of hers, a girl named Elizabeth Clere, was sent for, 'and the Queen made right much of her, and desired her to have a husband; and the Queen was right well pleased with her answer'. One example of her match-making is in a letter she wrote to a certain Robert Kent, on behalf of Thomas Shelford, one of her servants:

By the Quene
Welbeloved, we grete you and late you wite that our wel-beloved servant, Thomas Shelford, whom for his vertues and

the agreable service that he hath don unto us herbefore, and in especial now late in the company of our cousin of Suffolk, we have taken into oure chamber, there to serve us abowte our personne, hath reported unto us, that for the good and vertuous demening that he hath herd of a gentilwoman beying in your governance, which was doghter to oon Hall of Larkfield, he desireth full hertley to do hir worship by way of marriage, as he seith. Wherfor, we desire and praye you hertley that setting apart all instances or labours, that have or shalbe made unto you for any other personne what so ever he be, ye wol by all honest and leaful menes be welwilled unto the said marriage, entreting the said gentilwoman unto the same, trustyng to Godd's mercye that it shalbe both for His worship, and availle in tyme to come. And if ye wol doo yor tendre diligence to perfourme this oure desire, ye shal therin deserve of us right good and especial thanke, and cause us to showe unto you therfore the more especial faver or oure good grace in tyme to come.

Regrettably, this apparently had no effect either on Robert King or on the daughter of one Hall of Larkfield.

On 11 April 1447, at the age of eighty, Cardinal Beaufort died in his palace of Walvesey and was buried in Winchester Cathedral. There were many bequests in his will, mainly to religious institutions, for he had much to dispose of, and he left Margaret 'the bed of cloth of Damascus' and the arras from the bedroom she had slept in when she stayed on his estate at Waltham. The residue of his goods were to be used for charitable works at the discretion of his executors, specifically for the relief of religious houses that were in financial trouble, 'for marrying poor maidens, and for the help of the poor and needy, and in such works of piety as they [the executors] deem will most attend to the health of his [the Cardinal's] soul'. Knowing of this clause, Margaret applied to the executors on several occasions 'for the relief of the indigent', in particular on behalf of 'one Frutes and Agnes Knoghton, poor creatures, and of virtuous conversation, purposing to live under the laws of God, in the order of wedlock'. She asked the executors to assist these two 'in their laudable intention' with the alms at their disposal.

Margaret also interested herself in the future of Thomas Burneby, whom she describes as the 'sewer for our mouth'. A sewer was responsible for superintending the arrangement of the table, the seating of guests, and the tasting and serving of dishes. Burneby was eager to marry Jane, widow of Sir Nicholas Carew, who had left his widow no less than seventeen manors in her own right, a legacy which no doubt prompted much of the eagerness of her suitor. Margaret wrote to tell Jane how much Thomas really loved her 'for the womanly and virtuous governance that ye be renowned of'. She extolled his merits and then added that she hoped 'at reverence of us the lady will be inclining to his honest desire at this time'. Jane Carew obviously did not have enough reverence. She married Sir Robert Vere, brother of John, the twelfth earl of Oxford.

In the cause of one Thomas Fountaine, yeoman, Margaret wrote to the father of a girl named Elizabeth Gascarick saying:

We pray right affectuously that, at reverence of us, since your daughter is in your rule and governance, as reason is, you will give your good consent, benevolence and friendship to induce and excite your daughter to accept my lord's servant and ours, to her husband, to the good conclusion and tender exploit of the said marriage, as our full trust is in you.

Her trust was misplaced. Neither Queen Margaret nor William Gascarick was able to prevent Elizabeth from marrying Henry Booth of Lincolnshire.

Writing from her castle of Pleshey, one of her favourite country seats, on 11 March 1447 Margaret appealed to Edith Bonham, Abbess of Shaftesbury, asking her to intercede on behalf of her chaplain Michael Tregory and recommend him for the vacant see of Lisieux in Normandy, but Thomas Basin was chosen to be Bishop. A little while later she appealed without success to the Master of St Giles-in-the-Fields for admission to the leper-house of an unfortunate boy called Robert Upholme, 'aged only 17 years, late chorister unto the most reverend father in God the Cardinal, whom God assoil [absolve from purgatory] at his college at Winchester, who is now, by God's visitation become a leper'. Even her polite request to the Lord Mayor and Sheriffs of London on behalf of 'Lory, oure cordwainer' was ignored. She pointed out that he had a full-time job in fitting her and the ladies of her court with shoes and therefore asked that 'at such tymes as we shall have neede of his crafte, and send for hym, that he may not appere and attend in enquests in the Cite of London, that he may not be empannelled, but therein sparing him at reverance of us . . .'

She wrote many testimonials for her servants, referring on one occasion to the 'famous and clean living of her clerks' in the hope of getting promotion or preferment for them, but her pleas and requests were seldom even answered and she invariably had the greatest difficulty in persuading anyone to do anything on behalf of those she tried to help. She had all the enthusiasm of youth, and its impetuosity, She was too apt to rush in, with the best of motives, and, because she did not pause to consider what the effect or cost of interference might be, she often gave offence and aroused resentment which negated all her efforts.

Her surviving letters are all private and personal, having nothing to do with politics or affairs of state. She writes of money owed to her, on the care of her estates, on the training of a blood-hound and the preservation of her deer. Almost invariably she hopes that action will be taken 'out of reverence' for her as queen, but as the wife of a king like Henry she had no power to bring effective pressure to bear, and her correspondents knew this. To many people she, as a Frenchwoman, represented the enemy. The poverty in which she had grown up had made her acquisitive and grasping; it was known that she evaded Customs duties and was running various little rackets in the export of wool and tin. She was unpopular outside the circle of her friends at court and, though Henry loved her, he was too weak in character and resources to support her. She was treated with indifference and disloyalty on a scale which indicated clearly enough how low the sovereignty of the crown had fallen.

Nevertheless, during this time of increasing disillusion throughout the country she did succeed in one lasting achievement.

By the time Henry her husband was twenty he had made plans for a school and a college, one to be the 'nursery' for the other, and these took shape with the founding, in 1440, of 'the College of the Blessed Mary of Eton beside Windsor', and of the College Royal or King's College to Our Lady and St Nicholas at Cambridge in the following year. Eton had an establishment of one Provost, ten priests, four clerks, six choristers and twenty-five 'poor and needy scholars'. The annual cost of these colleges was

£3,400, and since Henry was always short of money the legacy of £2,000 left to him by Cardinal Beaufort in 1447 must have been a help.

This was an era of church and college building, and Henry VI's enthusiasm had been aroused by the founding of the College of All Souls which Archbishop Chichele had begun to build at Oxford in 1438. Seven years previously, in 1431, new universities had been founded by the English at Caen in Normandy and Poitiers in Guienne. Margaret, following Henry's example, and that of her parents who had done so much for education in Anjou, was the royal founder of Queens' College Cambridge.

The 'working' founder was a man named Andrew Docket, the Rector of St Botolph's, Cambridge, who in 1446 had obtained a charter to found a small college to be named St Bernard's, of which he was to be president. Since Margaret was often at Pleshey, only about forty miles from Cambridge, and owned a lot of land in the areas of Dunmow and Saffron Walden, he probably made it his business to find out about her and learned of her charitable pursuits. Early in 1447 he went to see her at Pleshey and asked her if it would be possible for his college to be moved nearer to the river and to King's College, and be renamed the Queens' College of St Margaret and St Bernard. The idea appealed to her enormously. She petitioned Henry for a new charter which was issued on 30 March 1448, and on 15 April 1448 her chamberlain, Sir John Wenlock, laid the foundation stone of the college chapel on her behalf. It was engraved with '*Erit Dominae nostrae Reginae Margaretae in refugium et lapis iste in signum*' (The Lord will be a refuge to our lady Queen Margaret, whereof this stone shall be the sign).

Henry gave her £200 to start things off and, this time with considerable success, she persuaded all sorts of people, including Suffolk, York, Dorset and Edmund Beaufort, Duke of Somerset, to contribute to the college fund she was raising. The initial establishment was to be a Master and Four Fellows. The chapel was not opened for worship until 1464 and the college was only half-finished when Edward Earl of March (Edward IV) drove Henry VI off the throne. For a time it seemed that despite all Docket's efforts – he was president for forty years – the project would have to be abandoned, but he persuaded Elizabeth Woodville, wife of Edward IV, to come to the rescue and the work begun by a Lancastrian queen was completed by her Yorkist successor.

Margaret gave permission for her armorial bearings to be used as the arms of the college, with the only difference that the college arms are surrounded by a green border. They were carved in stone and can still be seen over the inner entrance. She also gave an altar piece for the chapel. This consists of three paintings, 'Judas betraying Christ', 'The Resurrection' and 'Christ appearing to the Apostles after the Resurrection'. Though it is not known for certain who the artist was, the pictures are well within the capabilities and in the style of her father, King René.

Poor Margaret, writing with such urgency and enthusiasm the letters to which no one paid much attention, making busy plans with Andrew Docket, and wanting so much to be given just a little 'reverence' and affection, cannot have been very happy in the first years of her marriage. She seemed to be unable to bear the child she longed for, unable to make peace between her husband and her father and uncle, unable even to win respect, and after the unfortunate death of Humphrey Duke of Gloucester she must have realized how much the opposition to Suffolk's administration was growing. What she may not have been able to see was that sooner or later the antipathy which Suffolk provoked was likely to take a violent form.

5 Suffolk, Cade and Somerset (1449-1452)

When John Stafford, Archbishop of Canterbury, died in 1449 and was succeeded by John Kemp who had been Archbishop of York, the court party, which Margaret was doing her best to unite against all opposition, also included Henry Percy, the second Earl of Northumberland, Edmund Beaufort, Duke of Somerset, the Dukes of Exeter and Buckingham, and the Lords Stafford, Clifford, Dudley, Scales and Audley.

They formed an oligarchy; jealous of power, bent on the exploitation of any opportunity for private gain, and taking little thought for the morrow. They may well have believed that the opposition consisted only of a small group of envious noblemen, but in fact the feeling against most of them ran deep and wide. Thousands of ordinary people, merchants, artisans and labourers – many of whom were ex-soldiers – began to murmur against the weight of taxation. The tame surrender of lands won in France by untold effort and suffering aroused bitter resentment, and there was growing fear of the total breakdown of law and order. Already in many districts the King's Law no longer existed. Men of all classes, once they had made sure of powerful patronage, did more or less what they liked. Local squabbles became feuds which flared into open warfare without any attempt by the central government to assert its authority. Notorious vendettas, such as that between the Bonvilles and the Courtenays in Devon, went on unchecked. Judges and sheriffs could be bribed and juries could be packed, and far from trying to restore justice and peace, Henry and Margaret, chronically short of money, sold letters instructing judges in the favour they must show and telling sheriffs what verdicts juries were to give.

All Henry's attempts to borrow from the rich landowners who were his own courtiers, or to raise money by selling honours and privileges, merely made matters worse. Naturally, in these circumstances it was impossible to maintain adequate garrisons in France. French troops were massing on the frontiers of lands that could not be defended, and were raiding with impunity.

No political advantage had been gained from the surrender of Maine because, in the general climate of disobedience, the English, threatened by the army of Charles VII, retaliated by breaking the truce. They seized fortresses in Brittany and sacked the town of Fougères. This gave Charles VII the opening he had long awaited. He could now, with a clear conscience, ignore Suffolk's pleas for co-operation in a policy of peace and, with his efficient regular army, occupy by conquest lands which might have taken years to acquire by negotiation. Moreover, not only did he hold the operational initiative but he was able to attack English forces in no shape to fight because Henry could hardly find money for the soldiers' pay, let alone repair defences and provide weapons, equipment and supplies.

In July 1449 Charles declared that the truce was over, thereby adding immeasurably to Henry's financial difficulties. Normandy and Guienne had to be defended but there was no money for the troops in the garrisons. Rouen, the great city which had been so hospitable to Margaret on her way to England as a bride, fell to the French, and the English forces in Normandy were driven back north-eastwards to Formigny, twenty-seven miles beyond Caen and almost on the coast.

News of the loss of Rouen brought direct repercussions, affecting Suffolk's administration and also, inevitably, Margaret herself. Her friend the Duke of Somerset had replaced York as Governor of Normandy nearly three years previously, and he was now accused of cowardice, treachery and treason, although his garrison had consisted of only 1,200 men. Count Dunois had besieged the city with a large army and many French agents were active within the walls. There was no real attack. The disaffected population rose against the English, opened the gates to Dunois, and Somerset and Talbot were forced to withdraw with the garrison into the citadel. Talbot, the Earl of Shrewsbury, was a famous warrior. Even the mention of his name had hitherto frightened the French, for his great feats of arms were legendary in his lifetime, but there was nothing he could do against the main French army. Somerset capitulated on 4 November 1449 and was compelled to yield up several fortresses in Normandy as the price of his freedom. Talbot was given as a hostage. Somerset withdrew to the large castle on the hill overlooking Caen.

Neglect of the garrisons in France and the indiscipline which had led to the raid on Fougères had played into the hands of Margaret's uncle. All Normandy now lay open.

Of the popularity Suffolk had enjoyed in 1445 – for his firm line over peace negotiations – no trace now remained, and he came under concentrated attack for what was happening in France. The people held him to be directly responsible, and he must be called to account. Unpleasant rumours and accusations against him and against Margaret began to circulate, and when Parliament assembled on 6 November, two days after the fall of Rouen, the Commons ordered his imprisonment in the Tower as the preliminary to a formal impeachment. The direction of the political wind now being obvious, his colleagues began to think of their own skins. Bishop Lumley, Lord Treasurer, resigned even before Parliament assembled. Bishop Moleyns surrendered the Privy Seal, but gained nothing from his sacrifice. A month later, on 9 January 1450, he was murdered at Portsmouth by a party of sailors. It was said that they were taking revenge for the loss of Rouen, but there is another, more likely story that they accused him of cheating them out of their pay. The murder of a bishop, even of a political bishop, shocked many people and was an alarming indication of the state of anarchy creeping through the whole country. The crime was made to serve the ends of Suffolk's enemies for it was announced that just before he died Bishop Moleyns had stated that Suffolk had been solely responsible for giving Maine back to the French, and it was this surrender that had begun the present chain of events in France.

When Parliament reassembled on 22 January 1450 the charges against Suffolk began to take shape. He was accused of selling English territory in France to Charles VII and trying to get his son upon the throne by planning to marry him to Margaret Beaufort, the heiress of the Duke of Somerset and of the House of Lancaster (she was the great-granddaughter of John of Gaunt).

The Commons formally asked the Lords to commit Suffolk to the Tower while the remainder of the charges were framed, and it is said that Margaret, fearing for the safety of her friend and adviser, persuaded Henry to act on the recommendation of the

Lords and protect Suffolk from the mob. Suffolk went to the Tower and Margaret came under a more personal attack. Already hated for the part she had played in the surrender of Maine, and there is no denying that for good reason she had done what she could to secure peace, even on her uncle's terms, she now became the target of insult and slander. For example, one of the stories spread about was that King René was not her father and that she was the illegitimate daughter of Isabelle of Lorraine, conceived while her father was a prisoner-of-war in the hands of the Duke of Burgundy. In public, Margaret, with typical courage, gave no sign of the deep distress this caused, but in his *Chronicle* Mathieu d'Escouchy says she often wept bitterly in private.

Suffolk was impeached on 7 February 1450, and the number, complexity and contradiction of the charges against him reveal clearly enough the doubt in the minds of his accusers about being able to bring any specific indictment. He had certainly enriched himself at the expense of the crown, but this was normal practice; it was going to be very difficult to prove he was responsible for the surrender of Maine and Anjou and for the loss of Rouen. These were the principal charges. Henry listened patiently to the whole list, read over to him in Council on 12 February. He tried to reserve the case for his own judgement but at the end of the month the Lords, led by York, ruled that the impeachment must go forward. On 17 March Archbishop Kemp, the Lord Chancellor, announced that Suffolk had been banished for five years.

It was a severe sentence, involving the loss of offices, privileges and revenue, but the hunt was up and the mob was calling for blood. Suffolk managed to escape from the Londoners hoping to assassinate him as he left the Tower, and went to his estates near Ipswich. Here he called together all his relatives, dependants and friends and swore upon the Host that he was innocent of the charges against him, particularly those relating to the surrender of lands in France. This we know to be true. He then went to Ipswich where he and his most trusted retainers embarked in three small vessels. He sent one of them ahead, carrying letters to Calais where he had formerly been the Captain, to find out how he would be received there, but ships manned by his enemies were patrolling the Channel. The forerunner was intercepted, Suffolk's approximate whereabouts became known, and on 2 May, as he was sailing between Dover and Calais, the great warship

Nicholas of the Tower, belonging to the Duke of Exeter, Constable of the Tower and Lord High Admiral, came up astern and forced him to heave to.

Ordered on board the warship, Suffolk was greeted by the Captain with the ominous words 'Welcome, traitor!' There is a story that Suffolk then asked for the name of the ship and was at once filled with foreboding because he remembered the words of a soothsayer who had once told him that 'if he might escape the danger of the Tower, he would be safe'. It may be true.

He was taken to a cabin and confined there for the next two days and nights while the ship put back to Dover and communicated with his enemies on shore. He had to endure a mock trial by the sailors, who condemned him to death, but knowing from the beginning what was bound to happen he spent most of his time with his confessor. On the second morning he was lowered into a small boat lying alongside where a man in a mask awaited him. Instructed to 'die like a knight' and to place his neck on the gunwale, his head was finally hacked off by the amateur executioner after six strokes with a rusty sword. His naked body was thrown on the beach at Dover and his head set on a pole beside it. It remained there for several days, under guard, while the local sheriff sent to London for instructions on what was to be done with it. At length the remains of this unfortunate man were taken to his widow and buried with Christian rites in the church of Wingfield in Suffolk.

Margaret's reaction to the death of her friend, one of the first Englishmen she had known, was a blend of horror and fury. She knew, from all the stories reported to her, that he had been regarded as the 'Queen's darling', and she also knew there were two reasons why he had been killed. One was to prevent his recall to power and revenge and the other was to demonstrate the feeling against her. She and Henry mourned his death, but the people openly rejoiced at the murder of a man generally believed to have been responsible for all the nation's ills.

No investigation was ever made and the murderers were never formally identified. Thus it was demonstrated to all that the crown neither could, nor would, protect or avenge those who served it. The spectre of civil war came appreciably closer and assassins grew bolder. On 29 June, Bishop William Ayscough, who had married Henry and Margaret at Titchfield and, as a close friend of Suffolk and a member of his administration was more of a courtier than a priest, was dragged from the church at Edington where he was celebrating Mass, taken five miles away and done to death on a hill overlooking Westbury in Wiltshire. William Booth, Margaret's chancellor, and Lehart, Bishop of Norwich, were both threatened with a similar fate, but their lives may well have been saved by the distraction of Cade's Rebellion which began in June.

Meanwhile, much had been happening in France. As a result of decisions taken by the Parliament which assembled on 6 November 1449 a hopelessly inadequate force of 3,000 men under Sir Thomas Kyriel was sent over to restore the situation in Normandy, and these troops, added to the survivors from fortress garrisons in the province, made up an army of about 5,000 men. Kyriel, a veteran who had learned his soldiering from Henry V and the Duke of Bedford, took command, confident that in any set-piece battle he could thrash the French as they had so often been thrashed before.

On 15 April 1450 the French, under the Comte de Clermont, attacked his position at Formigny, and for the first time the hitherto virtually invincible Bowmen of England found themselves outmatched by a superior weapon, the French artillery. Clermont, with sound tactical sense, had placed his guns as far out on either flank as possible so as to take the massed formation of English archers in enfilade while part of his force worked round to the flank and rear of the enemy position. The guns created havoc. Part of Kyriel's force broke. The French closed in and, giving no quarter, perhaps in revenge for Verneuil, killed nearly 4,000 of their enemies.

After this overwhelming defeat the Duke of Somerset was unable to prevent the French from taking Bayeux and Avranches. Both fortresses were so badly in need of repair that they could not be properly defended, and he himself was driven out of Caen in June after a very feeble resistance. The English fell back on Cherbourg, Charles VII concentrated his forces, attacked it by land and sea and the port surrendered in July.

The whole of Normandy had been lost.

The year 1450 brought one disaster after another to Henry and Margaret. Any other man with Henry's responsibilities and a little more interest in current affairs might well have abandoned himself to despair, but Henry had the comforting conviction that all things are in the hands of God who will arrange matters in His own way. Margaret's faith was not quite so strong. Although she was beginning to realize that politics and politicians are not quite so black or so white as she had imagined at first, she believed that most of her husband's troubles were deliberately caused by his enemies who were simply jealous of the influence and authority of the court faction. These enemies must be overcome, if necessary by armed force, and it would then be possible to restore law, order and financial stability in the country. She never really had any doubt who was leading the forces of rebellion, or who was behind the strange character Jack Cade.

Cade was an Irishman, a one-time soldier in France and, according to some, an outlaw. He called himself John Mortimer, thereby trying to associated himself with the family of Richard Duke of York, whose mother's name had been Anne Mortimer. He collected a large, well-organized and well-disciplined force of men from the county of Kent, established a military camp on Blackheath and issued a manifesto. He protested against taxation and corruption and lawlessness in high places. He blamed the king's ministers, and proposed that the Dukes of York, Norfolk, Exeter and Buckingham should replace the present Council. He claimed, like so many leaders since, to be able to put everything right but did not explain in any detail how it was to be done.

No matter how much truth or wisdom there was in his manifesto, its publication, and indeed the very existence of Cade alias Mortimer were an affront and a challenge to Henry's sovereignty. Henry raised an army to deal with the rebels and rode in arms through the streets of London to lead it in person. The Londoners were delighted. Here at last was some display of the martial spirit of his father, but Margaret refused to let him go out to battle. As things turned out, she was probably right. Cade's force fell back on Sevenoaks and there, in a good defensive position, awaited the attack of a detachment of the royal army. On 24 June 1450 the detachment was defeated and its commander, Sir Humphrey Stafford, was killed. By the first week of July Cade had occupied the City of London and supervised the beheading, under the standard at Cheapside, of the extortionate and much hated Treasurer, Lord Say, and his equally unpopular son-in-law,

ENGLAND and WALES

Sketch map showing principal
places mentioned in the text

Linlithgow
EDINBURGH
Berwick
Holy Island
Bamborough
Roxburgh
Hedgeley Dunstanborough
Moor Alnwick

Hexham
Newcastle Tynemouth

Carlisle

Kirkcudbright

Appleby

Richmond

Isle of Man
Middleham

Tadcaster York
Towton
Clitheroe Ferrybridge
Castleford Pontefract
Wakefield
Ravenspur

Doncaster

Hoylake
Worksop Retford
Beaumaris
Denbigh Chester
Newark

Harlech Eccleshall
Blore Heath Burton Grantham
Market Drayton Kings Lynn
Tutbury Norwich
Shrewsbury Bosworth Stamford
Aberystwyth Leicester Peterborough

Coventry Ely
Wigmore Ludlow Huntingdon Bury St Edmunds
Kenilworth
Mortimer's Cross Leominster Warwick Northampton Cambridge Ipswich
Olney Walden
Hereford Tewkesbury Bedford Dunmow
Cheltenham Edgecote Stony Stratford Pleshey
Gloucester Dunstable Chelmsford
Cirencester Oxford St Albans
Watford Barnet
Wallingford Eton LONDON
Bristol Windsor Greenwich
Bath Reading Rochester
Devizes Sevenoaks Canterbury
Westbury Sandw
Deal
Salisbury Clarendon Dove
Shaftesbury Winchester
Cerne Abbey Southampton Calai
Titchfield Porchester
Exeter Boulogne
Weymouth Isle of Wight

Plymouth
Start Point

E N G L I S H   C H A N N E L

N

0 10 20 30 40 50 Miles

Scale

Cherbourg
Harfleur
Honfleur Rouen

Formigny
Caen

William Cromer, the Sheriff of Kent. In the meantime, at Margaret's instigation, Henry and his court had removed themselves to safety at Kenilworth. This unashamed running away caused much anger, and increased Margaret's unpopularity at a time when she needed all the support she could muster.

After the executions a number of Cade's followers pillaged several houses in the City. The Londoners took counsel with Lord Scales, commanding the garrison of 1,000 troops in the Tower, and on the following day, when Cade tried to come back into London from the Borough, there was a battle for London Bridge which lasted for six hours. At length, on 8 July, the rebels left London on the promise of pardon and the redress of grievances, only to return to Southwark two days later saying it would be ridiculous to give up without any guarantees. Impressed by the hostile attitude of the people of London they withdrew again, towards Rochester, and a price of 1,000 marks (a mark being two-thirds of an English pound) was put on Cade's head. Learning of this, Cade abandoned his rebel force and galloped across country towards the Sussex coast, hoping to escape by boat. He was pursued by a squire named Alexander Iden, who overtook him and slew him in single combat on 12 July.

In August Henry and Margaret went to Canterbury where the leading rebels were tried and punished. Although there were no outward signs of trouble, the people of Kent and Sussex had not by any means been subdued or reassured by the failure of Cade's Rebellion, and in Wiltshire the whole county was prepared to come out in support of the murderers of Bishop Ayscough. The presence of the king and queen in the troubled areas did little to placate rebellious spirits or restore order, as Henry had hoped it would, and it was in this oppressive atmosphere that Richard Duke of York decided to leave his post as the King's Lieutenant in Ireland and come back to England.

His uninvited return, coupled with Cade's claim to kinship – albeit illegitimate – with the duke, was proof enough for Margaret that York was behind the murders of the two bishops and all the trouble in the southern counties. It is possible, though by no means certain, that he did have some underhand connection with what had been going on, but it is equally possible that he was merely well informed and took advantage of the great wave of antipathy building up against Henry's government. York was quick to realize that in all probability quite a lot of Cade's initial influence and success had stemmed from his adoption of the name Mortimer, and his death and subsequent judicial mutilation* had in no way reduced the support York felt certain of attracting. Indeed, the lesson he learned from the rebellion in Kent was that the country, in recoiling from Henry's ministers, was turning to him. He landed at Beaumaris in Anglesea in the middle of August, and though he had brought only a handful of men with him from Ireland, he had a force of more than 4,000 by the time he reached the outskirts of London.

The court had early news of his approach, and Margaret's apprehension was based on York's claim to the throne. He was the direct descendant, admittedly through two women, his mother and great-grandmother, of Lionel Duke of Clarence, the *elder* brother of John of Gaunt from whom Henry VI was descended. Therefore, under the law of primogeniture, it could be said – and undoubtedly was being said by an increasing number of people – that Richard Duke of York had a more valid claim to the crown than Henry, and unless Margaret produced a child, York was justified in considering himself to be the rightful heir to the throne. Margaret had good reason to fear that the people of England might decide that in their own interests it would be better to let the heir take over now, without necessarily waiting for Henry's death.

Henry may well have thought this might be rather a good idea. He could retire to some peaceful spot where he could do a little hunting, to please Margaret who was more keen on it than he was, and spend most of his time in theological study and discussion, leaving all the fearful problems of ruling the country to someone who was really interested in them.

From Margaret's point of view, life without power and wealth was not worth living. The function of kings and queens was to rule. She could not imagine anyone of her own family yielding to any usurper without a ferocious struggle.

So, as York marched on London, gathering support as he came, she and Henry's ministers did their best to counter the new

* His head was stuck up on London Bridge and his quartered remains sent to various 'disaffected' towns in Kent as a deterrent to would-be rebels; a revolting example of the brutality of an age almost as barbarous as the twentieth century.

threat by making Somerset the Constable of England and letting it be known that he, as the direct descendant of John of Gaunt, was the true heir to the House of Lancaster.

The whole question of the succession was in fact prickly with problems. Somerset was the Lancastrian claimant, but York had two claims. Apart from his descent through his mother from Edward III's second son Clarence, he was descended through his father – Richard Earl of Cambridge, executed for treason by Henry V just before he sailed on the Agincourt campaign – from Edward III's fifth son, Edmund Langley, Duke of York.

A situation in which a king such as Henry VI sat upon a throne between rival claimants of the calibre of York and Somerset had all the necessary ingredients of civil war.

Edmund Beaufort, Duke of Somerset, had returned to England on 1 August 1450, bringing the defeated survivors of the siege of Cherbourg and a sad tale of military misfortune. Unfortunately, Margaret, now aged twenty-one, soon established with him the same sort of relationship as she had had with the Duke of Suffolk. Somerset now had her trust and confidence; feelings he did not apparently inspire in many other people although he was the most powerful man in the government. Outside court circles he was generally regarded as the incompetent commander who had failed to hold Normandy – though it is most unlikely that anyone else, in similar circumstances, could have done any better. The three main factors in his defeat were the lack of military resources, the determination of the ordinary people of Normandy to get rid of the English, and the excellence of the French army, particularly its artillery, which Charles VII had built up. Without manpower, material and money in large and regular quantities, sent out from England to maintain a high level of efficiency, no English commander had any hope of defending so large an area, but this was not taken into consideration by all those who were angered and humiliated by the loss of English possessions. They were even more furious when it became clear that Somerset's failure had had no effect on his political career.

Within two weeks of his return he was a member of the King's Council, and this was attributed to Margaret's influence. People felt she had openly rewarded the man who had been instrumental in giving their territory to her uncle and father. She had come to England ostensibly to bring peace and prosperity to both nations, now it appeared that she was the agent who had tricked them out of their overseas dominions, She and Suffolk and Somerset had all been in this together. Suffolk was dead. Somerset took his place in the minds of the people. Margaret was their evil genius. It was hard for her to counter the prejudice mounting up against her.

York disliked Somerset almost as much as he had disliked Suffolk, and for much the same reasons. His animosity had its roots in jealousy, and this was understandable in the light of the preferential treatment, both financial and in terms of promotion, shown to the Beaufort brothers, Edmund and his elder brother John (who had died in 1444) by Suffolk's administration. Since Henry and Margaret had no children, York, as the heir presumptive, considered he should play a leading role in national affairs, and Suffolk, angered by York's criticisms of the way the war in France was being fought, had for several years managed to keep York out of the King's Council. To make matters worse, John Beaufort had been promoted over York's head to a command in France and then elevated to a dukedom in 1443. York, serving at this time as the Governor-General in Normandy, was owed large sums by the Exchequer in arrears of salary, and when he asked for payment he was told to be patient. On the other hand, John Beaufort had been given £25,000 in advance. After York's quarrel with Bishop Moleyns in 1446 the principal command in Normandy was given to Edmund Beaufort (now succeeded to the title) and in 1447 York had been posted to Ireland, on an exceptionally long tour of duty of ten years, although, determined to deal first with his enemy Suffolk, he did not go there until 1449.

In York's opinion, Somerset had made a hopeless mess of affairs in Normandy, yet he had now been promoted again, and it was clear to York that unless he asserted himself and demanded his rights he would be pushed away into obscurity and Somerset would become the heir presumptive. Somerset's election to the King's Council was probably one of the reasons why York came back to London, but there was another, even more pressing.

Although by 1450 York was the most powerful magnate in the kingdom, owning large estates in most English counties and in central and south Wales, and having vast holdings in Ireland which included the earldom of Ulster and several other lordships, he was also in desperate need of money. His income was not in proportion to his acreage – his English and Welsh estates, for example, yielded only £3,500 a year – and when he was given operational command in France (in 1436 and 1437 and from 1440 to 1446) he was expected to pay his officers and garrison troops from his salary. By the end of his tour in 1446 the Exchequer owed him the enormous sum of £38,666. He offered to give up £12,666 on condition that the outstanding £26,000 was paid promptly. It was not; and the crown's debt to him increased by a further £10,000 of unpaid salary for his post in Ireland. He knew very well he was only one creditor in a long queue, and while he was away in Ireland he was likely to remain at the end of it. Without direct influence at court and personal pressure on Henry himself he could not hope for any relief. It therefore became essential for him to try and force himself into the King's Council, to obtain the means for satisfying his own creditors.

This is really why York came to London and why, when the full measure of Henry's bankruptcy became known to him, he set himself up in direct opposition to the House of Lancaster. Money was at the root of the trouble that was to tear England apart.

As his growing force moved through England, York was regarded by the people as a new leader, marching on the capital to remove the corrupt and incompetent government and introduce a new era of justice and peace. He received very little support from the nobility. They saw him as a usurper whose interest in reform was limited to his personal affairs, and at this stage his only supporters were the Duke of Norfolk and the Earl of Devonshire.

His wife Cicely was the youngest of the fourteen children of Ralph, first Earl of Westmorland, and thus one of the great Neville family which, by sheer weight of numbers, was spreading far and wide through the aristocracy, but her kinsmen were not inclined to accept York as a political leader. Concerned only with their individual interests, many of the barons did nothing and waited to see whether the House of York would serve them better than the House of Lancaster.

To Margaret, York was an enemy, and it was obvious to her that despite his placating assurances of good intentions, his aim was to seize the throne. It transpired later that she was perfectly right, but there is some doubt whether this was actually in his mind as he rode towards London. Despite all his failings, Henry VI had been on the throne for nearly twenty-nine years, and York must have known that at the moment he had nothing like enough support to offer a serious challenge.

Whether or not Henry shared Margaret's opinions it is difficult to say. He was certainly apprehensive, and determined to avoid civil war. He received York in audience at the end of September and, when York complained of the charges of treason being made against him, said that no formal indictments had been made and so far as he was concerned he regarded 'his cousin of York' as a loyal and faithful subject. York then spoke of the general grievance that there was no justice in the land, and added that a number of people whose actions appeared to be treasonable – and no doubt he was referring to Somerset – ought to be imprisoned and brought to trial. Henry side-stepped this by replying that it would be wrong for him to accept the advice of only one man, and in any case he proposed to set up a council to consider the whole question of the legal system. He hoped York would be a member.

With this, York had to be content. Since he was the great upholder of government by council there was nothing he could say when Henry turned his point against him.

A new Parliament met on 6 November 1450, in an atmosphere of considerable tension; London seemed to be full of armed retainers. Most people expected York to press for a decision on the succession, but he could get no support from the Lords, who had no wish to see Henry displaced by someone they regarded as a self-seeking trouble-maker. York then launched a major attack against Somerset, demanding his impeachment on the grounds of his failure in France.

Rioting broke out on 30 November. Westminster Hall was surrounded by a mob calling for action against the 'false traitors' and next day a gang of ex-soldiers attacked Somerset's lodgings at Blackfriars. He was rescued by York and Devonshire, and taken in Devonshire's barge down river to the Tower. This led to a rumour that he had been arrested but he went there for his own safety. York, determined to appear as the champion of law and order, would have lost all credibility if he had allowed the rabble to murder Somerset, even though he was his sworn enemy. Looters became active in the City, and York underlined his authority by ordering the instant execution in Cheapside of a man caught in the act. It was the equivalent of a declaration of martial law, and Henry's response was to lead a splendid procession of lords and their followers through the City as a demonstration of his own leadership and authority, and to indicate to York that he should mind his own business. Another royal gesture was the committing to prison of Thomas Young, the Member for Bristol, for proposing in the Commons that York should be formally recognized as the heir presumptive.

The Commons, strongly Yorkist and led by the Speaker, Sir William Oldhall, who was York's chamberlain, renewed the attack on Henry's ministers after the Christmas recess by petitioning for the banishment of about thirty people. Most of them were Margaret's friends and supporters and included Suffolk's widow, William Booth and Somerset himself. Again Henry evaded the issue with vague undertakings, but he gave his real answer by making Somerset head of the royal household and elevating Margaret's chamberlain, William Booth, to the archbishopric of York.

Parliament was dissolved in May 1451. On the surface it seemed that York had not achieved anything, and Somerset's position at court was even stronger than it had been in the previous year. Yet the real outcome of events that winter was that York could see his way ahead more clearly. He realized now that though Henry did not lack personal courage in a crisis, his actions were dictated by his advisers, and his chief adviser was his wife. Somerset was still his principal enemy at court, but Margaret was his main opponent. York saw, too, that the issue between him and Somerset could now only be resolved by armed conflict, and if he was to dominate the King's Council the only road to success lay across the battlefield.

Because of the opposition to him in the Lords, York left London and apparently did nothing for the rest of the year 1451. The calm in the capital after the rioting in the previous December seemed to reassure Henry, whose religion filled him with optimism and charity and encouraged him to believe in the fundamental goodness of mankind. Margaret, far more practical and shrewd, recognized the lull for what it was, a pause while poison gathered beneath the skin of society. The eruption would come, and she began to take precautions.

She and Henry spent most of the summer on a tour of southern and eastern England and the Midlands. They were accompanied by the royal justices, and Somerset made all the arrangements. Various people involved in the recent disturbances were tried and punished, and the king and queen returned to London knowing that the majority of the great nobles were still loyal to the crown. York remained on his estates in the Welsh Marches, and from his castle at Ludlow sent out a stream of propaganda aimed at attracting the attention and support of the ordinary people. If he was to fight he needed an army. He knew that battles are won, in the end, by soldiers, and if a commander is to be successful he cannot have too many of them.

In January 1452 he issued a proclamation blaming Somerset for the state of the country and announcing that with the help of his friends he would march against him. With the Earl of Devonshire and Lord Cobham as his chief supporters he set out from Ludlow on a second march to London. Henry, with his force, moved to Coventry to intercept him and sent messengers to tell York to meet him there. Ignoring this invitation York swung southwards, and with the royal army in pursuit went straight for London and found the gates closed against him. He had to go back up the river as far as Kingston to find a crossing place, for his next objective was Kent, where he hoped to enlist the malcontents who had followed Cade. He moved his army into a defensive position at Dartford, behind the river Darent. Henry drew up his troops on Blackheath.

Battle was avoided only by the united efforts of the Bishops of Winchester and Ely and the Earl of Salisbury and his son Warwick. All were resolved that the long war in France should not be followed by a worse conflict in England.

Although York had sworn that he 'would have the Duke of Somerset' the mediators were able to arrange a meeting between Henry and York on the strength of a promise by Henry that Somerset would be 'had unto ward to answer such articles as the Duke of York should lay unto his charge'. York was told by the delegation from the king that this meant Somerset would be arrested and brought to trial for his behaviour in Normandy, but York did not appreciate the basic weakness of his position. The people of Kent had made no move to join him and, trapped in the area between the Darent, the Thames and the Medway, his way back to the Welsh Marches was blocked by the royal army on Blackheath. Nevertheless, he had insisted, all the way along, that his quarrel was with Somerset and not with the king or his royal authority, and being a man of his word himself he did not doubt that of the envoys.

He therefore had a most unpleasant shock when, having sent his army home, he went into Henry's tent at Blackheath and found that Somerset was still very much in power while he himself was made a prisoner and forced to ride as such through London. At length, on 10 March, having taken a solemn oath of allegiance to Henry, publicly in St Paul's, he was set free.

This resort to trickery separated the court into opposing factions as well defined as those in the days of Cardinal Beaufort's long feud with Humphrey Duke of Gloucester, and Gloucester's vendetta against Suffolk. On one side stood York, the challenger, and on the other, Somerset, defending the position of authority which, had he been an upright man, might have been unassailable. In the middle was Henry, trying to keep the peace and yearning for a quiet life. Just behind, or on one side of Somerset was Margaret, his ardent supporter who felt that in his hands the House of Lancaster would be safe.

She had now lived in England for seven years and it was clear to her just how tenuous was her husband's hold upon the throne. Furthermore, the members of the court party were beginning to realize that their rank, offices and estates, being inextricably linked with the fortunes of Lancaster, might well be dependent upon this French girl of twenty-three who seemed to be capable of arousing extremes of affection and hatred. Margaret herself had lost all her illusions, acquired in her father's 'court', about honour and chivalry. She knew now that in politics there are no rules and only one motive – to gain and hold power – and this knowledge affected any tendency she might have developed towards con- ciliation and compromise. In trying to sustain her position and increase her authority in a world in which the place and function of females were clearly defined, her sex and her nationality were formidable disadvantages. Because she was a woman she was expected to remain in the background and do what she was told. Circumstances still forced her to act through third parties – her husband or his ministers – though she was reaching the point where she was able to separate her affections from her trust.

It was her misfortune that paradoxically her clarity of purpose

clouded her judgement of character, although, in surveying the
advisers available to her, it is not easy to recognize any, apart
perhaps from the old Duke of Buckingham, who were worthy of
implicit trust. Like her mother and grandmother before her,
danger merely strengthened her resolve and opposition was only
a challenge inviting attack.

Sadly enough, Somerset was just such a man as Suffolk had
been. It was almost as if he deliberately courted unpopularity by
the way he exploited the advantages of his position. He knew
what passions had been aroused by his quarrel with York yet he
made no attempt to close the widening rift threatening to split
the whole country. Leading Yorkists were excluded from the
King's Council, nothing was done about the growing number of
grievances throughout the land, and it seemed as if with arrogant
self-confidence this royal favourite, who had failed conspicuously
against the French, was looking forward to meeting his political
enemies on the battlefield.

6   Birth of an Heir (1451-1455)

After his successes in Normandy, Charles VII threw the full
weight of his army against the province of Guienne in south-
western France which had been in the hands of the English for
more than three hundred years. Practically no attempt was made
to defend it. Apart from the lack of money, Henry's ministers
and the nobility were all too preoccupied with the approaching
war in England to aid the under-strength garrisons of dilapidated
fortresses which were all that remained of the English empire in
France.

The French campaign began in earnest in the spring of 1451
and the weak and scattered English detachments were forced to
surrender one by one, often without a fight because resistance
was hopeless. Only Castillon, St Emilion, Libourne and Rioux
were carried by assault. The English concentrated what was left
of their forces in the area of Bordeaux. In the summer of the
following year the Counts of Dunois, Penthièvre, Foix and
Armagnac, leading separate columns, converged on Guienne
from four different directions. The town of Blaye on the Gironde
was made to capitulate, other towns declared for Charles, and by
the autumn the English forces had been penned up in the towns
of Bordeaux, Bayonne and Fronsac. It was then agreed that if
these garrisons were not relieved and reinforced by troops from
England by the festival of St John the Evangelist (27 December
1452) they too would surrender. Throughout the campaign such
reinforcements as had arrived were too few and too late to have
any effect, and no more came. Bordeaux and Fronsac opened their
gates on the appointed day but the garrison of Bayonne tried to
fight on and was reduced by Count Gaston de Foix.

Thus the last of the great heritage of Eleanor of Aquitaine was
lost, and England's sole possessions in France had been reduced
to the town and castle of Calais and a small area around them.
It is one of the ironic twists of history that Henry V's great

conquests had been made possible by the disunity in France, the rifts between the nobility and the ineffectiveness of a mad king. All these conquests had been lost because of the divisions between the nobility in England and the weakness of Henry V's son.

Yet the continental war was not over. In Normandy, and in most places in France, the expulsion of the English was regarded with deep satisfaction, but in Guienne there was a large proportion of English 'settlers', merchants and ex-soldiers, and plenty of people who were loyal men of Aquitaine but not of France. They began to realize they had little to gain and much to lose by being brought into the French national system and given French governors. Forgetting all their previous complaints against the English – whose rule, often enough, had been largely nominal – they remembered with regret the happy days when the red cross of England had waved over their prosperous ports and cities. Early in 1453 the lords of the Bordelais, chafing under recently imposed French regulations, decided to call the English back. A deputation consisting of the Sieurs of Duras, l'Esparre, Montferand, Rauzan and L'Anglade went secretly to London and, difficult though the situation was, Somerset explained to Henry the advantages to be gained in the conflict with the Duke of York if some effort were made to recover what had been lost in France.

A force of 5,000 men was raised and command of it was offered to the old soldier whom the French called '*le roi Talabot*'. Though in his eighty-sixth year the old man accepted it with enthusiasm. On landing in France the Earl of Shrewsbury was acclaimed as a deliverer, and the nobles of the province brought strong contingents to his standard at Bordeaux. In the heat of a long, dry summer the flame of insurrection ran unchecked through the countryside and once again the red cross appeared over most of the towns of Guienne.

Charles VII, whose main army was engaged in a campaign against the Count of Savoy, reacted swiftly. While his troops were marching westwards across France from the Alps he tried to avoid active operations by promising better government for the people of Guienne. Since they remained rebellious his force advanced against the towns on the Dordogne and the Garonne, putting down the rebellion with the characteristic severity which the French reserve for dealing with their internal problems. In July 1453 they besieged Castillon, about twenty-six miles up the

Dordogne, east of Bordeaux, and Shrewsbury led his force out to relieve it.

In the half-light of dawn on 17 July, Shrewsbury fell upon an enemy force, took it by surprise, cut it to pieces and, driving in the French outposts, launched an attack on the main besieging force in its trenches. The French position was strong and well-defended by bombards firing heavy stone shot, but Shrewsbury had nearly succeeded in carrying it when he was suddenly attacked in the flank by a relieving force led by the Count of Penthièvre. Pulling back from the siege-works Shrewsbury's men formed up in good order and prepared to fight their way back to Bordeaux, but at this moment Shrewsbury was struck from his grey percheron by a cannon shot. The French put in a savage counter-attack. Shrewsbury, unable to rise, was killed as he lay on the ground and his son was slain while trying to protect him. His troops fled, about 1,000 were taken prisoner and there was no one to rally the rest. Penthièvre followed up, laid siege to Bordeaux and two months later, on 10 October, the city was starved into submission.

Thus ended the last land operation of the Hundred Years' War, and thus died another of Margaret's close friends. Sadly, the death of gallant old John Talbot, Earl of Shrewsbury – to the French, one of the great heroes of the Hundred Years' War – and that of his son, passed almost unnoticed in England, though Margaret and Henry, in particular, were profoundly affected by the news. The men who had lost their lives in trying to regain the irretrievable were blamed for their failure, although it had been made inevitable by Henry and his ministers. Perhaps Henry realized this.

When Parliament met at Reading on 6 March 1453 it had lost the strong Yorkist flavour of the previous session. Margaret had learned a great deal since coming to England, and she had used her charm and personality to great effect in her recent tour of the midlands and the south with Henry. Whereas he impressed people with his innate courtesy and piety, she inspired them to give their support. In the Angevin tradition, she required not merely approval for her cause but active and whole-hearted participation, and though she seems to have had so little success with her written appeals – possibly because her correspondents resented her interference – she could be extremely alluring when she chose. It is a tragedy that her partiality, in the end so destructive, prevented her from applying her powers of persuasion to the enemies of her party. Both York and his son Edward Earl of March were remarkably susceptible to pretty women, and one with Margaret's attractions might even have prevented the civil war.

Certainly her persuasiveness, no doubt aided by Somerset's money and influence, had so telling an effect on the knights and squires she met on her travels in the country that one of the first actions of Parliament on assembling was to cancel the petition of 1450 to banish Somerset and his adherents from court. The Commons then went on to vote Henry the money he needed so badly and to provide him with resources to pay 20,000 archers for six months whenever he should require them for the defence of the realm. This force was to defend not just the throne but the country, because there was now a genuine fear that Charles VII, encouraged by his victories in Normandy and Guienne, might launch an invasion which, in the present stage of national defence, could be embarrassingly successful. Even if this threat did not come to anything, Henry had now been provided with an army which he could call out to defend himself against far more likely aggression from the Duke of York.

This represented a considerable triumph for Somerset and his party, and was a complete reversal of the trend of previous Parliaments – probably because the sudden appearance of rival armies at Dartford and Blackheath had shown the Commons just how close the country had come to civil war. No doubt many of them agreed with York's demands for reform but his quarrel with Somerset was obviously personal and vindictive, and there were signs that Somerset's administration might be pulling itself together. This was at the time when Bordeaux had just been recovered and a certain amount of action was being taken to protect English vessels in coastal waters from French pirates. Everybody, except York and his followers, was frightened of civil war, the ordinary people had no wish to become involved in any struggle for power between the great magnates, and York was seen to be the threat to the present armed and uneasy peace.

Thus, in the summer of 1453, the tide of opinion turned in Henry's favour and flowed strongly against York. He had lost not only the goodwill of the country gentry who filled the seats in Parliament but the support of those people who provided the rank and file of an army. They were not concerned with politics. They wanted good and stable government. York had never had much influence in the Lords, and those who supported him were fewer than ever. Norfolk had abandoned him and both Cobham and Devonshire had been imprisoned after his abortive attempt at a coup. Neither had yet been released. Even the Earls of Warwick and Worcester and Lord Cromwell were, at this moment, prepared to support the crown while there was any threat of civil war.

To Margaret, all this was eminently satisfactory. Her enemy stood alone, discredited and with no suggestion of any sort of Yorkist party behind him. On 6 March 1453 his Lieutenancy of Ireland was taken from him and given to the Earl of Wiltshire. York retired into private life. Then, within a few months, two events completely transformed the whole political situation.

In August 1453, about a month after Shrewsbury's defeat and death at Castillon, Henry suddenly became very ill. He suffered a shock, described at the time as a 'fright' but there is no explanation of what it was. All we do know is that he lost his memory and lay for long periods unable to speak or move. His contemporaries attributed his condition to necromancy – the obvious explanation then – and there has been much speculation since, on the lines that his stupor may have been form of schizophrenia, and so on. Inevitably his breakdown has been related to his grandfather's initial fit of madness, also believed to have been caused by a sudden fright – in the case of Charles VI of France, the strange appearance of the no doubt hairy and grubby hermit shouting at him in the forest,* but Henry had been under very great stress for a long time. For the previous three years he had been increasingly upset and depressed by such things as the baronial feuds, the murders of the bishops and Cade's Rebellion. Moreover he had been made to do a great deal of travelling, which he never enjoyed, in the hope that by showing him to the people order would be restored and loyalty regained. It exhausted him, although he was only

---

* There is another story that Charles VI's fit was started by a blinding flash of sunlight reflected into his eyes from a burnished helmet or the blade of a halberd, but there was a considerable difference between the initial symptoms. Charles tried to kill men in his escort; Henry became virtually unconscious.

thirty-two, and he was also very alarmed by the way things were so obviously getting out of control. The discrediting of York may have removed the immediate threat of civil war but it had not solved any of the problems still outstanding at the time when York came over from Ireland. The shock which tipped Henry over the edge into the chasm of depression may well have been the news of the débâcle at Castillon.

Henry had this breakdown while he was staying in the royal hunting lodge at Clarendon in Wiltshire, and Margaret and the ministers who were with her felt it was imperative to carry on as if nothing had happened. He might soon recover; but in any case, Margaret had a very special reason for keeping things going at all cost. For the first time in eight years of marriage she was pregnant.

It must have been an appalling situation for her. If her child was a boy, she carried within her the solution to the whole problem of the succession. York and Somerset might still be rival claimants, but on a lower plane of urgency, and York, by his recent activities and the failure of his attempt to put matters to the test of battle, had lost all support and was virtually out of the running. Even if she had a girl she would have shown she was not barren and the next child could be male.

Just when it seemed that so many pressing difficulties would be overcome, Henry's breakdown threw everything back into the balance. If he did not get well quickly a Grand Council would have to be called, and that might lead to a regency. There could be no question of Margaret herself, seven months pregnant, taking on such responsibilities until she had had her child and recovered from her confinement, and so York, as the heir presumptive, would probably be the regent. The very position he had sought to gain by battle would drop peacefully into his lap. And if he did become regent, by the time she was on her feet again he would be well entrenched and the House of Lancaster would be on the wane.

Everything depended on Henry's health. Margaret kept him out of sight at Clarendon and for two months Somerset and the other ministers behaved as if everything was perfectly normal. But servants see things, and people talk. The fiction that the king was merely indisposed could not be maintained indefinitely, and the longer the secret was kept, the greater was the danger of it being discovered.

Early in October the court returned to Westminster and on
13 October, attended by her great friend Eleanor Beauchamp,
Somerset's wife, and her ladies, Margaret gave birth to a boy.

It was now impossible to delay any longer the summoning of
the Great Council, and Somerset, in Henry's name, announced
that 'among other things that moved his Highness [to call it] one
was to set rest and union betwixt the lords of this land'. York
was not invited.

The Great Council assembled at Westminster and immediately
insisted that a belated summons be sent to York. The messenger
rode off on 23 October. When York arrived his behaviour was
faultless, and no doubt his restraint was a measure of his
uncertainty about his own position. Yet, soon after he had taken
his place in the Council, a number of peers began to seek his
company. Margaret had been afraid this would happen if he came
back into public life, and it must have been disturbing for her to
be told that Norfolk, Worcester – who had been made Treasurer
in the previous year – Warwick and his father Salisbury all
appeared to be friendly with him. Another shock must have been
the discovery that the King's half-brothers, Edmund and Jasper
Tudor, were apparently giving York their support.

Henry's mother, Catherine of France, showed scant interest in
him when he was little. No one knows exactly when she married
Owen Tudor; there was a lot of trouble about it because he was
only one of her late husband's squires who had risen to be a clerk
of her wardrobe, and it was all kept very quiet, but she went off
to live with him, bear his two sons and then die on 3 January
1437 at the age of thirty-five – the same age as Henry V when he
died. Henry could so easily have ignored his half-brothers but
his sense of family loyalty was strong. He made sure that the two
little boys were properly brought up. In 1452, worried by York's
opposition and feeling he might need all the friends he could find
among the nobility, Henry had elevated them both to the peerage;
Edmund became Earl of Richmond and Jasper Earl of Pembroke.
But there was no question, during the winter of 1453, of anything
in the nature of an alliance, and York's association with Richmond
and Pembroke did not even become a friendship.

Margaret's child was christened early in November 1453 and
given the name of Edward, possibly because he had been born
on the feast day of St Edward (the Confessor). It was a sensible

choice because just then the name was more popular than that of Henry. William Waynfleet, Bishop of Winchester, the friend and confidant of the King, performed the dual ceremony of baptism and confirmation in Westminster Abbey. The Duke of Somerset, Kemp the Archbishop of Canterbury and the Duchess of Buckingham were the godparents. The baby was wrapped in a velvet mantle embroidered with pearls and precious stones, and lined with fine linen so that tender skin would not be scratched; this christening robe cost £554 16s 8d.

A few days later, Margaret was churched at the palace of Westminster in the presence of ten duchesses, eight countesses, one viscountess and sixteen baronesses.

As soon as she was strong enough to travel she took her husband and child to Windsor, where it was easier to conceal Henry from prying eyes, and she was so successful in keeping the Yorkist nobles away from him that very few people knew what was wrong with him or what his condition really was. Occasionally word got out, as for example in a letter written to the Duke of Norfolk early in the New Year of 1454:

At the Prince's coming to Windsor the Duke of Buckingham took him in his arms and presented him to the King in godly wise, beseeching the King to bless him. And the King gave no manner of answer. Nevertheless the Duke abode still with the Prince by the King. And when he could no manner of answer have, the Queen came in and took the Prince in her arms and presented him in like form as the Duke had done, desiring that he should bless it. But all their labour was in vain, for they departed thence without any answer or countenance, saving only that once he looked on the Prince and cast down his eyes again, without any more.

At Windsor, on Pentecost Sunday 1454, the baby was created Prince of Wales, Duke of Cornwall and Earl of Chester.

The arrival of young Edward did little to decrease the odium surrounding his mother, and at a time when she herself must have been rejoicing it was made clear to her that few, apart from her particular friends, shared her happiness. The disasters in France were still at the root of her unpopularity, and when her child was born her enemies said Somerset was probably the father. The more charitable hoped that the birth of an heir to the throne might bind her more closely to England, for most people felt she was 'too well affected to France'. Many felt the Duke of York had a good claim to the throne, and since nothing could be worse than the present state of affairs, they looked to York as the hope for the future. To them the birth of Edward only made everything worse because there was now little chance of any peaceful succession by the House of York.

By the last week of November 1453 York had managed to establish himself as Henry's regent in all but name, and his supporters in the Commons had arranged for the 'Lancastrian' Parliament that had assembled at Reading to be prorogued until February. Just before Christmas, Somerset was arrested and deprived of the governorship of Calais. The appointment was given to Warwick. Calais could be a useful refuge in time of trouble, a base from which to arrange any necessary alliances with, for instance, the Duke of Burgundy, and it could be a springboard for military operations. York felt it would be as well to place it in the hands of an ally as trustworthy as the Earl of Warwick.

During this period of increasing tension, while the barons mobilized their forces and every lodging in London was filled with the armed followers of both factions, Henry lay in a stupor, speechless and sometimes hardly able to stand. Margaret recovered rapidly from her confinement and, giving most of her time to her new son and sick husband, she was careful to keep York constantly on edge, wondering if and when Henry would regain his reason and thus deprive him of his authority.

During the months of November and December she may either have been a little unsure of herself or preoccupied with her domestic problems, but, with the examples of Yolande of Aragon and Isabelle of Lorraine to inspire her, by the end of the year she had come to the conclusion that the regency during her husband's illness should be hers by right. Nevertheless, knowing how critical the situation was, and that any incautious attempt to snatch the reins of power might precipitate a revolution, for the moment she was content to await an opportunity. She held audiences and courts as queen but left all public affairs in the hands of the Great Council. She had plenty of reminders of the impending crisis. Humphrey Stafford, Duke of Buckingham, and one of her firm friends, gave orders for the making of 2,000 'bands' or scarves embroidered with the Stafford knot; badges for his private army. The elderly Kemp, acting as Head of State during the king's 'indisposition', told his servants 'to be prepared with all such habiliments of war as they knew how to use, in the defence of his person'. He was afraid of meeting the same fate as Moleyns and Ayscough.

In the middle of January 1454, when it became known that Parliament would reassemble at Reading on 11 February, Margaret decided to take matters into her own hands. She prepared a Bill which was to be her claim to the regency, for submission to Parliament as soon as the Commons met. It consisted of four Articles:

1. That she desires to have the whole rule of this land.
2. That she may appoint the Chancellor, Treasurer, Privy Seal and all other officers of this land, with sheriffs, and all other officers that the king should make.
3. That she may give all the bishoprics of this land, and all other benefices belonging to the king's gift.
4. That she may have sufficient livelihood assigned to her for the king, the prince and herself.

News of her intention to make this petition was not well received. This was the winter in which Charles VII recovered Guienne, and popular feeling in England was running very strongly against anything and everything French. Yet York and his friends regarded Margaret's petition as a serious challenge, and Lancastrians who had been much discouraged by the virtual disappearance of the king, the arrest of Somerset and the rapidly growing influence of the Duke of York, took heart and looked to Margaret as their leader.

Parliament met at Reading on the appointed date and immediately adjourned for three days, to meet again at Westminster on 14 February. In the meantime York was to act as the King's Lieutenant. Margaret put in her claim at once but the Commons, reluctant to come to grips with anything so controversial, delayed their decision for as long as possible by turning first to other business. They asked for information about the Great Council, reminding the Lords to have special care 'for the peace of this land'. There was much talk of peace but nothing much was done to disperse the looming threat of war.

The sudden death, from natural causes, of Archbishop Kemp on 22 March 1454 made it impossible to postpone any longer the appointing of a regent, although the Lancastrian party tried to hold matters up by saying Henry was getting better. On 3 April Richard Duke of York was formally appointed 'Protector and Defender of the Realm and Church, and Principal Councillor of the King'. Much care had been taken over the wording of this title, making sure there was no suggestion of sovereignty, and it was made clear that York's authority would cease as soon as the Prince of Wales came of age. There was no question now of York being the heir presumptive, and Somerset, although imprisoned in the Tower but busily sending out spies and agents all over the country to organize demonstrations of support in the hope of procuring his release, was no longer the Lancastrian heir.

Even so, Margaret, who by now had no illusions about political motives or loyalties, was well aware that much could happen before her son Edward grew up, and since it was generally understood that the regency would also come to an end in the seemingly unlikely event of Henry regaining his reason, she redoubled her efforts to protect the rights of the two people she loved best, both of whom were helpless. Henry still showed no signs of improvement and her son, whom she adored with a passion inspired by the sudden fulfilment of long-frustrated motherhood, lay in his cradle happily unaware of his place in history.

It is ironical that Margaret of Anjou, so reviled by many historians as the symbol of unrelenting hatred and cruelty, and accused of 'a savagery which belonged to nearly all the members of the younger House of Anjou', was in fact motivated by that most Christian of emotions, love. If only that love could have flowed in a wider channel she might have been a very much happier woman. Rudyard Kipling has written of the deadliness of the female of the species, and Margaret was really dangerous only when she was defending her family. Her attitude and her actions in the face of the threat posed by the Duke of York to the future of the House of Lancaster are not only understandable but logical. She knew that unless she protected, and if necessary fought for, the rights of her child he would never be King of England.

York wasted no time in taking advantage of the responsibility bestowed on him by Parliament. His brother-in-law Richard Neville, Earl of Salisbury, was made Lord Chancellor, and Thomas Bourchier, Bishop of Ely, took the place of Archbishop Kemp. As soon as he could, the new Protector and Defender of the Realm put an end to the feuds between the great families in the north by rallying his supporters in the northern counties and thus curbing the activities of the powerful Percy family; particularly Henry Percy, Earl of Northumberland, and his son Lord Egremont. Trouble in Somerset and Devon was checked by the arrest of the Duke of Exeter, chief Lancastrian noble in the south-west. Yet York took no action to bring either Exeter or Somerset to trial because there was too much support for the Lancastrians in London and the provinces. Having become the most powerful noble in the land by perfectly legitimate means he had no intention of prejudicing his future by inviting civil war.

Margaret, now the symbol and champion of the Lancastrian cause, knew that although Henry was in a state of mental and physical collapse he still had an enormous advantage over those who opposed his sovereignty. He was the anointed king whose father and grandfather had worn the crown before him, and the hostile feeling in the country had not been directed against him personally. There were very few people who, at this stage, were prepared to take definite steps to depose him. He was the rightful king, and York was not even any longer the rightful heir.

Margaret had also learned one valuable lesson from the failure of her petition for the regency; if she was to rule, she had to rule through Henry, and she therefore began to devote all her energies to restoring him to health. She decided, very wisely, that this could not be done either in London or Windsor, where politicians were still liable to disturb him. For example, when Archbishop Kemp died, the Lords sent a delegation to 'discover his wishes' on the question of a successor. It was really only a matter of getting Henry to approve their nominee, and though they did everything they could, over a period of several days, 'they could get no answer or sign'. Margaret knew how bad for him this sort of thing must be, and so she took him and her little son away to the peace and tranquillity of the staunchly Lancastrian city of Coventry, where she nursed her husband devotedly all through the year of 1454.

If her motive for trying to bring him back to health had been merely her own ambition, her own hunger for personal power, it is possible that by the autumn she would have given up. In March that year a medical commission consisting of John Arundel, John Faceby and William Hatclyff, physicians, and Robert Wareyn and John Marshall, surgeons, had been appointed to attend the king, but since no one knew how to treat mental illness there was not much the doctors could do. Henry made no progress, and for a long time his response to all Margaret's care was negligible. But she loved him, and never was her affection and compassion stronger than during these long and apparently hopeless months.

Then, at last, all her love and care and infinite patience were rewarded. The first signs of improvement were apparent as autumn turned to winter, and on 9 January of the following year, 1455, Edmund Clere wrote to his cousin John Paston:

> Blessed be God. The King is well-amended, and hath been since Christmas Day . . . on Monday afternoon the Queen came to him and brought my Lord Prince with her. And then he asked what the Prince's name was, and the Queen told him, Edward; and then he held up his hands and thanked God thereof. And he said he never knew till that time, nor wist not what was said to him, nor wist not where he had been while he hath been sick till now. And he asked who was godfathers, and the Queen told him, and he was well pleased.

It must have been marvellous for Margaret. After sixteen months of constant anxiety, while her enemies prospered and she was unable to intervene, everything she had hoped for began to happen. Bishop Waynfleet announced that Henry had recovered completely and had spoken to him 'as well as ever he did', but in fact, though Henry did make a remarkable recovery which must have been entirely the result of Margaret's nursing and her insistence that he be kept away from the stress of 'business', he was never quite the same as he had been before his breakdown. He was more frail, more dependent, and more easily upset.

Although from Margaret's point of view Henry's recovery brought so welcome a change in the pattern of her misfortunes, and must have seemed like a direct answer to prayer, there is no doubt that for the country it was a disaster. During the time of Henry's illness York had been ruling firmly and well, meeting the demand of the people for stable government by a council which included all the great peers of the realm and not just those of a faction which exploited power for personal gain. Since most of the lords met in council, and those most likely to cause trouble – for instance, Somerset, Exeter and Devonshire – were under restraint, the feuding in the provinces had virtually ceased. There was peace in the land and the fear of civil war had receded.

If the system had been allowed to continue; if Henry had remained a mere figurehead, wearing the crown as the rightful king but letting York deal with all the mechanics of government, there would have been no civil war. But to Margaret it was the duty of royalty to rule, and if for any reason the king could not reign himself, his queen must reign for him. This was strictly in the tradition of her upbringing, and the idea that any 'over-mighty subject' should be the real source of power was, for her, out of the question.

Nevertheless, it is perhaps conceivable that Henry's long illness might have influenced her to accept the delegation of some of the royal authority to a deputy, if only to make things easier for her husband, had it not been for two factors which made this impossible. One was the birth of her son and the other was York himself. The Prince of Wales was the heir to the throne, and Margaret considered it to be her duty to make sure he succeeded his father. York, having tasted power as the Protector was not likely to relinquish it willingly, and if he was able to continue as the equivalent of regent he would see to it that the succession was Yorkist. Margaret was convinced of this, and furthermore, York was a personal enemy. They hated each other, each seeing the other as the one great obstacle in their plans for the future.

Sincerely believing that all her efforts must now be concentrated on maintaining the rights of her husband and child, Margaret had no such word as compromise in her vocabulary. She was the leader of the Lancastrian party, and far from ever attempting, or even being able, to unite the court factions in loyalty to the crown, she led one against the other and there was no hope of peace. Philippe de Commines summed up the situation when he wrote of the civil war:

It was upon a difference that happened at court ... the King not having wisdom enough to compose it, it grew to that height ... and the Queen would have acted much more prudently in endeavouring to have adjusted the dispute between them than in saying 'I am of this party, and will maintain it'.

The crown, which should have remained above the level of squabbles between the barons, sank into the thick of them, and for this, despite her admirable motives, Margaret was responsible.

She did not delay. York's regency, or protectorate, was brought to an end and once again he was excluded from the King's Council. In February 1455 Somerset was released from the Tower and Exeter was freed a month later. On 6 March Somerset was once again given the captaincy of Calais. All the Yorkists were eased out of authority. Salisbury, forced to resign from the post of Lord Chancellor, was replaced by Thomas Bourchier, the Archbishop of Canterbury, who was always able to adjust himself to any political climate, and the Earl of Worcester was made to hand over the Treasury to the Earl of Shrewsbury, old Talbot's second son.

Later on in March, York left London and went to his estates in the north where, with the help of Salisbury and Warwick, he began to raise and equip an army. Margaret, aided principally by Somerset and Exeter, mobilized the fighting strength of Lancaster. All the great barons began to call up their retainers and prepare for war. Though some undoubtedly felt that matters of principle and honour were involved, the majority were prepared to join in because there might be something personal to be gained; in terms of the lands of an opponent or a position of influence at court. Others took up arms to defend what they had, fearing what might happen if their enemies should win.

Thus, at the beginning of the war there was no clear-cut conflict, no well-defined divisions of the baronage split between rival causes. It was not a question of the House of York seeking to topple the House of Lancaster from the throne. The fight was not between the king and his rebellious lords. The civil war began as a personal and bitter quarrel between Richard Duke of York and Edmund Beaufort, Duke of Somerset, over who should control the government. It might never have risen above that level if Margaret had not taken Somerset's part and, by so doing, in due course turned a brawl between barons into a dynastic war. Nothing happened for six weeks, and then Somerset called a meeting of the Great Council, to assemble at Leicester on 21 May; the declared object being to make provision for the king's safety. The supporters of York and the Nevilles were not invited. It thus became perfectly obvious that Somerset's real purpose was to collect together enough strength to enable him to arrest York, who was ordered to wait upon the king at Leicester, with a small following. York paid no attention to the summons. He knew the time had come. Gathering all his resources he set out, not for Leicester but for London, and he marched with such speed that when the court, on its way to Leicester, had travelled only as far as Watford, Somerset learned that York and his army, outnumbering the royal forces by three to two, were approaching St Albans, less than eight miles away.

The situation in the royal camp became somewhat confused. Quite a number of the nobles were by no means the enemies of York; they were simply accompanying the king on his journey to the meeting of the Great Council.

During the night of 21/22 May Henry held a council of war. Several nobles advised the king to remain where he was, at Watford, but the Duke of Buckingham advocated a move to St Albans, possibly because he was convinced that York would come to terms and, being now an old man, steadfast in his loyalty to Henry, he wanted to get the whole thing over.

The king's troops entered St Albans at first light and at once made preparations to defend it, although the old rampart and ditch had long since fallen into disrepair. The main roads through the town were barricaded with beams, and one can only hope that the houses of the unfortunate citizens were not torn down to provide the timber – soldiers have always shown a splendid disregard for other people's property when constructing defensive positions. Lodging for the king was found in St Peter's Street, little more than a hundred yards from York's army, encamped in Key Field, and parleying began almost at once. Buckingham acted for the king, and Mowbray Herald for the Duke of York. York, protesting his loyalty to the crown, insisted that his quarrel was only with Somerset and he demanded that 'such persons as he should accuse' be handed over to him. Henry refused. Neither side would yield. The Royal Standard was raised in St Peter's

Street; a symbolic act signifying that thereafter all who fought against the king were automatically traitors.

York's force advanced with banners flying and closed with the king's troops at the barricades. The initial attack was held, but Warwick, now aged twenty-seven, led his archers through the back gardens and broke through Buckingham's defences. In the mêlée of hand-to-hand fighting which followed, Somerset, mortally wounded, fell at the doorway of the Castle Inn in St Peter's Street, and the battle, having lasted about an hour, was over.

There is a story that Margery Jourdemayne, the famous Witch of Eye who had been hanged in 1441 for her part in the sorcery case involving Eleanor Duchess of Gloucester, had once told Somerset's fortune and advised him 'to shun castles'. Like the tale of Suffolk and the 'Tower', this may well be a legend invented some time afterwards, for in the days when the nobility lived in castles it would have been difficult to avoid them.

Henry took no active part in the fight, but he was wounded by an arrow in the neck, which caused him discomfort for the rest of his life. He was taken into the house of a tanner for the wound to be dressed, and there found by the victorious Duke of York. The duke knelt to beg forgiveness for taking up arms, and then rather spoilt the effect by congratulating Henry on the death of Somerset which would, he said, be a cause for rejoicing by all men. He then led the bandaged and unhappy king to a service of thanksgiving in the abbey of St Albans.

About 5,000 men fought in the first battle of St Albans and the casualties, mostly among the Lancastrians, amounted to about 120 men. Somerset, the Earl of Northumberland, Humphrey Earl of Stafford and Lord John Clifford were killed; Buckingham was wounded by an arrow in the face, and the Earl of Dorset, Lord Dudley and Sir John Wenlock were also wounded. York's Welsh troops sacked the town, so the ones who really suffered were the unfortunate people who happened to live there.

The civil war that most people for the past four years had tried to avoid had now begun, and though the local political results of what was little more than a skirmish may have been disappointing to the Duke of York, the engagement marked a point of no return in Margaret's personal fight for the survival of the House of Lancaster. From now on there could be no negotiation with those who threatened her husband and her son.

7 The Rout of Ludford (1455-1459)

The contemporary Burgundian chronicler Philip de Commines, writing of the dispute between the Dukes of Somerset and York, says that 'it occasioned many battles in England and a war which continued nine-and-twenty years; and in the end nearly all the partisans of both sides were destroyed'. This is strictly true if the first battle of St Albans is taken to be the beginning, and the battle of Bosworth Field in 1485 as the end, but the civil war was by no means continuous during all these years. After the engagement at St Albans there was little or no fighting for another three and a half years until the comparatively brief campaigns of 1459, 1460 and 1461. The next major battles were not fought until 1471, and they were followed by a long period of Yorkist rule, until 1485. A state of war between the Houses of Lancaster and York certainly existed from 1459 to 1471, twelve years, and there was a lot of other feuding and fighting between the barons, but the root of all the trouble was the inability of either House to produce an autocratic ruler who would stand no nonsense from the baronage. Not until the English nobility had very nearly succeeded in destroying itself was it possible for young Henry Earl of Richmond, first of the House of Tudor, to establish a government as autocratic and determined as that of Henry V.

In some ways it is a pity that this whole period was given the name of the Wars of the Roses – by Sir Walter Scott in his *Anne of Geierstein* published in 1829 – because this implies a comparatively tidy contest between participants as well defined as, for instance, the Cavaliers and Roundheads of the seventeenth century, and easily identified because all wore either the red rose of Lancaster or the white rose of York in their hats. It was nothing like so straightforward. Since many of the nobility and gentry who took part never failed to keep one sharp eye open to spot any personal advantage, there were frequent changes of side and so much double-dealing that no commander in the field could ever be sure who would desert him, or who would join him, even in the middle of a battle.

It seems probable that Margaret and the ladies of the court were left behind at Watford on the night before the battle at St Albans, and they moved up next day, when it was all over. There is no mention of her presence during the fighting but she certainly travelled back to London with her husband, who was now York's prisoner, although York was careful not to say so. The issue between Margaret and York had become clearer. He felt he had now established by force of arms what he considered to be his hereditary right to be the chief minister. She regarded him as the threat to her son's inheritance, and since victory at St Albans had given him confidence she was determined he would have no further successes.

So far, in their personal contest, he had done well, for she held him directly responsible for the deaths of Suffolk and Somerset, and there appeared to be no one among the nobles with enough rank or experience, influence or ability to take the place of either of them at the head of the Lancastrian party. Thus the faction fight, started by Cardinal Beaufort and the Duke of Gloucester for control of the monarchy, moved on into another chapter. Margaret felt she had no option. York had to be resisted and she personally would have to lead the opposition.

The tragedy of the situation was that it was really only Margaret's deep suspicion of York's motives that kept the contest going. There was no need to form a Lancastrian party. Henry was the sitting tenant on the throne. The House of Lancaster was the properly constituted and generally accepted authority in the state. No one at this stage disputed this. Henry got on very well with Richard Duke of York, on several occasions assuring him he had no doubts about his loyalty and that he looked upon him as his 'true liege man'. Moreover, he would have been perfectly happy to have York as his chief councillor and lieutenant, and what made the idea even more attractive was that York lacked the support among the baronage which he would have to have if he was aiming for the throne.

But Margaret was not going to play second fiddle to anybody, least of all to York.

When Henry and Margaret and York rode back into London

from St Albans they were welcomed by the citizens who were careful to show no partiality. The people of London lived mainly by trade, on which war usually has a disastrous effect, and they were prepared to declare for the winning side only when there was no longer any doubt who the winner was. From their point of view nothing had been decided at St Albans, and it was soon obvious they were right. Everything became more complicated and confused, largely because York's success at St Albans forced Margaret to accept the situation, and for the moment she could do nothing except wait for a suitable opportunity to retaliate. York still lacked support among the baronage, and Margaret was not prepared to invite his direct opposition or encourage his followers by making any overt move against the authority he had won in battle.

York filled the gap left by Somerset in the post of chief minister. The captaincy of Calais was given back to Warwick, and Wiltshire was replaced as Treasurer by Henry Viscount Bourchier. Lancastrians, exiled from court by this change in Yorkist fortunes, caused as much trouble as they could – the Bonvilles and the Courtenays fought a pitched battle near Exeter – and what small degree of authority Henry had possessed vanished into the ever-widening gulf between the two parties. The growing chaos in the central government encouraged two long-standing enemies, the Scots and the French, to see what advantages might be gained, and the possibility of attack from the north and invasion from the south led to a state of emergency on the northern border and extensive preparations for defence along the Channel coast. James II of Scotland, whose mother had been related to Somerset, used the death of Somerset at St Albans as a somewhat far-fetched excuse to launch a surprise attack on Berwick. It was beaten off by the new Earl of Northumberland.

In the south it had long been expected that Charles VII would carry the war across the sea, and York provided him with a motive. Arrangements for a marriage between York's eldest son Edward Earl of March and Charles's daughter Magdalene had recently broken down. York had then approached the Duke of Alençon, one of the main opponents of Charles's plans to make the French aristocracy more obedient to the crown, and Alençon was expecting York to bring over an army to support him against Charles. Charles was showing signs of intending to nip this in the bud by invading England. Margaret added more fuel beneath this bubbling pot by encouraging her father, her uncle and old friends like Pierre de Brézé to raid the English coast, thereby proving to the people of England that since the Yorkist ministers obviously could not protect them, the government should be in the hands of the Lancastrians. This reveals the unfortunate narrowness of Margaret's partisanship. She was apt at this stage to forget that whatever her private feelings might be, she was, whether she liked it or not, the Queen of England. Yet it is easy enough to say how people ought to have behaved when one has not been subjected to the pressures of their lives.

Parliament assembled on 9 July 1455, passed, with some reluctance, a Bill of Amnesty for the Yorkists who had fought at St Albans, and was prorogued on 31 July. It was to reassemble on 12 November, but before then Henry had another nervous breakdown.

It was not nearly so bad as the previous one and he was able, with great effort, to conduct a little business, but the country was in no state to risk any more political crises. York was again appointed 'Protector and Defender of the Realm and Church, and Principal Councillor of the King until he be discharged by the King in Parliament by advice and assent of the Lords Spiritual and Temporal therein'. This was a repetition of what had happened in 1454, with one exception. It was no longer enough for Margaret and the King's doctors to affirm Henry's recovery and so terminate York's protectorate. A great deal more formality was involved, possibly because Margaret was now far more of a political leader than she had been, even two years before, and most people believed Henry would not recover from this second collapse.

Yet he did, surprisingly quickly, and early in February 1456 York realized his second protectorate would soon be over unless he tooks steps to stay in office. On 9 February he and Warwick came to Westminster escorted by three hundred armed men. No one except Henry seems to have been in the least impressed, but Henry was their real target in a psychological operation. He, always the peacemaker, allowed York to continue as chief minister and, perhaps for the first time, the fundamental difference between the king's policies and those of the queen became apparent. Henry genuinely wanted to keep York as his lieutenant and chief

councillor. Margaret was determined that if Henry was not prepared to keep power in his hands, she would hold it in hers.

Henry's unfailing courtesy and his perpetual willingness to
turn the other cheek may well have earned his wife's respect,
but, to her profound regret, those qualities which most endeared
her husband to his people drove her into opposition to him.
Though she loved him and, so far as can be judged, never looked
at another man, she could not stomach appeasement.

On 25 February 1456 Henry came into Parliament and formally
relieved York of his protectorate. This was not a demonstration
of the royal authority, for under the terms of York's patent his
tour of duty as Protector was terminated with the assent of Lords
and Commons. The administration remained unchanged, but
while Henry made use of York, sending him north as his representative to persuade James II of Scotland to abandon his plans
to capture Berwick, and generally treating him with every sign
of confidence, Margaret did her best to engineeer the removal of
all Yorkist ministers. And so the year which could have marked
the beginning of effective and stable government was one of
unease and ill-feeling.

In his efforts to raise the crown above party dissension Henry
went out of his way to demonstrate his impartiality. On one day
in March he gave money to Eleanor Dowager Duchess of
Somerset, for the care of her small son, and on the next arranged
for the payment to York of arrears of salary outstanding from
his previous protectorate. He elevated George Neville, Warwick's
brother, to the see of Exeter, and in May did much to solve
York's pressing financial problems – dating back to his service
in France – by giving him control of all gold and silver mines in
Devon and Cornwall for a period of twenty years.

The Duke of Buckingham, the most loyal, moderate and
reasonable of men, did his best to act as mediator, as did Henry's
half-brother Pembroke, Chancellor Bourchier and his brother
Henry the Lord Treasurer, but as time went on and hopes of any
reconciliation grew fainter, the Bourchiers moved towards the
Yorkists while Buckingham and Pembroke joined Margaret.

During the summer of 1456 there was trouble in South Wales,
an area where many of the great landowners had estates, and
which, for this reason, had been in a state of indiscipline bordering
upon anarchy for years. Margaret herself may have had a hand

in it because there is reason to believe she asked Edmund Tudor, Earl of Richmond, to begin the covert mobilization of Lancastrian sympathizers there. But the outcome of a complicated train of incidents was that a Yorkist, Sir William (later Lord) Herbert, began a series of military operations, thereby involving the Duke of York. In October Henry summoned the Great Council to meet at Coventry, where he and Margaret had been staying since August. His motive was to try and patch things up and keep the peace. Margaret regarded the meeting as a trial of strength. When the Council met, York was accused of various vague offences relating to Herbert's siege of Carmarthen Castle, the capture of the Earl of Richmond and the subsequent seizure of Aberystwyth Castle. Buckingham, the mediator, and other peers asked Henry merely to reprimand the duke and impress on him that it was only the exercise of the royal clemency which had saved him from arrest. This prevented Margaret from taking the stronger measures she had planned. Then she put it to Henry that if Buckingham could not be relied upon to support her in any confrontation with York, then Buckingham's half-brothers, the Bourchiers, Lord Chancellor and Lord Treasurer, could not be trusted either. They would have to be replaced by men who were more dependable, and this, in Margaret's creed, meant Lancastrians.

On 5 October Henry Bourchier was dismissed and replaced by the Earl of Shrewsbury. A week later his brother the Archbishop resigned and Bishop Waynfleet was appointed Lord Chancellor. Since Laurence Booth, the brother of Margaret's own chancellor William Booth, had already become Lord Privy Seal at the end of September, she now, for the first time, had a complete grip on the administrative machinery of the state.

York withdrew from court and Warwick returned to Calais, thus expressing the disapproval of the Great Council for Margaret's political manoeuvring, but the relationship between York and Henry seems to have been entirely amicable. James Gresham, writing to John Paston on 16 October 1456, says that the Duke of York 'departed in right good conceit [esteem] with the King, but not in great conceit with the Queen'.

Margaret had no objection to Warwick's captaincy of Calais because it took him out of England, and she intended to keep him out by arranging for Pierre de Brézé to ensure he was busily

occupied in defending the port. In March 1547 she persuaded
Henry to renew York's appointment as Lieutenant of Ireland, but
York refused to disappear into exile again.

Having stayed in Coventry until the end of March, the court
moved to Hereford, spending April there and then going on to
Leicester. In his travels Henry did his best to restore confidence
and put people's minds at rest, but throughout the spring,
summer and autumn of 1457 the Yorkists made their quiet preparations for war. York had no doubt that a decision could only
be reached on the battlefield, whereas Margaret seemed to feel
that all could be resolved in the Council. She therefore used her
new authority to secure the advancement, and support, of anyone
she thought could be of assistance to her. She made a grave error
in always dealing directly with the Council instead of the Commons, for this made her unpopular with the knights from the
shires – the backbone of any army – and laid her open to the
charge, which York made, of governing unconstitutionally.

York, on Henry's behalf, had dealt effectively with James II of
Scotland on the question of Scottish designs on Berwick, and
when the threats of invasion were renewed, the duke suggested
an open declaration of war. Margaret's more romantic solution
to the problem, a double marriage, between Henry Duke of
Somerset and his brother Edmund and James's two daughters
Annabelle and Jeanne, received no support, and in the late
summer of 1457 her popularity, waning even among her own
supporters, received a really serious setback when her friend
Pierre de Brézé sacked the town of Sandwich.

For a long time Margaret had been appealing to her uncle for
French aid in the Lancastrian cause, and in May 1457 Charles VII
authorized the equipping of a fleet, to be commanded by de Brézé,
which was to have the operational tasks of dominating the
Channel by destroying Warwick's fleet, and preventing the
Yorkists from using Calais as a base for their operations against
Margaret. De Brézé sailed from Honfleur on 21 August, searched
for Warwick without success and then appeared off Sandwich at
six o'clock on the morning of Sunday, 28 August. He had about
sixty-six ships and 4,000 men, a formidable force which had
caused much alarm along the English coast when he had been
looking for Warwick. Having landed half his troops a mile or so
out of Sandwich he sailed in and put the rest ashore on the town

quay. There was little the townspeople could do, and next morning the French sailed away with a large number of prisoners – to be ransomed – and a great deal of booty. It was just the sort of raid that Edward III had carried out on the Normandy coast – though he had operated on a larger scale – but it was no consolation to the people of south-east Kent that the French were only wiping off old scores. It appeared to them that they had their own queen to thank for their misfortunes. Yet this was only partly true. Margaret was now in control of the government and de Brézé would not deliberately have embarrassed her. He must either have been ill-informed or he misunderstood the situation, for it seems clear that having failed to find Warwick's fleet he used his initiative and did his best to put Sandwich out of action because it was the base and source of supply for the Calais garrison.

Unfortunately for Margaret there were all sorts of repercussions. The merchants of London, whose livelihood depended on trade across the Channel, took steps to protect their shipping by equipping a punitive fleet. In October it set out to attack Harfleur but, finding it too well defended, went on to look for an easier prey. The ships had to sail a long way, right round past Ushant and down the coast of Brittany to the little port of La Pallice, near La Rochelle, but there was no real profit from the attack. The result of it was that for the next six years there was a peculiar maritime free-for-all, which was nothing less than piracy, in the Channel. It involved ships from France, England, Burgundy and Brittany, and even from Portugal and Castile. The chief damage to Margaret's cause was the realization by the people of southern England that she was prepared to seek help from the ancient enemy, France. On the other hand Warwick, the Yorkist, as the defender of the Channel coast, gained much popularity and many recruits. His propaganda was particularly effective in Kent, the county of vital strategic importance to the Yorkist garrison of Calais, because through it lay the road to London.

Despite all Henry's efforts for peace and security, things were no better by the end of 1457. The feuds in the provinces still continued, the worst of them being the Nevilles and the Percys in the north, and it was in the hope of bringing the peers of his realm off the battlefield and into the council chamber that he called another meeting of the Great Council, to be held in London at the end of January 1458. All the evidence indicates that this serious attempt to resolve differences and avoid a repetition of what had happened at St Albans was inspired entirely by Henry. He cannot therefore have been quite the mindless puppet, manipulated by Margaret, that some chroniclers would have us believe. He could see what was developing. He knew where the road his wife had chosen would lead, and it is yet another tragedy of the age that his aims, so much more noble and altruistic than hers, should have been frustrated by the woman he really loved who was convinced she was acting in his own best interests.

In the middle of January Warwick's father, Salisbury, rode into London with 500 retainers behind him and found lodgings in Fleet Street. On 25 January York arrived with 400 men at his back and moved into Baynard's Castle in the City. Early in February, after the announced date of the meeting, the Lancastrians came in; Exeter, and young Henry Beaufort, Duke of Somerset, whose main ambition was to avenge what he regarded as the murder of his father at St Albans, brought 800 men. The young Northumberland, Lord Egremont and Clifford, whose fathers had also been slain at St Albans, had a small army of 1,500, and all these had to be accommodated outside the City. The tension caused by so many armed men inside and without the City of London was bad enough for the nervous inhabitants, but Warwick made things worse when he appeared with his army of 600 soldiers in red jackets, wearing his badge of the 'ragged staff'.

The Lord Mayor feared the worst. He mustered his own resources and for the next two months no less than 5,000 armed Londoners were available to guard the streets in daylight while at night there were patrols supported by a strong inlying picket to prevent any disorders.

Henry and Margaret arrived at Westminster on 7 March. Henry led a procession to St Paul's to pray for peace, and having begged the lords to come to some peaceable arrangement he retired to Berkhamsted to let them sort things out between themselves. He was rather too optimistic. This was an age in which warfare was regarded by the nobility and gentry in much the same way that many young men in universities on the other side of the Atlantic look upon American football today. It was a good competitive sport; a bit rough perhaps, but protective clothing and an offensive spirit removed much of the personal risk. The nobility and gentry could afford good accoutrements, and they went into battle not just because they enjoyed a good fight but because there was always the chance of taking a prisoner whose ransom would augment or restore the family fortunes. Hitherto it had been part of the chivalric code that any man-at-arms (who could be of any rank from prince to esquire) knocked off his horse or defeated by an opponent, surrendered and was taken out of the battle as a prisoner to await the financial negotiations for his release. He might have the bad luck to sustain a mortal injury when unhorsed or hit on the helmet with a mace or battleaxe, but normally he was not deliberately killed because he was worth much more alive than dead. The introduction first of the longbow and then of artillery virtually put an end to this arrangement because neither the arrow nor the cannon shot was selective, but the general rules were still observed, and the spirit of the tournament lingered on. Only the common soldiers suffered, because, not being nobility or gentry, they were considered to be fair game for any man-at-arms, well protected by his armour, who felt murderously inclined.

For generations hot-headed young knights, eager to win a military reputation, had found their opportunity in the wars in France. This outlet no longer existed, and thus the Lancastrians and the Yorkists, glowering at one another in the council chamber, remembering old feuds and past insults, were in the mood for war. Few of them realized that one of the more unpleasant aspects of the fight at St Albans was that it had begun a blood-feud which was going to reverse the normal pattern of battle casualties. The horror of civil war lies in the element of personal hatred, often stemming from a desire for revenge. When the representatives of the two factions fought each other in this civil war there was no thought of ransom in their minds. They intended to kill their personal enemies or be killed in the attempt. The common soldiers were not their targets.

Although Henry passionately wanted to prevent the fearful conflict which nearly everyone else seemed to be accepting as unavoidable, his mental breakdowns and the effect of the arrow wound at St Albans had so reduced his strength that in the end he was borne along on the tide of events.

Nevertheless, his exhortation to the lords to resolve their differences with goodwill, and the skilful mediation of Bishop Waynfleet, the Lord Chancellor and Archbishop Bourchier, seemed to achieve the desired result. On 24 March Henry came to the Council to read out what had been agreed. It was mostly to do with money. York, Salisbury and Warwick, as the principal aggressors, were to build a chapel at St Albans and endow it so that masses could be said for the souls of the men killed in the battle. They were also to provide compensation for widows and children. Both York and Warwick were to renounce salary payments to a total of £4,000 so that adequate sums could be paid to the dowager Duchess of Somerset and to John Clifford. Salisbury was to pay compensation to the Percys, and Lord Egremont was bound over to keep the peace for ten years. Henry tried to reinforce this by giving him territories in Yorkshire on condition that he went away on a pilgrimage.

York, Salisbury and Warwick made no difficulties about agreeing to this because in effect they were only being required to write off debts which probably would never have been paid. Henry thought he had satisfied the demands of the Lancastrians, Egremont, Somerset, Clifford and Northumberland for vengeance for the deaths of their fathers; he was perhaps a little naïve to imagine that money can pay a debt of blood, but on the surface the arrangement seemed to be a generally acceptable compromise. The people, particularly the commercially-inclined Londoners, rejoiced at the promise of peace. On 25 March the hopes of the nation appeared to be confirmed by a public display of reconciliation between erstwhile sworn enemies in a magnificent procession to a special service in St Paul's. Poor Henry must have been so happy. In front of him in the procession, holding hands and no doubt smiling sweetly, went first Somerset and Salisbury and then Exeter and Warwick, while behind him Richard Duke of York held the hand of Queen Margaret. It was all immensely impressive and utterly false.

In front of God, the king and the high altar these enemies swore eternal friendship. Great crowds in the streets, warmed by feelings of relief and gladness, cheered the procession as it came and went. To the people it seemed as if everything had been amicably settled, but Margaret, York and Warwick were involved in something much deeper than a blood-feud barely three years old. It is most unlikely that any of them believed the Great Council had really decided anything; certainly not the main issue – whether York or Margaret would rule the country.

Although Margaret had done her best to have him replaced by the Duke of Somerset, Warwick returned to Calais, turned the fortress into an independent base for future operations, and began to prey on shipping in the Channel. His piracy made him very popular in London and Kent, and in particular his defeat of a combined French and Castilian fleet off Calais in May 1458 was regarded as timely revenge for the French attack on Sandwich. Margaret was disturbed because Warwick the Yorkist was showing up the shortcomings of Exeter the Lancastrian who, as Captain of the Sea, had failed to prevent de Brézé's raid and to control the narrow waters.

Warwick's next gesture was to intercept a convoy bound for Lübeck and order the captains to strike their flags to the English squadron commanding the Channel. They refused and he took them in to Calais. Such naval arrogance delighted the English. The government was acutely embarrassed and Henry recalled Warwick. But the Captain of Calais was thoroughly enjoying himself and had no intention of abandoning the lucrative governorship of the port. It was not only an admirable base but a political and military observation post from which he could keep in touch with what was going on in the rest of Europe.

The Great Council was summoned to meet again at Westminster in October 1458. By this time all the cordiality and hopefulness inspired by the reconciliation in the previous March had vanished. A sudden sharpening of the French invasion threat – largely because of Warwick's activities – had led to signs of a possible closing of the ranks to face the common enemy, and Henry hoped to exploit this flicker of unity. Though Warwick was not officially appointed Lord Admiral and Captain of the Sea to replace Exeter who, according to a contemporary, 'showed little capacity for this duty', he was asked to 'keep the sea', a function he performed so well that Charles VII changed his mind. This did not prevent Henry, under pressure from Margaret, from ordering Warwick to hand Calais over to Somerset.

Warwick, who came to London for the Council meeting, was evasive, and it seems that in November an attempt was made to assassinate him. The story is not clear, but apparently while Warwick was attending the Council at Westminster there was a fight between one of his men and a member of the royal guard, and this led to a subsequent attack on Warwick himself and his retinue by the rest of the guard. Warwick had to fight his way out and leap into his barge on the Thames which took him to safety in the Tower. From there he went straight back to Calais.

This seemed to indicate the direction events were taking. Both sides took heed and made greater efforts to prepare for war. Though it has been suggested that Margaret was involved in the attempt on Warwick's life – if indeed it was a planned attack – it seems unlikely. Since her failure, in April, to take the governorship of Calais away from Warwick she had spent a great deal of her time in her son's earldom of Cheshire, doing her best to inspire the fighting men of that county to take up her cause. She was not in London at the time of the meeting of the Great Council, which broke up almost immediately after Warwick's rapid departure for Calais.

The conflict between Margaret and Richard Duke of York now began to acquire an international flavour. In the spring of this year, 1458, York had made tentative moves towards enlisting the aid of Charles VII against the House of Lancaster, but, not surprisingly, they had come to nothing. Charles had a strong family feeling and in any case may well have felt under an obligation to Margaret for sending her off to England as a hostage for the peace treaty he had no intention of making. In the summer, Henry, seeking to counter any after-effects of York's diplomacy, sent a delegation over to the Low Countries to open negotiations with the Duke of Burgundy, and the whole situation became almost Italian in its complexity. The essence of it was that if York's plans, now becoming centred on the throne of England, were to succeed, it was vital there should be no alliance between the Lancastrians and the French. But Charles knew very well that whatever pact he made with either faction in England was bound to drive the other to make some sort of compact with his powerful and hostile 'vassal' the Duke of Burgundy, and if he picked the wrong one he could find himself in all sorts of difficulties. It was therefore to his advantage to wait and see, not committing himself until the picture became clearer.

Warwick then made his own approaches to the Burgundians. His subsequent attempts to persuade Pierre de Brézé that any arrangements with the Lancastrians would be most unwise because the real power in England was in Yorkist hands, and his efforts to thwart Henry's ambassador, Sir John Wenlock, merely added to the confusion and at the same time cancelled everything out. Nothing was arranged or agreed, and in any case both sides were soon so involved in events in England that neither had the time or the opportunity to negotiate with Charles VII or Philip the Good.

The break up of the Great Council after Warwick's escape destroyed all hope of another reconciliation. Margaret, blaming Warwick for what had happened, demanded his arrest. Both sides assembled their forces and, wanting to avoid accusations of aggression, each waited for the other to make the first move.

In September 1459 Margaret was in Cheshire when she heard that Salisbury was on his way to join York at his castle of Ludlow. With Henry's permission she sent a force under Lord Audley to intercept Salisbury and arrest him. Warned of Audley's approach, Salisbury waited for him at Blore Heath near Market Drayton, and the armies met on 23 September 1459. Drawn up behind defence works consisting mainly of sharpened stakes stuck in the ground and angled towards the enemy, the Yorkists beat off three determined attacks and might have been overrun had not a number of Audley's men deserted to the enemy. Lord Audley was killed, Salisbury withdrew under cover of darkness and joined York. A few days later Warwick also arrived at Ludlow with a contingent of trained soldiers from the Calais garrison; 200 men-at-arms and 400 archers.

Early in October York, Salisbury and Warwick wrote jointly to Henry protesting their loyalty to him and explaining they had assembled their army to protect the interests of the people of the country against the king's ministers who, despite constant petitions, had done nothing towards carrying out reforms demanded by all loyal subjects. They stressed that their action arose from their concern 'for the common weal of the people' and far from being rebellious, it underlined their virtue and goodness of heart.

There was some truth behind what they had written, but they could not deny that Salisbury had taken up arms to resist the king's lawful warrant for his arrest. Weak though Henry was as a ruler, he nevertheless became very upset by any deliberate flouting of the royal authority. It was easy for Margaret to persuade him he had no option now but to stamp out rebellion with a bold and determined attack on the Yorkist force, which had still received very little support from anyone but the Nevilles.

The royal army, much larger than York's, marched on Ludlow, and on 12 October reached the little village and bridge over the river Teme at Ludford, just to the south of Ludlow. Here, on the far bank, the Yorkists had prepared a position surrounded by the river and a moat flooded from it, and protected by stakes, earthworks and several pieces of artillery. Offers of pardon to all who would forsake the Duke of York were shouted across the river, doubtless aimed in particular at the regular soldiers from Calais who had all served under the Duke of Somerset before Warwick was given the command. That night an officer named Andrew Trollope came over to Margaret with a large body of men behind him. This defection left the remainder of York's army in danger of annihilation, and all three lords took the only course open to them if they were to live to fight another day. York, his second son the Earl of Rutland, and Lord Clinton, fled to the Welsh coast and thence to York's estates in Ulster. Warwick, his father Salisbury, York's heir Edward Earl of March, and Sir John Wenlock rode south to Devon. (Wenlock, for years a faithful Lancastrian, had recently changed sides.) Sir John Dynham met this party on the south coast and took them across the Channel. They arrived safely at Calais on 2 November (1459). Their troops dispersed as best they could, and though the incident became known as the Rout of Ludford they do not seem to have been pursued or molested.

Margaret's firm action appeared to have been very successful. The 'rebellion' had been crushed and its leaders forced into exile. Perhaps even more important, the Yorkists had been revealed as a rebellious minority with very little support from the country as a whole. The House of Lancaster was still the constitutional authority, and Margaret acted swiftly to consolidate her achievement.

8 Wakefield (1459-1460)

The Parliament summoned to meet at Coventry on 20 November 1459 consisted for the most part of knights of the shires nominated by the Lancastrian lords without any semblance of an election, and Margaret arranged for it to deal immediately with the problem of the Duke of York. It sat, not in judgement but in condemnation, and dutifully attainted all the leading Yorkists. York and his two sons March and Rutland, Warwick and his father and mother, Lord Clinton, Sir John Wenlock and Sir William Oldhall were all found guilty of high treason and condemned to death; although Henry, who abhorred violence and vengeance, reserved the right to pardon any or all, as he thought fit. It is typical of his sense of justice that he made sure no action was taken against the Duchess of York, Cecily Neville, and in fact he arranged for the sum of 1,000 marks to be paid to her every year for the rest of her life, 'for the relief of her and her infants who have not offended against the King'.

Margaret's next move was to compel all the remaining members of the Lords, even Yorkists like Norfolk and Bonville, to swear a solemn oath to be loyal and faithful to the king, protect the queen and uphold Edward Prince of Wales as the rightful heir to the throne. She then took the precaution of distributing lands confiscated from the declared traitors among her supporters such as Buckingham and Shrewsbury, Pembroke, Wiltshire, Northumberland, Exeter, Devonshire, Arundel and Andrew Trollope – the professional soldier who had changed sides at Ludford Bridge.

This may have done more harm than good. By tradition, inheritance was inviolable, and to interfere with it by Act of Parliament or any other means was to attack the very foundations of society. Many people may have felt that if Margaret could do this she could do anything, and no one's property was safe, and it also probably aroused considerable sympathy for the 'traitors'.

By the time the Coventry Parliament was dissolved on 20 December 1459 Margaret could gain some satisfaction from the knowledge that all possible steps, in law, had been taken against her enemies, but her actions were only the measure of her insecurity, and the equivalent of a public announcement of her firm belief that York's aim was to become King of England. In one way there was some advantage in this, for in making York's intentions clear she gained the support of all those who, though they might not favour the Lancastrian cause, had no wish to see York on the throne. It was the old story of preferring the devil one knows. Henry's administration was bad enough in all conscience, but York's might be worse. Admittedly, he had been a good second-in-command during his protectorates, but seconds-in-command can change radically if they get command.

Even so, for all her legal precautions, Margaret had learned by now that there is one thing which cuts through all the obligations of a solemn oath and peels off all the protection of Acts of Attainder – a sharp sword wielded by a determined man. She had to face the unpleasant facts that York was safely in Ireland, where he had been welcomed with enthusiasm, and that Warwick, now in control of most of the ships of the English fleet, was still in command in Calais. Both were plotting invasion. Soon they would co-ordinate their efforts and attack.

The preparations to deal with their invasion were expensive; taxation had to be increased, and the unconstitutional Commissions of Array which mobilized troops for the defence of the realm were bitterly resented. The extreme unpopularity of taxation and recruitment did little to help the Lancastrian cause and materially aided the Yorkists.

Margaret took what action she could with characteristic energy. Money was sent to various Irish chieftains who promised to cause trouble for York, but none of them earned it, and it was a little naïve of Margaret to expect them to. The Duke of Somerset, officially appointed to relieve Warwick as Governor of Calais, aided by Andrew Trollope who had a sound knowledge of the fortifications and surroundings of the port, landed in France in November 1459 with the object of ousting Warwick by force. Trollope prevailed upon the garrison of Guines, an outlying fortress in the defence system, to surrender, and this encouraged Somerset to hope that Calais too could be won by persuasion.

The garrison had previously been commanded by his father, and the contingent Warwick had taken to Ludlow had shown their loyalty to the crown; but they were professional soldiers and, as usual, rated pay above politics. Warwick had the support of the rich wool merchants in Calais who were prepared to pay to keep the port open for their commerce. Somerset was therefore at a disadvantage because he could offer no financial incentives to loyalty. He met with little success, and his attacks, launched from Guines against the main fortress, only weakened his force and strengthened the determination of the garrison to resist him.

In January 1460 Margaret began to assemble reinforcements for Somerset, under the command of Lord Rivers and Sir Gervase Clifton, and a small expeditionary force was fitted out in Sandwich harbour. This was reported to Warwick who sent a squadron under Sir John Dynham to deal with it. In the grey light of the winter morning of 19 January, Dynham, Sir John Wenlock and 300 men landed at Sandwich, taking the garrison completely by surprise and carrying off to Calais Lord Rivers, his wife and their son Sir Anthony Woodville, and the whole Lancastrian fleet except the *Grace Dieu* which had been damaged. When the alarm sounded, Woodville had dashed out of his lodgings without a helmet and with his breastplate under his arm. He had been knocked on the head and carried off to the harbour.

Warwick's reputation as a bold and able commander was greatly enhanced by this success, and on the other side of the Channel some of the crews of Somerset's ships, moored too close for comfort to Warwick's guns, felt their turn might be next. The captain of the *Trinity* went ashore under flag of truce and offered their services, the ships, and their cargoes in return for their lives. Warwick's acceptance contained hidden reservations. When the deserters from Somerset's fleet were paraded in front of him his officers removed from the ranks, and executed on the spot, all those who had followed Andrew Trollope into Margaret's camp at Ludford. The remainder were made to put on Warwick's badge. This, happening in full view of the garrison, was a salutary lesson in loyalty.

The court received the news of these disasters with apprehension. There was no means now of preventing a Yorkist invasion. The only questions were when and where it would come. At the end of January 1460 Margaret again got in touch with Pierre de Brézé and asked for help from France. An agent named Doucereau acted as courier between them, carrying extremely secret letters, and though there is no exact information of the price Margaret was prepared to pay for naval and military assistance, Philip of Burgundy certainly believed she had offered to sell Calais to the Dauphin. De Brézé, writing to Charles VII in his official capacity as Seneschal of Normandy in January of the following year, gives no details but says 'if those with her knew of her intention, and what she has done, they would join themselves with the other party and put her to death'. It is unlikely he would have used such strong language over anything less than an offer of Calais.

Margaret was never very interested in sounding public opinion or gauging reaction to a diplomatic proposal, and one cannot expect her to have understood how the English felt about their last outpost on the continent. No doubt it seemed perfectly reasonable to her to offer this fortified port which was in the hands of her enemies and being used as a base against her, in return for the help she needed; and it had the advantage of killing two birds with one stone. Her enemies would lose the base she had failed to take from them, and she would get French reinforcements. It may not have occurred to her that the English would regard such an arrangement as the most damnable treason. Like many women, Margaret was intensely practical and seldom allowed what she felt was mere sentiment to cloud her aims.

One can assume from de Brézé's remark to Charles that he thought the whole subject too dangerous to pursue, and for the moment nothing more was heard of it.

Meanwhile Margaret's son Edward was growing up, and she was doing her best to push him forward and establish him in the eyes of the nobility as the future king. With this object in view, although he was only six, he was formally appointed to various military commands, assigned to duties and frequently mentioned in official documents. His governess, Lady Lovell, was relieved of her duties in March 1460 because Margaret felt the time had come for her son 'to be committed to the rules and teaching of men, rather than stay further under the keeping and governance of women'.

Throughout the spring of 1460 Margaret and her ministers took increasingly unpopular measures to defend the country. The local gentry were instructed to raise troops to 'resist the rebels' and to arrest anyone suspected of having Yorkist sympathies. She sent Doucereau to ask de Brézé to do everything he could to damage Warwick's fleet, and her officers in English ports requisitioned all ships they could find, whether English or foreign, which could be converted into warships. She began to realize the vital importance of sea-power, now in Warwick's hands, and did all she could to counter it by a system of naval patrols and coast-watching by ground forces, but some of the people she relied on were not very trustworthy. For example, the Devonshire knight Sir Baldwin Fulford told her that for the sum of 1,000 marks he would set fire to Warwick's fleet in Calais harbour and burn his ships to the waterline. He was given the money and did nothing, and Margaret must indeed have been desperate – in view of the money already wasted in Ireland – to have fallen for such a confidence trick. Paradoxically, the efforts of the government to meet the Yorkist threat merely made the Yorkist cause more popular. Exeter, the admiral, put to sea in the spring but his ships were ill-found, short of provisions, manned by crews so unenthusiastic they could never have been relied on in any engagement, and there was little money to pay even those who were prepared to fight.

The trouble was that it was almost impossible to stir up public feeling against the Yorkists among people who disliked Margaret's government and resented her influence on Henry. A great many felt it might be a good thing to return to the conditions of York's protectorate, when the hand of government had been strong and there had been peace and growing security.

In March 1460 Warwick set off from Calais with a strong fleet to go to Ireland and plan the joint operation he and York were about to undertake. He was sailing back to Calais in May when his ships were sighted off Start Point in Devon by vessels of Exeter's naval force. There was no pursuit and no battle. Exeter had no wish to be embarrassed by the spectacle of wholesale defection by his men, who might well insist that he went with them, and Warwick did not attack for the good reason that he did not wish to damage ships he hoped would soon be his. Yorkists in England used the non-event as a demonstration of Warwick's loyalty to the crown, explaining that Warwick would not deliberately assault the royal authority, as represented by

Exeter; and no one was left in any doubt of the weakness of the forces of the crown.

In June Margaret tried to send more reinforcements to Somerset, still attempting to besiege Calais. Five hundred men, commanded by Sir Osbert Mountford, Warden of the Cinque Ports, collected at Sandwich, an unwise choice for an assembly area in view of what had happened only six months previously. Warwick's supporters in Kent sent him information and on 24 June Sir John Dynham and Sir John Wenlock made another raid, took a large number of prisoners, created what havoc they could, and carried Mountford back to Calais with them.

There is a story that since Mountford had once served under Warwick he was beheaded on the following day as a reminder to the Calais garrison of their commander's strict views on fidelity, but he may have died of wounds received during the raid. On the day after that, 26 June 1460, Warwick and his father, and York's eighteen-year-old son Edward Earl of March, with a force of 2,000 men, took swift advantage of the successful raid on Sandwich by landing there, before the Lancastrians could repair the extensive damage done to the fortifications or seal this gap in their coastal defences.

Henry and his Council were at Coventry and Margaret was on a recruiting tour in the northern counties when news of the invasion reached them. Archbishop Bourchier, once again adjusting his allegiances to suit the needs of the moment, welcomed the invaders, albeit a little warily, when they came to Canterbury. The Men of Kent and the Kentish Men joined Warwick in considerable numbers as he marched along Watling Street towards London. Elsewhere, most people waited to see what would happen, since the consequences of hastening to join what turned out later to be the wrong side could be fatal. The Common Council of London were in a quandary. Warwick and his rapidly increasing army were actually advancing upon them and a decision had to be taken. The city gates were guarded, all strangers were interrogated, and a deputation went out to tell the rebel leaders not to try and come in.

Warwick protested that he was not a rebel; he remained entirely loyal to King Henry VI and his quarrel was with Henry's ministers – a familiar tale. He made it clear that whether the Londoners liked it or not he would enter the capital and was quite prepared, and equipped, to deal with resistance. Wisely, the City Fathers did not resist. Warwick crossed London Bridge on 2 July 1460, losing several of his men in doing so, for they were crushed to death in the unruly mob forcing its way into the City. He then issued a manifesto setting forth his accusations against Henry's advisers and stating they had plundered the people, oppressed the Church, misappropriated public money, conscripted men into the royal army and even tried to betray the country into the hands of foreign rulers for political advantage – he must have heard some rumour of Margaret's correspondence with de Brézé. He added that the government acted unconstitutionally and tried to put the king's will above the law. It was all a very thinly disguised attack on Margaret.

No doubt she and Henry expected something of this sort, but with this document came a letter from an unexpected source, a papal legate – or so he described himself – named Francesco Coppini.

Coppini's task, which he said had been given to him by the Pope, was to reconcile the Yorkist and Lancastrian factions in England and persuade Henry to raise a contingent for a crusade against the Turks. It was, perhaps, a little ambitious, and Coppini was not the best choice for such a mission because his real aims were not related to the wishes of the Holy Father. He wanted a cardinal's hat and he also wanted to further the interests of his real patron, Francesco Sforza, Duke of Milan.

It seems that Coppini had first come to England early in 1460, but there is doubt about the exact date. He never really had any chance of success with his so-called papal mission. Henry and Margaret were both far too preoccupied with the problems of the Yorkist invasion, and in any case no one for years had been in the least interested in papal exhortations to win back the Holy Land from the infidels. Furthermore, as no doubt he himself realized, by this time the state of affairs between Lancaster and York had gone far beyond any hope of reconciliation. Coppini was not a very competent legate and he even succeeded in irritating the pious and courteous Henry, who in the end became so suspicious of him that he told him to go back to his master. It may well be that Coppini, ebullient and loquacious, talked too much and made himself very unpopular. He did not get his cardinal's hat, the Pope's adamant refusal lending colour to

Henry's belief that he had no papal authority – and Charles VII subsequently accused him openly of fomenting trouble in England. Suspicious of Coppini, Margaret helped to speed him on his way, and on his journey back to Italy he went to Calais. Here he met Warwick who saw the possible advantage of exploiting the way Coppini had been treated in England. He received the papal legate with great courtesy and deference, and persuaded him to remain in Calais until, in a few weeks' time, the Yorkists took over from the Lancastrian administration in England. Warwick felt he would now have the papal support and blessing in the conquest of England and it would also be possible for him to make useful alliances with Milan and Burgundy. Moreover, since the Dauphin Louis (later Louix XI) had quarrelled with his father and had taken refuge in the court of the Duke of Burgundy, the prospects of winning the support of the next King of France were very good indeed.

Hence, when Warwick, Salisbury and the Earl of March crossed to Sandwich on 26 June they took Francesco Coppini with them, and when they reached London Coppini wrote an open letter to King Henry. In it he stressed that he was in no way associated with the rebels; he was an entirely neutral agent of the Holy Father, acting purely as a mediator to prevent bloodshed. He went on to say that if only Henry would stop listening to his advisers and listen to him instead, all could be arranged. It would be possible, in his own words, 'to avoid these evils and arrange a union'.

In fact there was no hope of anything of the sort. On 3 July, the day after entering the City, Warwick sent one of his officers, Thomas, Bastard of Fauconberg, a scion of the Nevilles, on ahead with the infantry, making for Coventry. Assisted by the Londoners whose only motives were to preserve their city, maintain their trade and keep well out of any battle, Warwick himself made plans to lay siege to the Tower, held for the king by Lord Hungerford and Lord Scales, and then, with Archbishop Bourchier, Edward Earl of March and Coppini, he rode north with the mounted men-at-arms. He left his father behind to reduce the Tower.

Buckingham, commanding the royal army, and King Henry waited for them at Northampton in a strong position within earthworks and a pallisade, defended by artillery and archers. It was a very wet July. The roads, such as they were, were heavy with mud, and it was a long, unenjoyable march for Warwick's force, augmented by 400 archers from Lancashire who joined him at St Albans. On 9 July he came up to Henry's position and camped just out of range of the guns.

There was some attempt at a parley. Buckingham commented on the presence of the Archbishop and Coppini in the enemy force: 'Ye come not as bishops to treat for peace but as men in arms.' Coppini said they had come with Warwick for their own protection since 'they that be about the King, be not our friends'. The two priests only succeeded in delaying the fighting for a few hours, and since Warwick's men were tired after their long march, this may have been their object.

The battle was fought next day, in a torrential downpour that put out all the matches so that 'the King's ordnance of guns might not be shot' and not one of them got a round off. The Lancastrian Lord Grey of Ruthyn deserted with his men in the middle of the battle and the Yorkists broke through the defences he left unguarded. On Warwick's orders, no mercy was shown to the Lancastrian leaders though no attempt was made to pursue the ordinary soldiers when they broke and ran. Henry remained in his tent, and the Duke of Buckingham, the Earl of Shrewsbury and the Earl of Egremont and Lord Beaumont were all killed just outside it, trying to protect the king.

Henry was taken prisoner but treated with all honour and respect, Warwick and March and all the other Yorkists assuring him they had never at any time intended any disloyalty. They had come to remove the corrupt and incompetent administration, establish good government and the rule of law, and recover the estates which had been taken from them after the affair at Ludlow. Henry was taken to London on 16 July and lodged in the bishop's palace. Three days later the Lancastrian lords defending the Tower surrendered on terms, and the unpopular Lord Scales, trying to slip away to sanctuary at Westminster, was recognized by some Thames boatmen and brutally murdered.

Margaret had played no part in Warwick's brief and successful campaign for she was still recruiting Lancastrian support in the north. She had last seen Henry in June, when they bade each other an affectionate farewell at Coventry, and he sent her off to Eccleshall in Staffordshire before moving with his court down to Northampton. She was still in Eccleshall when a messenger brought her news of the defeat, and knowing perfectly well that all would be lost if she and her son fell into Warwick's hands, she at once fled with him into Cheshire. There are all sorts of stories about her flight onwards into Wales.

Near Malpas she was nearly taken prisoner by John Cleger, a servant of Lord Stanley, and her own followers robbed her of her possessions and her jewels. Her baggage was looted and, while the thieves were quarrelling over their shares, a boy of fourteen named John Combe of Amesbury carried her and her son away from danger, all three mounted on the same horse.

At length, after a long, dangerous and exhausting journey over the mountains they reached safety in the fortress of Harlech, dominating the great sweep of Tremadoc Bay. From here she later went on to Denbigh where she was joined by Exeter, the unsuccessful admiral, and a number of other lords made fugitive by Warwick's victory at Northampton. The news of her husband's defeat and capture merely strengthened her resolve and gave her the courage and determination to keep the Lancastrian standard flying.

Ensconced in London and in direct control of the king, Warwick seemed to have all his objectives within his grasp. He began to plan his next moves, while Margaret, more than two hundred miles away, planned hers.

She felt she could count on support from Wales and the north and west of England, but her adherents were widely scattered and disorganized. Somerset still had a military force of sorts at Guines. Her two immediate tasks were to mobilize her resources in England and Wales, and to tell Somerset to contact Pierre de Brézé and get him to ask her uncle Charles for naval and military aid. And there was another possible source of help; her relationship to the French king and the long history of friendship between France and Scotland might make it possible for her to come to some arrangement with James II of Scotland.

Her resolution inspired the remnants of the old Lancastrian Council with new energy. Exeter went to the north of England and, although hunted by his enemies and often in great danger, prepared an army for rapid mobilization when the time came. Margaret herself, and her husband's half-brother Pembroke, made everything ready in Wales. She wrote to her uncle asking him to give de Brézé the authority, money and resources to help her, and to send her a safe-conduct so that she and her son could visit the French court and explain in person what was needed.

But Charles was too crafty a politician to act hastily. He wanted to see the results of Warwick's victory, and when the Count of Charolais came to him and said he was prepared to lead a French army to England to help Margaret, Charles was evasive and said he had not yet made up his mind to do anything quite so drastic. He did, however, allow Somerset to take his troops back to England through Dieppe, and he sent Margaret the safe-conduct she wanted. His messengers, the Sieur de Janlis and Jean Carbonnel, reached Harlech too late, Margaret had just left for Scotland.

James II, never slow to find an excuse for cancelling pre-vious agreements or treaties, considered that Henry's defeat at Northampton freed him from all obligations. Early in August he attacked Roxburgh, but on 10 August 1460 he was killed accidentally when one of his own siege guns blew up. Never-theless the siege was brought to a successful conclusion by his widow, Mary of Gueldres.

Encouraged by this, the Scots began a series of offensive operations all along the border.

Margaret arrived in the Scottish capital early in December 1460, and Mary of Gueldres, acting now as Queen Mother and Regent for her infant son James III, received her and Prince Edward with kindness and sympathy. Alive to Scottish ambitions, Margaret let it be known that she, still Queen of England and therefore, at least in her own opinion, Regent for her husband while he was in enemy hands, was prepared to make substantial concessions in return for Scottish aid. In this she received support from her uncle who sent an embassy to the Scottish court as soon as he learned where Margaret had gone. All went well until another embassy arrived, this time from the Burgundian court and led by the Seigneur de la Gruthuyse, representing Philip the Good and the Earl of Warwick. Margaret, knowing how much depended on help from Mary of Gueldres, and how important it was to have a sanctuary on the other side of the northern frontier if the need arose, walked warily among the snares of diplomacy, but it was clear to her that without some startling success to swing local opinion in her favour, her negotiations in Scotland were doomed and her cause lost.

Thus, the news from England, when it came, must have convinced her that God was on the side of the anointed king.

Far to the south, Warwick in London, waiting for the Duke of York to join him from Ireland, had, like Margaret after the Rout of Ludford, been taking steps to secure his grip on the administration. His brother, George Neville, Bishop of Exeter, was appointed Lord Chancellor after the dismissal of Bishop Waynfleet, all the Lancastrian government officials were replaced by Yorkists, and the Yorkist nobility were instructed in writing to possess all castles and fortifications and arrest anyone who opposed them. Parliament was summoned for October 1460. Not until the first week in September 1460 did York sail from Ireland, after all these preparations had been made. He landed at Hoylake in the Wirral of Cheshire and travelled slowly down, through Shrewsbury, Ludlow and Hereford, and then across to Coventry and Leicester and various other towns, conducting a sort of Assize on what he claimed was the King's commission, to 'punish the towns by the faults to the King's laws'. It sounds as if he was hunting Lancastrians.

By the time he reached London on 10 October his purpose was clear. Hitherto he had displayed only the arms of York, but as he drew nearer to London his standard had become that of the royal arms of England and his advance resembled a royal progress. He had come to claim the throne.

Parliament had been in session at Westminster for about three days when he arrived and had already repealed all Margaret's careful enactments passed by the Coventry Parliament in the previous year. Warwick and Salisbury, and York's own son the Earl of March, had been waiting for him since the middle of July, but his extraordinary behaviour seems to have taken everyone by surprise. He strode into the royal apartments at Westminster and rudely ordered Henry to leave. Henry must have been shattered and completely at a loss. Always so courteous and considerate himself he had no idea how to deal with anyone uncouth enough to address him with anything but respect.

York then went to the House of Lords where his peers, having heard reports of his journey to London, awaited him in icy silence. He marched straight up to the empty throne. Everyone watched him. No one moved and no one spoke. His nerve must have failed him at the last moment because instead of seating himself, which had obviously been his intention, he merely laid one hand upon it and stood there, surrounded by an aura of hostility that must have been almost tangible. Archbishop Bourchier broke the tense silence. He came forward and asked the Duke politely if he wanted to go in and see the king. York then made his well-known reply: 'I know of no person in this realm the which oweth not to wait on me, rather than I on him.'

He withdrew from the chilly atmosphere of disapproval and dislike and returned to the king's apartments. Henry had meekly moved into those reserved for the queen. York must have been very conscious that something had gone badly wrong, and the fact that there had been no acclaim, indeed no response of any kind, from the crowded House of Lords indicates that Warwick and Salisbury must have been just as surprised as everyone else. Otherwise Warwick would either have rallied sufficient support beforehand or advised York not to attempt any sort of coup. In fact York's actions must have been a considerable shock to Warwick who had been so busy asserting and stressing his loyalty to Henry VI.

York changed his tactics, either on his own initiative or because his friends prevailed upon him to do so, and a week later, in the Lords, he put forward his formal claim to the throne, based on his descent from the second son of Edward III. It was rejected, but after a lot of argument – backed by York's indisputable military strength – it was agreed that Henry VI would remain king until his death and then his heir would not be his own son, Edward Prince of Wales, but Richard Duke of York. York was then declared to be the heir apparent; he became Prince of Wales and Earl of Chester with an annual income of 10,000 marks.

It was an extremely unpopular arrangement. York did not inspire either trust or affection, and both Warwick and his own son Edward Earl of March told him they thought he had been extremely unwise to make what they felt was a ridiculous compromise without having first brought the military situation under control. All he had done was to rob the rightful heir of his birthright, thereby alienating all those who felt strongly about long-established rights of inheritance. He had also guaranteed the

continuation of the civil war because everyone knew how
Margaret felt about her husband and her son and that she would
now fight to the death. He had raised all sorts of difficult constitutional issues which could have been avoided by straightforward military conquest, and they pointed out that it was
nonsense to argue that Henry's spineless abandonment of his son's
heritage proved there must be some substance in the scurrilous
ballads claiming that Edward was 'a false heir born of false
wedlock' – even though Warwick, for political reasons, had long
been saying that both Margaret and her son were illegitimate. It
was no secret to anyone that Henry was still a sick man, exposed
to extreme Yorkist pressure and quite unable to cope with the
problems that beset him unless he had his wife's support. Since
she was now so far away it was not surprising that he had given
way to the demands of his captors.

Yet what worried Warwick and the Earl of March most of all
was the lack of support for the Duke of York in the House of
Lords. This meant there was now a dangerous swing of public
opinion away from the Yorkists just at the time when they needed
powerful backing. This, coupled with the threat of Margaret's
two armies, one in Wales under the Earl of Pembroke and the
other raised by Exeter in the north, created a very unpleasant
situation which could have been avoided if York had had the
sense to wait until the main issues had been decided on the
battlefield.

Somerset now abandoned his abortive siege of Calais and
joined Exeter in Yorkshire where they plundered Yorkist estates
to provide the means of maintaining the Lancastrian army they
had collected. York gathered up his troops from the London area
and marched north to stamp out what he regarded as the last
defiant flickering of the Lancastrian cause, and he completely
misjudged the temper and morale of the enemy force. This consisted of the Percys, the Dacres, the northern branch of the
Nevilles and the Cliffords, and the following of the Earl of
Devonshire; a formidable array which York was marching to
attack with a force inadequate for his purpose. Though in
numbers it was greater than that of the Lancastrians it was considerably inferior in quality, and he, as its commander, was in no
sense a military genius.

On 21 December 1460, cavalry patrols from the two armies

met and skirmished near Worksop, and York pushed on to his castle at Sandal, two miles from Wakefield. He then realized he was in danger of being cut off and so he sent for his son March to reinforce him. A few days later, on 30 December – at the time when Margaret was staying with Mary of Gueldres at Lincluden Abbey in Scotland – the Lancastrian army appeared in battle order to the north of the castle. Without waiting for his son, York accepted the challenge and led his force out of the castle. Somerset, commanding the Lancastrians, charged him while he was trying to form up. The battle was brief and bloody. York and his son Rutland were killed in action and Salisbury, taken prisoner, was later executed at Pontefract. The Lancastrian victory was complete.

Various stories have been told about this battle, most of them unpleasant and few of them true. Waurin, in particular, gives elaborate details of Margaret's speech to her troops and how she rode through the ranks on a white palfrey encouraging them to die for her cause. Many chroniclers have described how, after the fighting, the captured Duke of York was beheaded on the field and his head, on Margaret's orders, set above a gate of the city of York adorned with a paper crown. Margaret was in Scotland and did not hear about the battle for several days. York's heap was certainly displayed but he was killed in battle. There is another tale about the brutal Clifford pursuing York's son Rutland, who was only a boy, and stabbing him, at the same time making the unfriendly remark, 'By God's blood, thy father slew mine, and so will I do thee.' This is all quoted as evidence of the blood feud, but it seems clear that the boy, fighting bravely in the general press, muddle and uproar of the battles of those days, was just another casualty. Yet the blood feud is evident in the beheading of Warwick's father.

This battle marked the extinction of the older generation of the nobility. The sword of vengeance passed into the hands of younger leaders who, mourning the deaths of gallant fathers, undoubtedly, from now on, increased the hatred and savagery of this sanguinary struggle. Yet for Margaret it was the startling success she needed so badly to persuade the Scots she was capable of waging effective war against her husband's enemies – who were really more her foes than his.

Suddenly, once again, everything had changed.

9 Towton (1460-1461)

News of the battle of Wakefield must have travelled fast, for on 5 January 1461, at Lincluden Abbey, Margaret signed a treaty of alliance with Mary of Gueldres. In return for armed assistance against Warwick, Margaret agreed to surrender Berwick to the Scots.

Charles VII, hearing of the death of Richard Duke of York, although still cautious, came out a little further into the open by declaring, on 3 February, that Lancastrians could use the ports of Normandy without safe-conducts. He also gave instructions to de Brézé to fit out a fleet and take control of the Channel away from Warwick. Within a few days de Brézé and his officers were busy at Rouen, mounting cannon on the decks of ships.

Margaret's treaty with the Scots was ratified by a council of Lancastrian lords headed by Somerset, Exeter, Northumberland, Westmorland and Devonshire. It probably never occurred to her that her enemies and many other people in England could now accuse her - and them - of treason and treachery, and that by negotiating with nations which for centuries had been regarded as enemies, she was making things extremely difficult for herself. She had the Angevin attitude to affairs of state. International agreements were solely the concern of the monarchs and senior ministers who negotiated them and were nothing whatsoever to do with the common people, who could not be expected to understand such matters. Unfortunately, what she still did not understand was the intensity of the hatred, the mutual enmity between the English and French, and English and Scots. It was not something to be expunged by a signature on a document, it was part of the national heritage. Margaret made her arrangements with Mary of Gueldres and with her uncle simply because, as a practical woman with her aims clear before her, they were to her immediate advantage. Often she was headstrong and impetuous, not given to analysing the long-term effects of what she was doing, yet, for all her drive and energy and determination, her principal misfortunes can be attributed to a fatal tendency to delay just at the moment when everything depended on swift action.

This is a criticism stemming from hindsight. We are apt to forget that in England at the time of this civil war one of the commodities most difficult to obtain was accurate information. The first news of a battle often came from someone who had fled before it was over, carrying some wildly exaggerated story to cover his own cowardice. Rumour fed on rumour, and even the reports of the rival military commanders were coloured by self-justification, excuses or self-glorification which concealed or enhanced the plain facts. It could take a long time to sort out what had actually happened, and without any system of communication except mounted scouts or couriers, and no maps, it was extremely difficult for any commander to assess the effects of his activities. Indeed it is surprising how much opposing commanders knew about each other, and if they were sometimes slow to exploit success it was because it was not at all easy for them to discover what was happening on what Wellington was later to describe as 'the other side of the hill'.

No final decision had been reached at the battle of Wakefield. York and Salisbury were dead, but two far more able Yorkist commanders, their sons March and Warwick, were very much alive, and they held the King a prisoner in London. Everything now depended on an immediate follow-up to take advantage of the Lancastrian success before the Yorkists could adjust to the change in circumstances brought about by York's death. Somerset should have marched south with every available man and attacked Warwick whose resources had been greatly depleted by having to provide the army which York had lost at Wakefield; and it was essential to do this before Warwick could be reinforced by the Earl of March, now in Wales.

The one man who seems to have understood the military situation was Francesco Coppini, the tiresome Italian, still in London. As soon as he heard that York was dead he advised Warwick to remain on the defensive until Easter, and at the same time he wrote to Margaret, putting Wakefield into perspective. He described it as a trifling victory, gained more by York's incompetence than Somerset's skill, suggested she should not attach too much importance to it and would be well-advised to make peace while she, as the victor, was still in a strong position.

Margaret and her son set out from Scotland at the head of the army provided by Mary of Gueldres. Somerset remained in Yorkshire and did nothing until she joined him on 20 January 1461. Three weeks had been wasted.

Meanwhile, Warwick, refusing to panic, assured his potential allies on the continent, Philip of Burgundy, the Dauphin Louis and Sforza, that all was well. There had, he admitted, been an unfortunate incident at Wakefield, but this sort of thing had to be accepted every now and again as part of the fortunes of war; it would make no difference to the ultimate Yorkist victory. They believed him. Philip of Burgundy sent over a contingent of eighty Burgundian 'hand-gunners' to join his army as mercenaries. Their peculiar firearms, said to be capable of shooting lead bullets, arrows a Flemish ell long (27 inches) and wildfire,* were apt to cause more alarm among friends than foes, but they were a new development in the art of war and Philip was proud of them.

A Burgundian embassy came over, soon after these troops, and was another indication of Philip's faith in Warwick. This was not shared to any great extent by the people of London, but being commercially-inclined they believed in insurance. They gave Warwick 2,000 marks and released from their jails any of his troops who were in them. The Duke of Norfolk and Lord Bourchier sent him troops, so did Lord Bonville, Sir Thomas Kyriel and Sir John Neville. Away to the west Edward Earl of March, the new Duke of York, was raising an army in Wales. He had been at Shrewsbury when he heard of his father's death.

As the result of Margaret's appeals, Charles VII's acquiescence and Pierre de Brézé's activities, Jasper Tudor, Earl of Pembroke, and the Earl of Wiltshire had collected in France a mixed force of Frenchmen, Bretons and Irishmen. They landed in South Wales and marched northwards, calling all Lancastrians to their standard. This was a direct challenge to Edward Duke of York, now nineteen, who was already on his way to join Warwick in London before Margaret's army, coming down from Yorkshire, could

---

* 'Wildfire' was usually a cloth dipped in highly inflammable substances, very easy to light but almost impossible to put out, attached to an arrow. In warfare, it was the descendant of 'Greek Fire' and the ancestor of napalm.

threaten his left flank. He had the ability to think fast and react swiftly, and he also possessed the attribute which distinguishes the effective commander, an offensive spirit tempered with a proper caution. To prevent Pembroke and Wiltshire from linking up with Margaret he turned back south-westwards immediately, met them and brought them to battle at Mortimer's Cross, midway between Wigmore and Leominster, on 2 February 1461.

Early that misty morning Edward's men were alarmed by the appearance in the sky of what seemed to be three suns but Edward turned the vision to his advantage. 'Be of good comfort and dread not,' he said. 'This is a good sign, for these three suns betoken the Father, the Son and the Holy Ghost, and therefore let us have a good heart, and in the name of Almighty God go we against our enemies.'

His men-at-arms must indeed have been heartened, for they charged and routed their Lancastrian enemies and their foreign allies. The pursuit continued as far south as Hereford, where the unfortunate prisoners were collected. Among them was the handsome old man Owen Tudor, second husband of Catherine of France, father of Jasper — who had escaped — and grandfather of the future Henry VII. He could not believe he was really going to be beheaded until he was taken to the market place, saw the axe and the block and felt the ripping off of the collar of his red velvet doublet.

'Ah!' he said, whether in sorrow or regret we know not, but certainly not in fear. 'That head shall be on the block that was wont to lie on Queen Catherine's lap.'

He had loved her very much and one likes to think he felt he was about to join her.

After a victory which had revealed his considerable talents as a soldier, Edward hastened to London.

Margaret and her army — if the ill-assorted and ill-disciplined mob that accompanied her can be dignified by the title — came south down the Great North Road cutting a swathe of rape and murder, plunder and devastation several miles wide. This was the Scottish idea of 'living off the country'. It was a motley host, consisting of forces from Scotland and Wales, levies summoned by Commissions of Array from the northern counties (which deserted at the earliest opportunity), and the private armies of the nobility. The strength of it cannot be judged with any accuracy; contemporary estimates of 200,000 and 100,000 are typical exaggerations. The only thing the troops had in common was the badge of the 'white ostrich feather on crimson and black', the insignia of the Prince of Wales. Churches, abbeys and villages, and towns such as Grantham, Stamford, Peterborough and Huntingdon were ruthlessly sacked and despoiled, in sharp contrast to the movement of the armies of both sides in previous campaigns. Hitherto the commanders had done everything they could to control their troops and create as good an impression as possible on the line of march.

The people of the eastern counties mobilized in their own defence with a speed and enthusiasm that Commissions of Array had never been able to inspire. Town walls were closely guarded and mobile forces stood in readiness to attack at the first sight of foraging parties.

All this was extremely damaging to Margaret, uniting the eastern counties against her and encouraging those in the south to resist the horde she brought with her by joining the Yorkists. Rumours played a large part in the feeling against her; one was that the Scots were to be allowed to plunder indiscriminately in the south as a reward for their services. Warwick took immediate advantage by issuing letters patent to all local authorities ordering them to raise troops and join the king in the defence of the country against the 'misruled and outrageous people in the north part of this realm, coming towards these parts to the destruction thereof, of you and subversion of all our land'. Naturally there was a great response and many Lancastrians felt Margaret had made an irretrievable mistake.

She had left the city of York in the last week of January, and early in February 1461, Warwick accompanied by Norfolk, Arundel, Bonville and Sir Thomas Kyriel, each commanding detachments from Kent and East Anglia, marched north. His army reached St Albans on 12 February and began to block all possible routes Margaret might take to London.

From the information he had, Warwick assumed Margaret would come down either the Baldock or Sandridge roads which joined at Barnard's Heath on the north side of the town. He therefore drew up his army in two divisions astride the heath, but he took the precaution of stationing an outpost of 200 mounted archers at Dunstable, eleven miles away to the north-

1. Margaret of Anjou. From a miniature painted by her father, René d'Anjou, in his *Livres des Heures*. This is believed to be the only authentic portrait in existence.

(*Photo: J. F. H. Davies*)

2a. Isabelle de Lorraine. From a miniature painted by her husband, René d'Anjou, in his *Livres des Heures*.

2b. René d'Anjou. A self-portrait on wood.

Margaret's Mother and Father.

2c. Yolande d'Aragon. From a stained-glass window in Le Mans Cathedral.

2d. Louis d'Anjou.

Margaret's Grandmother and Grandfather. (*Photos: J. F. H. Davies*)

3a. Henry VI. By an unknown artist.
(*National Portrait Gallery*)

3b. Edward IV. By an unknown artist.
(*National Portrait Gallery*)

3c. Charles VII of France.

3d. Louis XI of France.
(*Photos: J. F. H. Davies*)

4a. The Marriage of Henry VI and Margaret of Anjou.
(*Photo: J. F. H. Davies*)

4b. Philip the Good, Duke of Burgundy and his son, Charles the Bold.
(*Photo: J. F. H. Davies*)

4c. Edward Prince of Wales, son of
Henry VI and Margaret of Anjou.
(*British Museum*)

west up Watling Street. He also placed a lookout on the top of the abbey tower in St Albans and left a further guard of archers to cover his rear, through the town, in case Margaret did change the axis of her advance and come at him along Watling Street.

These dispositions were all reported to Margaret on 14 February by a certain Captain Lovelace of Kent, who was serving in Warwick's army.

Margaret thereupon changed her route, swinging round to the west, intending to turn the flank of Warwick's main position on the heath and approach through the town, behind him. On 16 February his outlying picket at Dunstable, posted to give him early warning of any such move, was surrounded, and his scouts 'came not home to bring no tidings how nigh that the Queen was, save one who came and said she was nine mile off'. Warwick was reluctant to change his battle positions on this meagre information because he could not be certain the action at Dunstable was not a feint designed to make him face the wrong way. Yet he strengthened his rearguard, and when Andrew Trollope led the initial Lancastrian attack at first light on the following morning, climbing up the steep hill towards the rear of Warwick's army, he was driven back by a storm of arrows which inflicted heavy loss.

Trollope withdrew behind cover, made a quick appreciation, sent parties to infiltrate through the streets on his left and get round behind the enemy archers, and then attacked again. Outflanked, the Yorkist detachment rejoined the main body on the heath, but they had made time for Warwick to turn about and prepare to meet the main Lancastrian attack from the town instead of from the north-east. Snow began to fall, driving into the eyes of Warwick's archers and putting out the spluttering saltpetre 'matches' of his handgunners and artillerymen. The Burgundian mercenaries were not a success. Several of their weapons blew up, sending jagged lumps of metal whistling through the Yorkist ranks, and no less than eighteen of them died a ghastly death when the wildfire they were trying to discharge blew back in their faces.

The Lancastrians charged and Captain Lovelace chose this moment to change sides, taking many of the Kentish Men with him. This had a serious effect on the morale of Warwick's troops who, despite Warwick's assurances that reinforcements were on their way, lost all heart in the early afternoon, turned and fled. The Lancastrian cavalry went off in pursuit. King Henry was found sitting under a tree, guarded by the old veteran Sir Thomas Kyriel and Lord Bonville. It is said that Henry had promised to protect them if they would stay and look after him. Both were executed later, and Waurin tells a distasteful story that Margaret 'blooded' her eight-year-old son by making him preside over a court martial, condemn the two old soldiers and then witness their execution. Yet, since so many of the horror stories of this civil war, Waurin's in particular, have been discredited and shown to be no more than malicious inventions, there is no reason to believe there is any more truth in this than in the tale of Margaret's vindictiveness at Wakefield.

It was a great day for Margaret. She and Henry had been separated for seven months, and now, with a victorious army behind her they were reunited, their enemies scattered, and the road to London lay open. Her bitter enemy York was dead and Warwick was a fugitive. As she and Henry and their son stood in Lord Clifford's tent the prince's chancellor, Dr Morton, handed Henry a book of orisons. Henry blessed his son and knighted him, and then they went outside and Prince Edward knighted thirty of his warriors. The first was Andrew Trollope, another veteran of the French wars, limping from an injury to his foot. As he rose he said, 'My lord, I have not deserved it for I slew but fifteen men. I stood still in one place and they came to me. But they bode still with me.'

In terms of the civil war as a whole, the second battle of St Albans was no more decisive than any of the previous engagements. Everything rested on the advantage taken of it.

Edward Duke of York was still on his way from the West Country, making for London. The obvious thing for Margaret and Henry to do was to get to London before he did and establish the court at Westminster without delay. If Edward and his victorious army from the Welsh Marches were to win the race, all might be lost.

Once again, hesitation and delay proved fatal; and the root of the trouble this time was the Scottish element in Margaret's army. No one could control it, and the citizens of London knew only too well what would happen if it was allowed into the capital. The Lancastrian leaders advised strongly against any movement

into London and the Common Council of the City, though tact-
fully congratulating Margaret on her victory and assuring her of
their loyalty, were on the alert to prevent it. Even the appearance
of a small body of Margaret's cavalry outside the walls was
enough to cause the closing of the gates, the boarding up of
shops and the calling out of guards upon the walls.

A week after the battle at St Albans, on 24 February, it became
known that Warwick, with the remnants of his army, had joined
Edward Duke of York at Oxford and both were hurrying towards
London at the head of their combined force. It became imperative
for the Lancastrians to occupy the City, but the delegation from
Margaret's army was unable to come to any arrangement with the
Common Council and the citizens demanded that their gates
should be opened to the young Duke of York.

On 26 February 1461 Warwick and Edward rode into the City
and were welcomed as if they had brought a relief force to raise
a siege.

There was nothing Margaret could do except withdraw to the
city of York, taking the king and the prince with her. Her army
straggled back up the Great North Road, looting and pillaging
as it went, and she renewed her appeals to her uncle for help from
France. She had learned nothing from the unfortunate example
of foreign aid from the Scots, and apparently she did not realize
that although the Nevilles and their supporters were ranged
against her she could still count on rather more than half the
forces of the English nobility to support the king.

The scene in the House of Lords when Richard Duke of York
had placed his hand on the throne had been a clear enough
indication of the general feeling against him. Instead of exploiting
this and employing it to defeat York's claim on the grounds that
not only was the claim illegal but also that, as Shakespeare wrote
subsequently, 'not all the water in the rough rude sea can wash
the balm from an anointed king', Margaret had either antagonized
or embarrassed many of her most devoted adherents by bartering
English interests in exchange for help from abroad. She misunderstood the whole situation, and by failing to make a really
determined effort to reoccupy the palace of Westminster she had
left the field open for the Yorkists who had now reached the
point where a critical decision had to be taken.

Edward's father Richard was dead and Parliament was not in

session, so there could be no question of reviving the arrange-
ment, made before the battle of Wakefield, whereby the Duke of
York ruled in Henry's name. There were only two alternatives;
either any idea of a Yorkist succession must be abandoned, and
Henry brought back to London as king, or Edward Duke of
York must become king at once. Only one of these was feasible.

On Sunday, 1 March 1461, a large crowd of soldiers and
citizens assembled in St John's Field, Clerkenwell, to hear
Yorkist orators declare that since Henry was no longer fit to
reign, Edward should be proclaimed king in his stead. The
throng of people roared approval. On the following Wednesday
there were processions to Westminster and St Paul's and further
acclamation. The sceptre of St Edward was placed in Edward's
hands and his lords did homage to him as the rightful king.
There was no coronation; Margaret and her army were still in
the field, and though the fact of usurpation might be disguised
by cries of the mob, it could only be established by force.

Warwick marched north with the vanguard of Edward's army,
leaving London on Saturday, 7 March. The main body of Welsh
and Kentish infantry left a few days later, and on 13 March
Edward followed, at the head of his cavalry. The total strength
of his army was in the region of 20,000 men, a large one by the
standards of those days. Margaret's force numbered about 26,000.
It had been considerably increased by men who were loyal to the
principle of hereditary monarchy and felt it their duty to resist
Edward's blatant usurpation. Just at the time when Edward was
leaving London, with the intention of forcing Margaret to a
decisive battle, her army encamped at Tadcaster, eight miles from
York.

Edward reached Pontefract, found that the Lancastrians had
destroyed the bridge over the Aire at Ferrybridge, and a detachment of his troops spent most of Friday, 27 March, building a
pontoon replacement. That night Lord Clifford galloped into the
town with a troop of horse. He caught the Yorkists in their beds
and cut down anyone he could find. The Yorkist detachment fled
back to Pontefract and, fearing a dawn attack, the whole of
Edward's force stood to arms. Nothing happened. Next morning
Edward decided to go back and recapture the abandoned pontoon
bridge, which was vigorously defended by Lord Clifford's men.
They were at length outflanked by a column under Fauconberg

which had crossed the river at Castleford, some miles upstream Clifford's little force withdrew and ran into an ambush in which Clifford was killed. The survivors galloped back to warn Somerset, commanding the Lancastrian army, how close the Yorkists were. Fearing a surprise attack and taking no chances, Somerset deployed his army that evening in open ground, since known as Bloody Meadow, between the little river Cocke, in spate from much recent rain, and the Tadcaster–Ferrybridge road, just south of the village of Towton.

On the same day, Saturday, 28 March, Edward and Warwick led their army across the Aire by the pontoon bridge, and in the evening marched some eight miles due north towards Tadcaster; but, not being quite sure where the Lancastrian army was, they halted their force in the area of the little village of Saxton, in the darkness. The troops got what sleep they could, lying on the frosty ground, and as soon as it was light they could see Somerset's position, on a slope above them and about half a mile away to the north. Both the young army commanders – Somerset was only twenty-four, nearly five years older than Edward – drew up their troops in two divisions on a broad front. Each forward division consisted of archers, and the rear ones of infantry and mailed men-at-arms. Fauconberg commanded the Yorkist archers, and Northumberland and Sir Andrew Trollope those of the Lancastrian army. In Edward's force, to the rear of the infantry 'battalia', was a cavalry squadron led by Sir John Wenlock and Sir John Dynham. It had the dual role of discouraging any Yorkist from fleeing during the battle and of pursuing the Lancastrians if they turned and ran. Far behind the Yorkists and still on the road from Ferrybridge was the Duke of Norfolk, leading his contingent. Norfolk does not appear to have been a very keen soldier. He was late now, and he had managed to miss the first battle of St Albans altogether.

Determined that this battle would end the civil war, Edward gave orders that the enemy was to be given no quarter, and Somerset issued the same instructions to his men. Neither Margaret nor Henry was on the battlefield, they had both remained in York, twelve miles away to the north-east.

It was a bitterly cold morning, and though the wind was in the south-west, the first flakes of snow fell while the troops were being drawn up in battle order. Suddenly the sound of church bells from nearby villages reminded both armies that the day was Palm Sunday, and there was a pause while they stood in silence, looking at each other. No doubt many men felt that peculiar sickening tautness in the stomach, the blend of fear and excitement that comes to most men in the few moments before they have to go into action. The Lancastrians, benefiting from Somerset's reconnaissance on the previous day, had the advantage of the ground for they held the line of a wide ridge some fifty feet above Saxton village, looking down upon their opponents. The morale effect of height is considerable, but as the wind grew stronger, blowing what was now thick snow in their faces, they could hardly see the enemy.

At nine o'clock both armies advanced towards each other. The leaders of the Lancastrian archers peered into the snow, trying to judge the distance, and Fauconberg, a very experienced soldier, told his men to shoot one volley of 'heavy' arrows, normally used only at close range. These, carried by the following wind, caused casualties among the Lancastrians and made them believe the range to be much shorter than it was, thus their initial 'arrow storm' fell short. Gathering up the enemy arrows the Yorkists shot them back and then closed in. Soon, exhausted by hand-to-hand fighting, the archers began to withdraw, making way for the heavy infantry, and the fight became a murderous contest, often enough between men seeking revenge for the death of relatives in earlier battles. The badges or tabards of the nobility and gentry made them comparatively easy to identify and they were the main targets on both sides. It is said that the Lancastrian Lord Dacre, moving back from the forward area for a moment's rest, took off his helmet and was at once shot through the throat by a young archer sitting in a tree, who recognized him as the man who had killed his father.

The battle went on into the afternoon, those in the rear of each division coming forward to relieve or replace those in front, and there was no sign of weakening on either side until Norfolk and his body of fresh troops appeared, coming up the Ferrybridge road on the left of the exhausted Lancastrians. The sight of Yorkist reinforcements was too much for them. They broke and fled. Many were drowned in the river Cocke but most of the army got back to Tadcaster, about three miles away, only to find the bridge over the flooded river had been destroyed by Somerset's orders – to discourage his men from running away. The Yorkist cavalry rode down the fleeing Lancastrians, turning the pursuit into a bloody shambles on which there is no need to dwell.

The Earl of Shrewsbury and Sir Andrew Trollope were found among the slain, and round them lay eleven barons and forty knights. Northumberland reached the city of York but died there, of his wounds. The Earls of Devonshire and Wiltshire were taken prisoner, only to be beheaded later. Henry Beaufort, Duke of Somerset, and Henry Holland, Duke of Exeter, both escaped and found refuge with the Percys of Northumberland. Margaret, Henry and their son Prince Edward fled to Scotland.

The victorious Edward rode into York on the morning of Monday, 18 March. The heads of his father, his younger brother and his uncle were still stuck up above Micklegate. They were removed, buried with the bodies at Pontefract, and replaced by the heads of Devonshire, Lord Kyme and Sir William Hill. Wiltshire was beheaded at Newcastle. To all outward appearances the Lancastrians had been completely crushed, a military solution had been found to a political problem. Edward had justified his coronation and the Yorkist winter of discontent had been made glorious summer by the son of York. Quite probably this would all have been true if the Lancastrian cause had been in the hands of anyone but Margaret of Anjou.

To her, the disaster of Towton was but a backward swing of the hinge of Fate, from which her unconquerable spirit drew the energy and inspiration needed for continuing the conflict. The battle would go on until what she regarded as a rebellion had been stamped out. Edward knew very well that while Henry and his son were still alive the Lancastrians had a focus, and in Margaret they had an indefatigable leader. If the crown was to fit securely on his head he had to find all three and dispose of them. There was no alternative.

He therefore sent out parties of light cavalry to comb through all the country northwards to the Tyne. Beyond lay the great estates of the Percys, where there could be no pursuit. The hunt pressed so close that Margaret was forced into headlong flight, and her plan to halt at Newcastle and use this northern fortress as the headquarters from which to rally and reform her forces had to be abandoned. She was compelled to ride on to Berwick and seek sanctuary with the Scots. She wasted no time in bewailing her ill fortune in this apparently hopeless situation; she was far too busy planning her next move.

Edward celebrated the festival of Easter in the city of York, with a magnificence in marked contrast to the pious humility of the man he had deposed. He then rode south, to his coronation.

Philippe de Commines, who met Edward and therefore could describe him from first-hand knowledge, says 'he was a very young prince, and one of the handsomest men of his age, at the time when he had overcome all his difficulties; so that he gave himself up wholly to pleasures, and took no delight in anything but ladies, dancing, entertainments and the chase'. He was also a man of great presence; of enormous size in comparison with his contemporaries for he was nearly six feet four inches tall, very broad and muscular, brown-haired, fair complexioned, with an open, engaging expression and a great deal of charm. By nature he was friendly, easy-going and generous, and, like other kings notorious for their amorous adventures, his success with women added to his popularity. Under pressure, particularly that of battle, he seemed to change completely, becoming alert, shrewd, quick-thinking, swift to take advantage of any opportunity, ruthless and vindictive. He and Margaret were well matched opponents, worthy of each other's mettle. It is one of the many tragedies of English history that this pleasant young man, reaching his twentieth birthday, and this woman of such beauty and charm, now just thirty-one, had to be enemies. He fought for his crown. She fought for her child's right to that crown, and upon such great issues there could be no compromise.

10 Invasion (1461-1463)

From Berwick, Margaret and her family went first to Linlithgow, and then lodgings were found for them at the convent of Black Friars in Edinburgh. Her first audience with the Queen Mother, Mary of Gueldres, was far more of a success than she really had any right to expect. She and Henry were penniless refugees at a time when it seemed obvious that Edward Duke of York had established his right to be king of England by conquest, the most potent of arguments. So far as most people could see, Margaret, sheltering in a foreign country and with her previous supporters being executed, proscribed or imprisoned, was in no position to challenge the usurper. It says much for her powers of persuasion – and no doubt for Mary's respect for hereditary monarchy – that Margaret was able to make a treaty of alliance. It was to be effective immediately and consolidated by the betrothal of her eight-year-old son to the baby sister of the young James III of Scotland.

On 25 April 1461, in accordance with Margaret's former undertaking and in the name of King Henry VI, Berwick was surrendered to the Scots and at once became an operational base for a Scottish force driving deep into the northern counties of England. Warwick managed to turn the invaders back at Brancepeth in County Durham, and in June his brother Lord Montague relieved the Scottish siege of Carlisle. Edward of York was being made to realize that the Lancastrian threat hung heavy over the border lands. Though popular in London he knew that elsewhere he was regarded as a usurper, and that what Yorkists saw as a dark cloud in the north was, to the Lancastrians, a bright ray of hope. Something had to be done, but since no English king had ever succeeded in conquering Scotland he was wise enough not to try. He fell back upon diplomacy, invoking the aid of his friends across the Channel.

First of all he sent a delegation to Edinburgh, asking Mary of

Gueldres to surrender to him 'Harry, late usurpant King of our said Realm, Margaret his wife and her son'. This was refused. He then arranged for Philip of Burgundy to intervene, and once again the Seigneur de la Gruthuyse arrived in Scotland bearing letters from Philip and from the Dauphin Louis. In a short while the Seigneur had virtually destroyed all Lancastrian influence at the Scottish court. Mary of Gueldres was persuaded to withdraw her troops from their expeditions in England, and though, probably for personal reasons, she allowed Margaret to regard Scotland as a refuge, there was no longer any hope of combined Scottish and Lancastrian operations against Edward.

Even so, despite all Edward's efforts, the Lancastrian cause in England was by no means dead. The beheading of the Earl of Devonshire at York, after the battle of Towton, had caused intense resentment among his followers in Devon and Cornwall, where the old confidence trickster Sir Baldwin Fulford and Sir William Holland were busily spreading anti-Yorkist propaganda, and in many other places the embers of Lancastrian loyalty needed only a slight breeze from the proper quarter. Although by the middle of June 1461 Edward seemed to have established his authority, his control was still precarious. It was made even more so during a brief visit he paid to Stony Stratford on his way down from the Midlands at the beginning of June, though no one could have foreseen the complications that were to arise.

At Grafton – afterwards Grafton Regis – near Stony Stratford lived Lord Rivers, the faithful Lancastrian whose second wife was the beautiful Jacquetta of Luxembourg, widow of Henry V's brother John Duke of Bedford. Lord Rivers and Jacquetta had a daughter, Elizabeth Woodville, who had married Sir John Grey. He had been killed, fighting for Margaret, at the second battle of St Albans, and his estates had been confiscated. Hearing that Edward was close by, Elizabeth Woodville, just as good a Lancastrian as her father, arranged to be taken to meet him, and there are several versions of the story in which a girl who had inherited her mother's renowned beauty, knelt in supplication before the handsomest man of his age whom, allegedly, no woman was able to refuse. It seems that Elizabeth begged Edward to restore her husband's lands to her, so that she would have something to live on. He said he would be delighted to oblige her if she would co-operate in the time-honoured way. She refused and was absolutely adamant. Her path to any man's bed led first to the altar and therefore there was no point in pursuing his suggestion.

This was a new experience for Edward. The more she refused him, the more he wanted her – a not uncommon reaction. Much to everyone's surprise her father was suddenly pardoned for his Lancastrian activities. Edward, frustrated but deeply affected by his meeting with the lovely Elizabeth, went on to London. As will be seen, the seeds of his quarrel with Warwick, the man who had put him on the throne, had been sown.

A few days later, on Friday, 26 June 1461, Edward was crowned as King Edward IV by Archbishop Bourchier in Westminster Abbey.

He was not looked upon as a soldier king who had delivered the country from the tyranny of the House of Lancaster. On the contrary, he was tolerated, in the nature of an experiment, as being possibly a better alternative. Henry VI had failed largely because he was too trusting. He believed people when they made promises, took oaths and gave him assurances. It cannot be said that affairs of state got out of his control, because all his life his ministers had seen to it that he had no real authority, but no one disliked him because he had not been a success. He apparently disliked no one, and in this way he was so very different from Margaret. Her hatred was passionate. She hated the Yorkists with the same fierce intensity with which she loved her child, and it was her partisanship and the methods she used to enlist aid in defeating her enemies that made it so easy to whip up popular feeling against her. Yet she never allowed the hatred directed against her personally to deter or deflect her. In her son and in her fight for his inheritance she found the sources of her energy and her hopes, and indeed, the whole reason for her being.

Edward IV's coronation appeared to be a great success. He marked it by elevating a large number of Yorkists to the peerage, where Lancastrians were still in the majority. He also called back from the court of Burgundy his two younger brothers, George and Richard, sent there for safety by his mother Cecily in the previous year. They were made royal dukes, of Clarence and Gloucester, later described by Shakespeare as 'false, fleeting, perjured Clarence' – a reasonably accurate delineation – and 'Richard Crookback', which is erroneous. Both have been the subjects of historical arguments ever since.

As soon as the crown was on his head, Edward seemed to relax and leave most things to Warwick and the Nevilles. Warwick, a man of thirty-three, took full advantage of his position and never let Edward forget how powerful a subject he was. But Edward was in no mood to fight his friends, he had had to fight quite enough to win his throne. He made it his business to get on well with Warwick.

Margaret, spurred to greater efforts by news of the coronation, turned again to France for help. In July 1461 she sent Lord Hungerford to the French court, and Somerset to Burgundy, with letters for Charles VII and de Brézé, the Count of Charolais and the Dauphin Louis.

When Hungerford and Somerset landed at the port of Eu on the Normandy coast on 2 August, they heard to their dismay that Charles VII had died only eleven days before, on 22 July, and the Dauphin, accompanied by the Duke of Burgundy, the Count of Charolais, Francesco Coppini, the Bishop of Salisbury and a large entourage, was now at Avesnes, on his way to his coronation as Louis XI at Rheims.

Charles VII was fifty-eight when he died, having come to the throne at the age of nineteen. His long reign had been extraordinarily successful – after a very difficult start – and he left behind him a country contented, powerful and free, except for the blemish of Calais, from the English enemy. The end of his life had been clouded by conflict with his son. They had disliked one another for years, but latterly the Dauphin had openly sided with his father's enemies and gone to live with the Duke of Burgundy, the man whom Charles, with justification, regarded as the real stumbling block to French unity – the great aim of the House of Valois. Louis XI, who later earned the nickname of the Spider, lived in a web of intrigue, and in pursuit of his father's aim of 'la France arrondie' would stoop to any means. He was a man of great personal charm – when he chose to exercise it – and a fluent liar whose word counted for nothing. He justified all his deceit and double-dealing with the cynical apophthegm 'he who has success also has honour'.

The little party of Lancastrians at Eu had every reason to be apprehensive because they could hardly expect friendly treatment from Louis, the declared ally of Burgundy and supporter of the

Yorkists. The first blow to Somerset and Hungerford was the dismissal and banishment of Pierre de Brézé for having been so loyal a servant of Charles VII. Only a week after Charles's death, the Sieur de Lambarde was sent to take possession of Rouen where de Brézé, as Seneschal of Normandy, had his headquarters, but de Brézé refused to obey the banishment order and hid in the Normandy woods near Mauny. A few months later he surrendered himself and was imprisoned in one of the underground dungeons below the keep of the massive castle of Loches. Somerset and Hungerford and their followers, a party of about forty people, were arrested. Somerset and six men were sent to Arques under guard, Hungerford and the remainder were taken to Dieppe.

Edward IV was delighted by the news of Charles VII's death. It seemed to solve so many problems. He had been finding it difficult to tread out the Lancastrian embers; the Scots and Lancastrians still held fast to the northern castles of Alnwick, Bamborough and Dunstanborough despite all Warwick's efforts to dislodge them, and there was still trouble in Wales. These worries now seemed to count for little against the splendid news that instead of being an active enemy providing naval and military support for the Lancastrians, France had suddenly become a friendly power. Philip of Burgundy appeared to be willing to arrange a formal alliance and Mary of Gueldres wanted a truce. Sir John Wenlock was sent off at once with an embassy to Philip, and Warwick was authorized to make terms with the Scots.

To Margaret, in Scotland, the news from abroad came as a series of heavy blows. The whole edifice of Lancastrian alliances and diplomacy was collapsing. Her ambassadors had been arrested, France had suddenly become an enemy, the death of her uncle had tumbled all her plans into ruin and she would have to start all over again. Yet in fact her affairs were nothing like so disordered as she may at first have imagined. She had not seen Louis for many years; he had been a young man of twenty-two when she left France to marry Henry, and she had no means of knowing what he was like now he was thirty-eight, and, as so often happens when a subordinate succeeds to high command, Louis XI was very different from Louis the Dauphin.

Instead of fighting his father he now had to fight for his vision of a unified France. He knew that the authority of the king was directly related to the amount of control he could exercise over his vassals, and that if France was to be strong he must make sure her neighbours were weak. Before his father's death he had been friendly with Sforza; now he saw the advantage of curbing the ambitions of Milan by having an Angevin king, John of Calabria, on the throne of Naples. He had no intention of being faced by a strong, united England across the Channel, still less could he countenance the possibility of an Anglo-Burgundian alliance of the sort which, in the time of his grandfather Charles VI, had brought disaster to France. It was clearly in his interests, which were also those of France, to foster the civil war in England, but there was a great need for caution, an attribute he did not possess at the beginning of his reign. He very nearly gave his secret game away in Paris, soon after his coronation, when he asked Philip of Burgundy if he would be prepared to break the truce he had made with Edward IV. Philip refused, angrily, and until he left the court in October 1461 Louis dared not give a hint of his intention to open negotiations with Margaret.

As soon as Philip had gone home, Louis sent for Somerset and Hungerford and received them at Tours. Much to their surprise, for they had been virtually under house arrest for more than two months, they were welcomed as friends. Louis talked a great deal and said very little, yet his whole attitude indicated a sympathetic regard for Margaret's problems.

Meanwhile Margaret herself, completely out of touch with all this diplomacy, had no idea what was happening, and all she could do was wait impatiently in Scotland for news from her ambassadors or for them to return. All the news from England was bad, and as time slipped by she was afraid that Edward was strengthening his hold on the country and the crown.

In February 1462 Philip of Burgundy became seriously ill. Edward was so alarmed by the possible effects of his death that he ordered all his subjects to pray for his recovery. Charles Count of Charolais was known to be a supporter of the Lancastrians and his accession to the dukedom would change the direction of Burgundian sympathy. The prayers were effective. Philip did not die, but he never completely recovered.

During the winter of 1461–1462 the Duke of Somerset's agents were active in the southern counties of England, and though they reported the existence of pockets of Lancastrian loyalty they advised against any attempt at rebellion. At length, in March

1462, Somerset and Hungerford returned to Scotland. Somerset's report on the state of affairs in England convinced Margaret that her only hope of restoring her son's inheritance depended on invasion, not rebellion. She sent more messengers to France, this time to her cousin Charles of Orleans but, too impatient to wait for them to return, she set sail herself from Kirkcudbright in April, and on 16 April arrived in Brittany.

It was the first time she had set foot in her native country for seventeen years. In many ways it must have been a happy homecoming. François Duke of Brittany received her as royalty and lent her 12,000 gold crowns. She then went to Angers and saw her father and his new wife, Jehanne de Laval. Her own mother, Isabelle of Lorraine, had died nine years earlier, on 28 February 1453, after a long and painful illness in which she had been nursed and cared for her by her daughter Yolande and son-in-law Ferri de Vaudémont. She and Margaret had written to one another frequently, but they had not met since the parting at Bar le Duc.

Margaret then rode across the hills to the Chateau de Brézé and thanked Pierre, recently freed from Loches, for his unfailing support. Louis XI, told of Margaret's arrival, ordered the governors of Rouen and Caux to receive her with all the respect due to her rank, and at the end of May, Margaret and Louis at last met in the Great Hall of the castle of Chinon, that royal residence where she had made so great an impression on the court, and perhaps on Cardinal Beaufort, all those years ago. Nobody could ever tell what Louis really felt, or what was in his secret mind, but he greeted his cousin with every appearance of being glad to see her, and a little while later they stood side by side at the font in the castle chapel as god-parents for the infant son of the Duke of Orleans who had been born in March. The baby grew up to become Louis XII.

When Edward heard about all this his first reaction was to disbelieve the report, and when it was confirmed he wondered what on earth was going on. Louis's representative, the Sieur de Lambarde, had recently given him to understand that Louis was enthusiastic about forming an Anglo-French alliance, yet here was evidence that he was negotiating with Margaret, the enemy. Edward therefore gave careful instructions to Sir John Wenlock, the head of the delegation that was to negotiate the French alliance, telling him to use the greatest caution and discretion;

promising nothing and discussing everything in the most general
terms until he could 'break and open the intent of the Frenchmen'. At the same time he began an intensive psychological
operation against Margaret, letting it be known that she was
making plans to launch 'such cruel, horrible and mortal war . . .
as heretofore hath not been used among Christian people'.
According to him, Henry VI had agreed to give up all English
rights to the crown of France and territories such as Guienne,
and to abdicate in favour of Charles of Anjou. Edward's main
object was to arouse such anger and fear throughout the country
that the people would accept the extra taxation needed to support
operations against the Lancastrians and their allies.

Early in June 1462 Jasper Tudor and Sir John Fortescue,
Henry's chancellor, arrived in France to help Margaret in her
negotiations with Louis. Talks were held in the castle at Angers,
so familiar to Margaret, and on 23 June a secret agreement was
signed at Chinon. This was the preliminary to the main treaty,
discussed, agreed and finally published at Tours five days later.
In the secret agreement, in return for a loan of 20,000 *livres
turnois*, Margaret undertook that if Henry VI should ever
recover Calais, her nominee, probably Jasper Tudor, would be
appointed captain of the fortress, under oath to deliver the town,
castle and port to Louis within a year unless, during that year,
Henry VI had repaid the loan. In Louis's opinion the chance of
being able finally to eject the English from the soil of France was
well worth the loan which, from the present state of English
finances, would probably never be paid, but for obvious reasons
neither he nor Margaret wished to broadcast their arrangement.
The open treaty was a truce between Lancastrians and the French
which, perhaps a little optimistically, was to last for a hundred
years. It dealt mainly with details of safe-conducts, travel in
France and England, and undertakings not to make alliances with
rebellious subjects of either signatory.

In addition to the treaty, Louis issued public proclamations
telling his subjects to favour the Lancastrians and have no trade
or other dealings with Yorkists while they continued to acknowledge the person described as 'Edouard de la Marche' as king of
England. He paid the loan at once and promised Margaret a
force of 2,000 men which she could take back with her to
Scotland. The troops were to be led by Pierre de Brézé, with

whom he had apparently resolved his differences, and, as a final gesture, Louis gave the royal consent to the marriage of Pierre's eldest son Jacques to Charlotte de Valois, the daughter of Charles VII by Agnes Sorel.

In the middle of July Margaret arrived in Rouen from Tours. She was accompanied by Somerset and the Archbishop of Narbonne, who was the brother of Pierre de Brézé's wife, Jeanne Crespin. Margaret was given an enthusiastic welcome by the city which had entertained her for a week when she had travelled to England as a bride, and then she began her preparations for her invasion of England. In August Louis and de Brézé rode together through the streets of Rouen where the crowds shouted their approval for the reinstatement of their popular Seneschal.

Edward reacted strongly to the Treaty of Tours. By the end of July he had commissioned a fleet of seventy vessels and a force of 12,000 men, deployed at Dartmouth, Portsmouth and Southampton, and it was his intention to carry fire and the sword to the coastal waters and territory of France. At the end of August his punitive expedition, commanded by the Earl of Kent, crossed the Channel and, beginning at the Breton port of Le Conquet, not far from Brest, ravaged the coast as far south as Bordeaux throughout the whole of September and October. Louis realized he had misjudged Edward. He had assumed that as soon as Edward heard of the preparations being made at Rouen he would concentrate his fleet in the Channel and man his coastal defences. Instead, the English king had seized the initiative, and it was the French who were on the defensive. In an attempt to draw Kent back from the coast of Guienne Louis encouraged Margaret to try and gain control of Calais. Margaret went to Boulogne and her agents tried to subvert the garrison of Calais by promising to settle arrears of pay, but once again the wool merchants came to the rescue by lending Edward £41,000. Calais remained in Yorkist hands, Margaret had to return to Rouen and Louis's enthusiasm for the Lancastrian cause began to wane.

Margaret, Pierre de Brézé and his son Jacques sailed from Harfleur with a fleet of fifty-two small vessels on 9 October 1462. They still had the force of 2,000 men provided by Louis, augmented by others who had joined the expedition for excitement or loot. Margaret believed that the landing of this force in the north would be the signal for Lancastrian risings all over England

and this would bring the Scots in on her side. She had miscalculated. She was able to land garrisons for the fortresses of Alnwick, Bamborough and Dunstanborough but when her troops came ashore at Tynemouth, the size of her 'army' and of the ships carrying it, failed to convince anyone that she was capable of anything more than the typical French 'nuisance raid'. Local Yorkist forces withdrew initially and then counter-attacked with such determination that Lancastrian sympathizers in the area kept very quiet and Margaret had to re-embark her troops.

She sailed north, making for Berwick, but her ships were scattered in a great storm. Four of the largest, loaded with most of her military supplies and money, went down. Four hundred French troops, blown ashore on Holy Island, had to surrender to the Yorkists, and she and de Brézé, in a very small fishing boat, were lucky to reach Berwick alive.

Meanwhile Edward's main army was moving north by forced marches.

On 24 December 1462 the garrison at Dunstanborough, led by Richard Tunstall, Philip Wentworth and the priest Dr Morton, surrendered to Warwick's large force, and so did that of Bamborough, commanded by Somerset, Lord de Roos and Sir Ralph Percy. Lord Hungerford, Sir Robert Whitingham and Jacques de Brézé continued to hold out in Alnwick. Dunstanborough and Bamborough had been surrendered on condition that there would be none of the usual executions, and Edward and Warwick kept their word. In fact, Edward made extraordinary concessions. Somerset, having taken an oath of allegiance, was allowed to remain at court and four months later, in April 1463, he was restored to full status as the Duke of Somerset. Sir Ralph Percy was also given back 'all his estates and honours' and appointed to command Dunstanborough and Bamborough in the Yorkist cause.

Early in January 1463 Pierre de Brézé came down from Scotland with an army of 10,000 men commanded by the Earl of Angus to rescue his son from Alnwick, but it was purely a relief expedition. The fortress was evacuated, all arms, ammunition and military supplies were carried off or destroyed and the Scots withdrew, having made no attempt to offer battle to Warwick's army. As soon as they had gone, Warwick occupied the deserted castle.

Margaret's failure in the north was merely the echo of another failure in South Wales, the other hitherto sure stronghold. Here the Yorkist Herberts had virtually cleared the country of Lancastrians and taken Jasper Tudor's castle of Pembroke. The elusive Jasper himself had escaped once again, but his titles and estates were taken from him and Lord Herbert became the new Earl of Pembroke (Yorkist).

This period of Margaret's struggle to win support for the House of Lancaster is a sobering illustration of human nature in the realm of power politics. It is a world in which sentiment plays no part, where every move is calculated in terms of the profit to be gained by it. Magnanimity is interpreted as weakness, generosity as a symptom either of fear or of a desire to ingratiate.

Margaret's abortive attempt to invade Yorkist England had widespread repercussions, all unfavourable to her. Mary of Gueldres and her court, having gained Berwick, were not prepared to give any more help without adequate reward, and this meant they had to be sure the Lancastrians would win in the end. This now appeared to be unlikely. Louis had learned that to aid Margaret was to incur Edward's wrath in an active and most unpleasant form. Philip of Burgundy was a firm believer in the basic principle that one should never reinforce failure. To all four rulers, Mary of Gueldres, Edward IV, Louis XI and Philip of Burgundy, Margaret was a trouble-maker whose value lay only in the way in which she could be used to their personal advantage in their dealings with each other. None of them was particularly interested in the ultimate fate of her, her husband or her son.

The Count of Charolais, still loyal to Margaret largely because his father would not help her, was somewhat of a worry to Louis who was afraid of a complete reversal of Burgundian foreign policy when Duke Philip died. If Burgundy became hostile to France, his plans to recover Calais might be upset because the Duke of Burgundy owned the fortress towns on the Somme which lay across the route to the north coast. Louis therefore decided to invoke the clause in the Treaty of Arras of 1435 which gave the King of France an option to purchase these towns. Provided peace could be maintained he felt he had a reasonable chance of being able to complete the purchase before Philip the Good died. He was therefore anxious to end the undeclared war with Edward IV and ensure that Burgundy made no hostile move.

He was reasonably sure of Burgundy because of his carefully cultivated friendship with the de Croy family who were in positions of great influence in Philip's court – an influence made stronger by the discord between Philip and his heir. Louis now wanted a truce with England, and Edward, after his successes against the Lancastrians in Wales and the north, had no reason to quarrel with Louis. Much to the surprise of them both, Philip of Burgundy offered to act as mediator, and it was agreed that English, French and Burgundian ambassadors would meet at St Omer on 24 June 1463.

Ever since the virtual collapse of the Lancastrian effort in England and Wales, Margaret had known she was utterly dependent on foreign aid. The news of this proposed meeting was therefore profoundly disturbing. She might find herself in a hopeless position if her cousin began to treat with her enemy and it was no longer possible to play Burgundy off against either. Yet, for a brief while, it seemed as if her luck had turned and the meeting at St Omer might not take place.

In May 1463 Edward's second Parliament forced him to prohibit the importation of certain Burgundian goods in retaliation for recent restrictions imposed by Philip on English trade with Flanders. This had a considerable effect on their relationship. In the same month, de Brézé, with Margaret in Scotland, received letters from France indicating that Louis still secretly supported Margaret. This was enough to affect the balance of opinion in the Scottish court where the Bishop of St Andrews backed Margaret and Mary of Gueldres was chiefly concerned with backing the winner.

With a Scottish army behind them Margaret and de Brézé marched south and recaptured Alnwick castle. Sir Ralph Percy unhesitatingly betrayed King Edward's trust by handing Bamborough castle over to them. Edward, detecting the hand of Louis behind Margaret's activity, postponed the St Omer meeting, and to Margaret this in itself justified her little invasion. It was only a small incursion, not strong enough to encourage the northern counties to rally to Henry VI. The Earl of Warwick hurried north, retook Alnwick and Bamborough and drove Margaret back into Scotland.

Unfortunately this second fiasco convinced Mary of Gueldres that her most sensible course of action would be to get rid of

Margaret as soon as possible and make peace with Edward. She told Margaret that she and her family and followers must leave Scotland. Almost at the same time Louis made it clear that because of this second failure he could not offer her a refuge in France.

Even in this desperate situation Margaret does not seem to have been unduly disturbed. She now saw that at all costs she must disrupt the St Omer meeting. This should not be too difficult. Amidst all the cross-currents of distrust, commercial rivalries and mutual recriminations for recent hostilities it was not going to be at all easy for the English, French and Burgundian ambassadors to reach any amicable agreement. Her personal intervention ought, so she hoped, to make it impossible.

In the third week of July 1463 she collected her few possessions and a small party of her closest supporters, which included her son Edward, Pierre and Jacques de Brézé, Henry Holland, Duke of Exeter, Sir John Fortescue and Sir Edmund Mountfort. She said goodbye to Henry, the man she loved and for whom she fought so untiringly. They parted at Edinburgh.

They were never to see each other again.

Henry, with a few followers, rode south to Bamborough which had once again declared for him as soon as Warwick's back was turned. Here, in the fortress on the huge rock beside the wintry northern sea, he lived in penury for the next eight months, until May 1464, when the tide of war again swept down on him and yet again he was forced to flee. Only this time he had nowhere to go.

Margaret and her party sailed away from Scotland and landed at Sluys early in August. She had only ten florins in her purse and was deeply in debt to Pierre de Brézé. (A florin was an English gold coin worth about one third of a pound.) As soon as she landed she sent a messenger to Philip the Good, asking permission to come and see him. The news of her arrival at this critical time must have been a shock to Philip, and he sent Philippe Pot, a member of his staff and an experienced diplomat, to meet her and explain that he was too busy to see her. Margaret was in no frame of mind to accept such a reply. She said she had explicit instructions from Henry VI, the rightful King of England, to see the Duke of Burgundy at all costs, and see him she would.

Philippe Pot tried to warn her of the dangers of the journey.

St Omer, the place of the meeting, was dangerously close to Calais, and the Yorkist garrison might waylay her and take her prisoner. He felt it was his duty to point out that she was not popular in Flanders, her presence was resented and no one could guarantee her safety. None of this had the slightest effect on Margaret. In the clothes of a peasant woman, riding in a country waggon drawn by four horses, accompanied by her son and three women servants, and with the faithful Pierre de Brézé acting as coachman, she set off to find Philip of Burgundy.

It is possible that the famous and much discussed incident of the robber occurred on this journey. Waurin, Chastellain, de Clercq and Gregory all recount the story, so does Monstrelet, and though their versions are reasonably consistent in some respects, all are vague about the time and place. Later historians have given their interpretations, and differ as much as the old chroniclers. For example, Hume places the tale in the forest to the north of Hexham in Northumberland and says that Margaret was fleeing through it after the battle of Hexham on 15 May 1464 – at a time when we know she was on the continent. He quotes Monstrelet as his source, but Monstrelet's actual account is quite clear. He gives the date as August 1463 and specifically mentions Pierre de Brézé. We know that Margaret had several dangerous journeys and escapes, from Eccleshall into Wales, for example, after the battle of Northampton, and to Scotland after Towton, but de Brézé could not have been with her. Monstrelet says:

I must mention here a singular adventure which befell the Queen of England. She, in company with the Lord de Varennes [one of Pierre de Brézé's titles] and her son, having lost their way in a forest of Hainault, were met by some banditti, who robbed them of all they had. It is probable that the banditti would have murdered them, had they not quarrelled about the division of the spoil, insomuch that from words they came to blows, and while they were fighting she caught up her son in her arms and fled to the thickest part of the forest where, weary with fatigue, she was forced to stop. At this moment she met another robber, to whom she instantly gave her son and said, 'Take him, friend, and save the son of a king!' The robber received him willingly and conducted them in safety towards the seashore, where they arrived at Sluys, and thence the Queen and her son went to Bruges, where they were received most honourably. The Queen left prince Edward at Bruges and went to the Count de Charolais at Lille, who feasted her grandly, whence she set out for Bethune, to hold a conference with the Duke of Burgundy.

The exact details of this adventure will probably never be known but Monstrelet's account does at least fit into the pattern of events. Margaret did go on to Lille, where Charles Count of Charolais welcomed her affectionately, lent her 500 crowns and sent her on to St Pol-sur-Ternoise. His father had gone there because he realized that since Margaret was determined to see him he had better meet her, but not at the town where the peace conference was to be held. That is why he had chosen a place some twenty miles away to the south. From what he knew of Margaret he was afraid that if he tried to avoid her she would suddenly turn up at the conference and spoil everything. He was probably right.

Travelling on the direct road from Lille to St Pol, Margaret had to pass through Bethune, and in view of all the harsh things she had said about Philip in the past, it must have surprised her and disarmed her a little perhaps, to find an escort of his archers waiting for her there. He had sent them to protect her from any possible kidnapping raid from Calais. At their meeting at St Pol he listened sympathetically to the Lancastrian case and promised to bear it all in mind when he went to St Omer. He reminded Margaret that he was only one voice at the conference. Much would depend on how her cousin Louis felt.

Philip was in fact much more than just sympathetic. Before he left for Hesdin, about twelve miles away to the west where he proposed to stay during the conference, he gave Margaret a valuable diamond and 2,000 gold crowns, 500 gold crowns to de Brézé and 100 to each of Margaret's women. He also arranged for the Duchess of Bourbon and her daughters to entertain Margaret at St Pol until she went back to stay with the Count of Charolais at Bruges.

With good reason, Edward's delegation was suspicious of Philip's real intentions when they learned of his meeting with Margaret, and Philip did not make things any easier by remaining at Hesdin, saying he had promised to meet Louis there, and refusing to attend the main conference at St Omer. The general atmosphere of animosity and suspicion was at length broken down, largely by Louis himself, who could be extremely urbane and persuasive, and on 8 October 1463 all delegations signed a treaty which was in fact a truce, to last one year, in which Louis undertook not to help the Lancastrians. Louis, as usual, was playing all sorts of different games at the same time. During the conference he had so improved his relations with Philip's minister, Antoine de Croy, that he had persuaded him to accept the first payment for the Somme fortresses.

Margaret, waiting at Bruges to learn what agreement had been reached at Hesdin and St Omer, was disappointed but not discouraged when she heard the news. Nothing definite had been arranged, and there was to be another conference on 21 April 1464. Anything could happen before then, and for the moment there was nothing more she could do. The only problem was her own immediate future. She could not return to Scotland; Philip did not want her to remain in Burgundy, and in view of the truce with Edward IV, Louis obviously could not offer her asylum in France. Her father suggested she should spend a few quiet months on one of his estates in the duchy of Bar and offered her a pension of 6,000 crowns. She accepted and said goodbye to de Brézé and Charolais.

De Brézé went off to Hesdin to try to bring about a reconciliation between Philip the Good and his son Charles. He was unsuccessful, and went on to join Louis at Eu. Louis greeted him effusively, but there was something in his manner which warned de Brézé that Louis did not care for his friendly association with the House of Burgundy.

11   Exile (1463-1470)

The little walled town of Saint Mihiel, lying in the valley of the Meuse, guarded the only bridge over the river between Verdun to the north and Commercy in the south. It was a quiet place, famous for its monastery dedicated to St Michael, where nothing very much ever happened except for festivals and processions on saints' days, and the market once a week.

Margaret came here in the autumn of 1463, little knowing it was to be her home for the next seven years. Only twenty-one miles away, in the deep valley on the other side of the wooded hills to the east, was Pont à Mousson, on the Moselle, where she had been born. She arrived with a certain amount of pomp and stir, attended by a royal escort of troops provided by Philip of Burgundy who, like her cousin Louis XI, was extremely relieved to see her go off to this remote and peaceful corner of the duchy of Bar. With her came her son Edward, the Duke of Exeter, Sir John Fortescue and a small band of English exiles. Out of the pension provided by her father who, as usual, could ill afford to spare it, she rented a house and her little 'court' moved in and made themselves as comfortable as they could. There was no question of maintaining any sort of state, and Margaret's household differed very little from any other reasonably large house in the town. In a letter to the Earl of Ormonde, then in Portugal, Sir John Fortescue described it:

> We are all in great poverty, but yet the Queen sustaineth us in meat and drink, so we be not in extreme necessity. Her Highness may do no more to us than she doth. Wherefore I counsel you to spend sparingly such money as you have, for when you come hither you shall have need of it.

Fortescue, a distinguished lawyer and judge, spent much of his time educating Prince Edward, teaching him how to rule England when he succeeded his father, and it was for Edward that he wrote his famous *De Laudibus Legum Angliae*. He also wrote a treatise on the legitimacy of the Lancastrian succession. He must have been a great comfort to Margaret because he never seems to have had any doubt that his pupil would accede to the throne, and Margaret had need for such confidence. He was clear-headed, shrewd and cautious, a counter-balance for her impulsiveness and prejudices. Both of them knew very well that against the combined military skills of Edward IV and Warwick there was no hope of inspiring the Lancastrians in England merely by landing some small token force. If Henry was ever to be rescued from Bamborough and restored to the throne, his supporters would need a display of genuine strength which could only be obtained by a firm military alliance with either Louis of France or Philip of Burgundy.

Having no money with which to run a court and maintain the agents and couriers essential for keeping in touch with current events, Margaret had great difficulty in obtaining information, and being right away in Saint Mihiel she was cut off from the usual flow of rumours which might have given her some idea of what was going on. Yet, when she had had time to consider her position and her next moves, she saw there were one or two hopeful factors. Louis and Philip were not backing Edward because they thought he had a better claim to the throne than Henry VI, their support was simply a matter of political expediency, and any new move in the game could change everything. In fact Louis, that restless plotter, almost before the signatures on the agreement made at St Omer and Hesdin were dry, was secretly trying to persuade the Duke of Brittany to support Jasper Tudor in his planned expedition to Wales, and had sent his ambassador Guillaume Cousinot to see Henry at Bamborough. It was some time before Margaret heard about any of this, but she did find out that after her meeting with Charles of Charolais at Bruges, the count had written to Henry saying he would always remain faithful to the House of Lancaster. She therefore had good reason to believe that when Charles succeeded his ailing father in the dukedom, she might count on Burgundian support.

Early in 1464 the whole situation seemed suddenly to change completely and the growing despondency of the exiles at Saint Mihiel changed to eager expectancy with the news that Somerset, who had apparently gone over to the Yorkist enemy after the campaign against the northern castles, had quarrelled violently with Edward and fled from his court.

Edward had done his best to secure Somerset's allegiance. By Act of Parliament Somerset had been restored in 'name, state, style, honour and dignity'; he recovered the lands lost by his attainder and Edward had even provided him with large sums of money. But the Lancastrian loyalty of the Beauforts was too strong, and it seems that Somerset's conscience was the real bar to a friendship Edward tried hard to foster.

Somerset rode first to Wales, to make contact with Humphrey Neville, and then joined Henry in his poverty at Bamborough. As he travelled through the country he re-lit the flame of Lancastrian revolt against the Yorkist power, and the news spread fast and far. Jasper Tudor came over from Brittany and his supporters flocked to him in Wales. The massive fortress of Skipton in Yorkshire was seized by Lancastrians, and this was the signal for risings in Cheshire and Lancashire.

Guillaume Cousinot brought all this information with him when he came back from Bamborough, carrying letters Henry had written to Margaret and also Louis, René, Charles of Charolais and François Duke of Brittany. In all his letters Henry asked for immediate military aid, completely disregarding the time it would take to mount any expedition, but it was clear that even though he had shut himself up in the remote Northumbrian stronghold, he knew – no doubt from Somerset – what was going on outside. He instructed Margaret to waste no time in forming a triple alliance with Charolais and François of Brittany in order to prevent Louis from signing a treaty with Edward at the next meeting at St Omer. He asked her to send him guns and gunners from Anjou, to persuade Charolais to despatch Burgundian artillery, and to raise money to pay for a Lancastrian army which Somerset would lead.

For the moment, Margaret took heart from her husband's excitement and enthusiasm. This, at last, seemed to be the sign for which she had been waiting, but her own commonsense, and no doubt the wisdom and experience of Fortescue, soon made her realize that even if there was to be a resurgence of the Lancastrian cause there was nothing that she, far away in Saint Mihiel, could do to promote it.

Edward would not waste time in dealing with another threat to his throne and, though events might move swiftly, news usually travelled slowly. For all she or Fortescue knew, it might already be too late. In any case, to bring Charles of Charolais and François of Brittany together in an alliance might take months. Furthermore, her father was in no position financially to supply troops from Anjou, and even if she could raise money or arrange for a Burgundian expedition, it was unlikely that ships would escape Edward's coastal patrols. He already knew, through his agents, of Henry's correspondence and had doubled his precautions against invasion. The time factor, apparently ignored by Henry, was all-important. If help was to be effective it must be despatched immediately.

Sadly, and with great disappointment, Margaret was forced to the conclusion that at this stage she could play no part in any turning of the Lancastrian tide, and that between them Henry and Somerset must do what they could, without her help. From her point of view, although the situation in England might be very promising, at Saint Mihiel it had not really changed. She could only wait impatiently to learn the outcome of Somerset's return to his true allegiance.

Somerset, comparatively safe, for the time being, in the Percy stronghold of Bamborough, stayed where he was for the first three months of 1464, until at Easter he heard that the Scots were proposing to convert their one year truce with Edward into a permanent treaty. Fearing that he would soon be caught between both armies, he tried to seize the initiative by attacking the force commanded by Warwick's brother Montague which was escorting the Scottish ambassadors to the peace conference at York. Lord Montague won the first engagement, at Hedgeley Moor on 25 April 1464, where Sir Ralph Percy was killed, and at Hexham, two months later – on 14 May – Somerset's gallant little force was completely overwhelmed. Somerset, Lord Hungerford, Lord de Roos and several knights, all taken prisoner, were beheaded at once. Later, at York, Edward witnessed the execution of Sir Philip Wentworth, Sir William Tailboys and fourteen of Henry VI's personal attendants. Sir Ralph Grey, who had been the captain of Bamborough Castle, was later decapitated at Doncaster.

But Henry VI, the one Lancastrian Edward really wanted, was not caught. He had not been on either battlefield, but had been

taken to Bywell Castle on the Tyne, about eight miles to the east
of Hexham. From here he was whisked away by his faithful
followers when news of the battle came, and for nearly twelve
months this unhappy man, miserable without his wife and hating
the wretchedness and discomfort of being a fugitive on the run,
disappeared, and few people knew for certain whether he was
alive or dead. He was hidden in such places as Appleby in the
Lake District, Bolton and Clitheroe. Finally, in July 1465,
betrayed by a monk, he was captured by the servants of Sir
James Harington at Furness in Derbyshire, while on his way to
Wales. With him were two priests, Dr Bydon and Dean Manning.
The latter had formerly been one of Margaret's secretaries and
Dean of Windsor.

All three were taken to London and imprisoned in the Tower.
This time there was no pretence of loyalty to the anointed king.
Warwick himself with a large escort guarded the captives on their
way through London, ready to discourage any manifestation of
support, and it was made clear that Henry was a prisoner. His
feet were bound to his stirrups by leather thongs. Again he disappeared from public view, this time for five years. The two
chaplains were released. Edward knew the value of his prisoner.
While Henry was in the Tower he was no longer a focal point
for the Lancastrians who, though everywhere defeated, were by
no means extinguished. Since Henry had lost none of his
popularity as an individual it was announced that he was being
well treated and comfortably housed in accommodation suitable
to his rank. It subsequently transpired that this was not true at
all, but it is possible, and indeed one cannot help hoping, that
Henry may have found some relief within the walls of his prison.
He was no longer being hunted through the northern hills, he
had no more responsibilities and he could at last give a proper
amount of time to his devotions.

Years before, Blackman had written, 'the lord King himself
complained heavily to me in his chamber at Eltham, when I was
alone there with him employed together with him upon his holy
books and giving ear to his wholesome advice and the sighs of
his most deep devotion. There came all at once a knock at the
King's door from a certain mighty duke of the realm, and the
King said, "They do so interrupt me that by day or night I can
hardly snatch a moment to be refreshed by reading of any holy

teaching without disturbance".' There were no such interruptions in the Tower. He must have wondered whether Edward was going to kill him, but he had no fear of death and probably would have felt only sorrow at the thought of not seeing Margaret again until they met in Heaven.

To Margaret, already grieving for the loss of the faithful Somerset, Hungerford and de Roos, the news of the capture and imprisonment of Henry was another burden, although, after many rumours of his death, it must have been a relief to know he was still alive. She badly needed the stimulus of action, but there was nothing she could do. So many of her adherents were now in their graves; there was little encouragement to be gained from either France or Burgundy where she was regarded as a nuisance, and no one in England seemed to have enough influence or enthusiasm to revive and lead the Lancastrian cause. She was forced to wait and watch for an opportunity to disrupt the political affiliations between Louis XI, Philip the Good and Edward IV. She never lost hope, but in the summer of 1465 there was more bad news to test her endurance and her resolution. She heard that her staunchest ally, Pierre de Brézé, had been killed at the battle of Montlhéry, on 16 July, while commanding the army of Louis XI against a victorious Burgundian force led by Charles Count of Charolais. His death was another bitter blow, for she had lost not only a life-long friend but the one reliable ally who could represent her at the court of France. It was another sorrow at a time when there was no sign of any light along the horizon of her hopes. Nevertheless, unknown to her, events in England and the repercussions of them in France, were creating a situation which was to give her and her Lancastrian supporters good reason to believe that everything might come right in the end.

On the last day of April in the previous year, 1464, Edward IV had gone to Stony Stratford on the pretence of a hunting expedition, and early in the morning of May Day, unable to acquire her by any other means, he had secretly married Elizabeth Woodville, older than him by five years.

Edward had good reason to keep very quiet about what he had done. He had been virtually taken over by the Nevilles, to whom he owed his throne, and had been made to feel he could do nothing without first consulting the greatest of them, the Earl of Warwick, with whom he had not discussed Elizabeth. Moreover, there was a deep-rooted creed held by all classes throughout the country that the girl chosen by the king to be his queen must be a virgin. This, Elizabeth Woodville was not, and she had two sons to prove it. It was bound to be a shock to the Nevilles to discover that Edward had a mind of his own.

During this time, Warwick, pressing for a close alliance with France, was negotiating with Louis XI for the marriage of Edward to the fourteen-year-old Bona of Savoy, one of the sisters of Louis's queen, Charlotte of Savoy. Philip of Burgundy, fearing the political effects of such a union, was offering one of his nieces, and in March 1464 ambassadors from Spain had been trying to arrange for Edward to marry Isabella of Castille.* Feeling far more secure in his own kingdom after the victories at Hedgeley Moor and Hexham, Edward considered that he was no longer so dependent on French support and showed little enthusiasm for an alliance with France. He knew Louis wanted to involve England in his quarrel with Burgundy – on the question of the sovereign rights of the French crown over its nominal vassals – and anything of this sort would affect the all-important wool† trade with the Low Countries. Edward was therefore determined not to upset Philip the Good and, being sensitive to the hostility of most Englishmen to France, he had no intention of repeating what he regarded as Henry VI's mistake by marrying a Frenchwoman.

Warwick, his common sense eclipsed by delusions of grandeur, determined to force Edward into a decision. He made plans for an elaborate embassy, which he would lead, to meet Louis at St Omer on 1 October 1464, and in September, just before his departure, at a meeting of the King's Council in the royal abbey at Reading, Edward was required to authorize Warwick to draw up the marriage contract for Bona of Savoy. Thus, on 14 September, Edward was forced to admit he was no longer free to marry the French girl.

* She subsequently married Ferdinand of Aragon, and between them Ferdinand and Isabella united Spain, finally defeated the Moors at Granada in 1492, and sponsored Christopher Columbus.

† Wool was by far the most important of English exports and the only source of wealth greater than agriculture. Furthermore, the prosperity of the Flemish towns was based on the art of weaving cloth and depended on the wool from England. As an economic factor, wool was thus vital to both countries.

Warwick was furious. Edward had made him look a complete fool in the eyes of the French court, and all the plans for the meeting at St Omer and the alliance had been overturned. Even so, he acted with caution and concealed his wrath. He and Edward's brother Clarence led Elizabeth by the hand and introduced her to the Council in the abbey at Reading where she was greeted as England's queen, and Edward tried to repair their friendship by elevating Warwick's brother George Neville to the Archbishopric of York.

Louis XI was not the sort of man to indulge in the luxury of anger but he was very disappointed by the failure of his plans for an alliance with Yorkist England. Margaret was absolutely delighted. Here at last was the sign of a break in the clouds. She wrote to Louis, reminding him of their agreement at Chinon and the Treaty of Tours three years before, and asking him either to give his active support or allow his nobles to do so. Her letter impressed him. 'Look,' he said to Prospero Camulio, the ambassador from Milan, 'Look how proudly she writes!' She then went to Paris herself but Louis by then was too engrossed in attempts to acquire Brittany and Burgundy to be anything but vague and sympathetic. Another year (1465) went by, and events in England moved slowly towards a climax.

The new queen was crowned in Westminster Abbey, and one chronicler describes the celebrations afterwards as 'unusually magnificent', then she lost no time in establishing herself and her family among the aristocracy. Edward tried to emphasize that on her mother's side his wife's ancestry was as good as his own, and her cousin Jacques of Luxembourg, head of the House of St Pol, brought an imposing entourage over for her coronation, but the Woodvilles were a new family of little renown. Within a short time, with Edward's support, Elizabeth had arranged for three of her five sisters to be married to the heirs of the earldoms of Arundel, Kent and Essex. Of the other two sisters, Catherine was married to the Duke of Buckingham, still in his minority, and Mary Woodville was married to the heir of Lord Herbert. Elizabeth's brother, John Woodville, in his twenties, was married to the Dowager Duchess of Norfolk who was nearly eighty, then Thomas Grey, Elizabeth's elder son by her first marriage, was provided with the heiress of the Duke of Exeter, and this brought the Queen into direct conflict with the Nevilles.

The Lancastrian Duke of Exeter was in exile. Commines says he personally saw the unfortunate Henry Holland 'following the Duke of Burgundy's train, bare-foot and bare-legged, begging his bread from door to door', and his wife, left behind in England was scarcely any better off. Elizabeth Woodville was thus able to 'buy' their daughter for the sum of 4,000 marks, but Warwick wanted her for his own nephew. Edward's influence decided the issue. The Nevilles were even more infuriated when Lord Rivers, Elizabeth's father, was made an earl, given the office of Treasurer and then made Lord High Constable.

Outwardly all this appeared to be a disgraceful example of the misuse of royal patronage and influence, indicating that Edward was completely in the hands of a beautiful but unscrupulous woman who was determined to satisfy the greed of a horde of relations. People found it very difficult to understand how a man like Edward, who could have filled the royal palaces with women, could be so besotted about one. But Edward knew exactly what he was doing. Hitherto oppressed by the sheer weight of the Nevilles he was resolved to build up his own party around him, dependent upon him and therefore loyal. His mistake was that he chose the Woodville family which, unlike the Nevilles, had virtually no support in the country, possessed no private armies and by now were generally disliked because they had come so far in so short a time.

Warwick could see what was happening. He realized that Edward was no longer a tractable young man who would do what he was told. He was showing dangerous signs of taking all power into his own hands and ridding himself of the Nevilles. Thus the seed sown at Grafton, when Edward first met Elizabeth, was now coming into flower, and between the King and the Kingmaker discord was turning into strife. The conflict between them was simply one for power, and to Warwick the issue was simple enough. If, after all that had been done for him, Edward wanted to be independent he would have to go, and the rightful king, the gentle Henry VI, would have to be restored to the throne.

Margaret, waiting with enforced patience for a really promising change in the diplomatic climate, could never even have guessed that such thoughts were in Warwick's mind. He was the dire enemy of the House of Lancaster, and from her point of view it was unthinkable that she could ever have any dealings with him. It is unlikely that at this time Warwick thought of including Margaret in his plans. She had been away for nearly two years and had apparently dropped out of the political scene. If Henry VI was to be brought back to the throne he would be only a figurehead; wearing the crown while Warwick ruled the country, and the Kingmaker knew that if Margaret returned from exile he would find himself in much the same position as Richard Duke of York during the protectorates. If he was to seize power it would be far better to leave her where she was. Meanwhile, though Warwick's relationship with Edward became more and more strained, there was as yet no open breach.

For the first three years of his reign Edward had been content to let Warwick handle all matters of foreign policy. Warwick had set his heart on the lasting treaty with Louis, but Edward did not trust the French king and inclined towards an association with Philip the Good, largely because of the importance of the wool trade. The issues and the options were now becoming complex, and Edward found himself in a position of considerable influence in the international web of intrigue.

Charles Count of Charolais, now reconciled with his father, wanted Edward's support in the contest of the princes against Louis. Louis needed Edward's help against the princes. In return for an Anglo-French alliance Louis would be required to abandon Margaret in her struggle against Edward. On the other hand, Charolais had always been a firm supporter of Margaret and was the one political leader in whom Margaret placed all her trust. Thus, whatever Warwick may have thought, Margaret had by no means dropped out of politics.

The Woodvilles, jealous of the Nevilles and in direct opposition to them because of Warwick's influence with Edward, favoured an alliance with Burgundy and, despite all Warwick's activities in preparing the treaty with Louis, in October 1466 Edward undertook to sign one with Charolais. But at the last moment neither Philip the Good nor his son would revoke their prohibition on the sale of English cloth in Flanders – made to protect their own manufacturers – and so Edward, trying to force Charolais's hand, showed renewed interest in negotiations with Louis. In this involved game of playing Burgundy against France, and vice versa, Edward was in the happy position of being able to send sincere, high-level embassies of Woodvilles to Burgundy and Nevilles to France, each claiming they represented the will of the king of England, while in fact Edward had no serious intention of committing himself completely to either.

Louis XI, the Spider, trusted no one and firmly believed that every man has his price. As a negotiator he was infinitely more devious and crafty than any of his contemporaries. He was a small, dark man whose large eyes, set wide apart under thin, level eyebrows, seldom gave any indication of his real thoughts, and whose charming, ready smile was merely one of the many weapons in his diplomatic armoury. He made it his business to know what was going on in the other courts in Europe, and therefore he knew that Warwick, who had no male heir, had a plan for his daughter Isabella to marry Edward's brother Clarence and thus, since Edward's Queen had not produced a son, there was a chance that a Neville might yet sit upon the throne. Louis also knew that Edward had expressly forbidden the marriage, thereby drawing attention to the rift between himself and Warwick and underlining his growing independence from the Nevilles.

In 1467 Warwick led a delegation to the court of France, then at Rouen, arriving there on 1 May. In a long series of discussions with Louis he promised to do everything in his power to prevent Edward from making any treaty with the Burgundians and to disrupt the negotiations, then in progress, for the marriage of Charolais to Edward's sister, Margaret of York. From correspondence between Prospero Camulio and Sforza it seems that during these discussions Louis suggested a partnership between Warwick and Margaret with the object of restoring Henry VI to the throne. Louis was not at all happy about the way things were going. It seemed unlikely that Edward would ratify any treaty arranged by Warwick, and in any faction fight between the Woodvilles and the Nevilles, Edward would take the side of his wife's family.

If this happened, Warwick would lose all his influence, and since he was obsessed by power, he would make no concessions to the Woodvilles. He would fight. Under the threat of an Anglo-Burgundian alliance against him, virtually the only counter-measure Louis could take was to foment trouble in England which would keep Edward out of continental affairs.

It seemed that the time had come to make further use of Margaret.

On 5 May Louis sent Ferri de Vaudémont to fetch his sister-in-law and her son Prince Edward and bring them to stay with him for a while at Chartres, and this was a clear indication that he had little hope of reaching any agreement with Edward IV. There is no evidence that Margaret accepted this invitation, and it is unlikely she would have done so while Warwick was at the French court.

Warwick's delegation, laden with expensive presents, sailed back to England from Honfleur at the beginning of June, and when Warwick reached London he found Edward had been busy while he was away. A truce had been signed with Brittany, it was clear that an agreement would soon be signed with Burgundy, and other arrangements were being made for an alliance between Edward and Henry of Castille, Louis XI's great enemy in Spain. When Louis's ambassadors arrived to follow up the progress Warwick had made at Rouen, Edward himself was barely civil to them. Furthermore, Warwick's brother George Neville, Archbishop of York, had been dismissed from the post of Lord Chancellor, and certain grants which Warwick had hitherto received from the crown were not renewed.

News of the death of Philip the Good, on 15 June 1467, heightened the tension, and negotiations for the marriage of Margaret of York took on a new significance when Charolais became Charles the Bold, Duke of Burgundy.

The French ambassadors were sent home, taking with them gifts of hunting horns and leather bottles which were a very poor exchange for the gold plate and precious stones they had brought with them. On 1 August, the day they left London, Charles the Bold confirmed the treaty he had discussed with Edward in the previous October.

Louis was not particularly surprised by this turn of events, but Margaret was shattered. Ever since coming to France at the beginning of her exile, when Charles had been so kind and reassuring, she had longed for the day when he would succeed to the dukedom and she would have a powerful ally on the continent. The shock of his treaty with Edward was like a blow in the face, but after four years of exile at Saint Mihiel Margaret was out of touch with the situation which had arisen as the result of her cousin Louis's determination to achieve *La France arrondie*.

By embracing the Lancastrian cause Charles would have thrown Louis and Edward together in an alliance too strong for the Confederation of Princes to withstand. Louis, with the excellent regular army bequeathed to him by his father, and supported by naval and military operations on the coast of Flanders, would overwhelm Burgundy and then turn to deal with Brittany. (At the news of the Anglo-Burgundian treaty Louis was able to mobilize 1,000 men-at-arms – with all their attendant squires and followers – and 16,000 archers, within a few days.) No matter what he may have felt about Margaret, Charles had no option but to continue the foreign policy of his father and protect Burgundy by an alliance with England. With her mind concentrated upon her own problems and her own aims, Margaret could see only that she had been abandoned by the one man, apart from Pierre de Brézé, she had trusted completely. Yet she soon realized that the hope of the Lancastrians still lay where it had always lain – with the odd man out. Faced with the Anglo-Burgundian treaty, Louis had to take steps to render it ineffective, and this could be done only by renewing the state of civil war in England.

But this was not so easy as it might sound. Everything depended upon Warwick, for with Henry VI a prisoner in the Tower, Margaret in exile at Saint Mihiel, and Edward firmly in control in England, there was no other instrument for reviving the Lancastrian cause. If Margaret were again to be given money and troops for an invasion, there was no reason to suppose it would be any more successful than her previous effort with de Brézé in October 1462. Louis appreciated that in present circumstances a civil war in England could not be engineered from outside, there would have to be a popular rebellion under a recognized leader. Warwick was the only military commander with any hope of success, and all Louis's hopes were pinned on him. Yet, despite his friendship with Warwick, carefully developed and tended during the treaty negotiations at Rouen, there were many obstacles to be overcome.

Margaret and Warwick were known to be implacable enemies who, somehow, would have to be reconciled before there could be any chance of a Lancastrian revival. There was another problem in that although the enmity between the Woodvilles and the Nevilles had seriously affected Warwick's loyalty to Edward IV, at the end of January 1468 Warwick allowed his brother the Archbishop to heal the breach between him and Lord Rivers, and when the three of them went to Edward's court at Coventry in the same month, outwardly all was peace and goodwill.

On Saturday, 25 June 1468, Edward's sister Margaret of York arrived at Sluys, and on Sunday, 3 July, she and Charles the Bold, Duke of Burgundy, were married at the little village of Damme, outside Bruges. Louis called up more troops and prepared for war. He attacked Brittany while at the same time fostering a revolt in Liège to keep Charles occupied. The wedding celebrations at Bruges were rudely interrupted. Louis forced François of Brittany to sign the treaty of Ancenis, abandon all his allies and swear to be a faithful servant of the French crown. Charles assembled the forces of Burgundy, but Louis made the mistake of thinking he could deal best with Charles by diplomacy and not by force of arms. He went under safe-conduct to see Charles at Peronne, where Charles seized him and locked him up in the castle. At length, largely on the advice of his minister Philippe de Commines, Charles agreed to respect the principle of the safe-conduct and released Louis on condition that he would recognize the Anglo-Burgundian alliance – now cemented by the recent wedding at Bruges. In return, Charles promised not to help the English if they invaded France.

Louis agreed readily to all proposals, but in the pursuit of his aim to destroy the power of the great princes and unite France, he never considered himself to be bound by any promise or treaty or agreement. Charles, who attached slightly more importance to an oath, felt that the agreement at Peronne had clarified the whole situation. Louis was no longer a menace to the independence of Burgundy – which had been the reason for the Anglo-Burgundian alliance – and therefore the alliance was no longer really necessary. There was certainly no need for him to give Edward any active support, nor in fact did he now have to enforce the commercial aspects of the treaty which had been in dispute for years.

Thus Louis had in effect achieved his immediate object of destroying the Anglo-Burgundian alliance. He now proposed to demolish the significance of the marriage of the Houses of York and Burgundy by turning Edward IV off the throne of England.

His policy was based on a simple appreciation. By restoring the House of Lancaster he could be certain of a firm alliance between England and France, arranged by Margaret and Warwick. This would isolate Burgundy. Furthermore, by establishing staple towns* in Normandy and giving special rights to English merchants trading with Bordeaux he could ruin Burgundian trade and force Charles to accept the sovereignty of France.

In October 1468 he announced his intention to give all possible assistance to his cousin Margaret Queen of England.

For Margaret, this, at last, seemed to be the end of the long exile. She moved her threadbare little court from Saint Mihiel to Rouen, and beside her rode Sir John Fortescue, for whom this move was the culmination of years of teaching and preparation. Under his guidance both Margaret and her son Edward knew what parts they had to play.

By the time the news of Margaret's arrival in Normandy reached Edward IV it had become considerably exaggerated, and he was given to understand that she was waiting at Harfleur for a favourable wind to propel a formidable invasion fleet across the Channel. He at once abandoned plans he was making for a combined operation against Guienne and began to patrol the Channel. Margaret's ships failed to appear, and after making one or two raids on the coast of Normandy, Edward's fleet concentrated at Spithead at the end of November and was laid up for the winter of 1468–1469.

Edward's reaction to the threat across the Channel was to plan a counter-invasion of south-western France which would draw all Louis's resources away from the north coast, but his plans were upset by a rebellion in Yorkshire in June 1469.

Ever since his reconciliation with Edward IV and Lord Rivers, in January 1468, Warwick had apparently been living a quiet and peaceful life as a member of Edward's court, and the only ripple on the surface of a seemingly amicable relationship had been Warwick's forthright refusal to have anything to do with the marriage of Edward's sister to Charles of Burgundy. He had always been, and still was, totally opposed to the Burgundian alliance, and he had developed an intense personal dislike for

* A 'staple' town was one appointed by royal authority, in which a body of merchants was granted exclusive rights for the handling of specified goods for export.

Charles. But, as Louis seems to have been aware, under the surface Warwick was deeply involved in plots against Edward and for furthering his long-standing design for the feckless young Duke of Clarence, now twenty-one, to marry his elder daughter Isabella. The Reverend Thomson says that 'the fair Isabella inspired the young prince with a sincere and, for a time, incalculating passion', and this may have been so, but in terms of impetuosity and unreliability Clarence had much in common with the Good Duke Humphrey of Gloucester.

At the end of 1468 there had been a small Lancastrian revolt in Lancashire which Edward had to suppress, without knowing it had been organized by Warwick, and in fact the king still trusted the Kingmaker to such an extent that in the spring of 1469 he gave permission for Warwick and his wife and daughters to live at Calais, where Warwick still held the official post of Captain.

It is probable that Warwick's allegiance to Edward was finally destroyed by the marriage of Margaret of York to Charles the Bold. It was so deliberately calculated to destroy Warwick's dream, amounting almost to a fixation, of a secure alliance with Louis XI. From then on he was Edward's enemy, though he took great care to hide his feelings.

In June 1469 the flag of rebellion was raised by Robin of Redesdale in Yorkshire, and not until he learned that Robin's sponsors were Nevilles did Edward associate the rising with Warwick. He at once summoned the Earl to court, only to be told that he, Clarence and Isabella, and George Neville the Archbishop, had all sailed secretly to Calais from Sandwich in the middle of June. Edward's own mother, Cecily Duchess of York, had sailed with them, but her reason for going was to try to prevent Clarence from splitting the House of York from top to bottom by marrying a Neville. She had failed. On 11 July, by papal dispensation, the Duke of Clarence was married to Isabella Neville, and news of the wedding was followed almost immediately by a manifesto issued by Warwick, Clarence and the Archbishop saying they were returning to England to present to the king 'reasonable and profitable articles of petition', and calling upon all loyal subjects of the king to join their cause.

Once again, it was rebellion in familiar guise, and the cause was simple jealousy of the Woodville faction and its influence over the king. It had nothing to do with the contest between the Houses of Lancaster and York.

The conspirators crossed the Channel on 16 July, landing at Sandwich, and from here they marched across Kent, gathering supporters as they went, through London and towards the Midlands where they intended to link up with Robin of Redesdale. Robin, having recovered from an initial defeat at the hands of Warwick's brother Lord Montague, came south, while Lord Herbert (the Yorkist Earl of Pembroke) and the Earl of Devonshire hastened across from South Wales with the object of reinforcing Edward who, with a small body of troops, was in the Nottingham area. The junction was never made. On 26 July Lord Herbert was forced to give battle at Edgecote, six miles north-east of Banbury in Oxfordshire; he was killed and his army was routed. In the pursuit which followed, Lord Rivers and his son Sir John Woodville – father and brother of Edward's queen – were caught in the Forest of Dean. So was the Earl of Devonshire. All three were taken to Northampton and beheaded. Edward's force melted away. He went first to Nottingham Castle and then, apparently trying to get back to London, was captured at Olney in Buckinghamshire by Archbishop Neville. He was taken to Warwick Castle.

Despite all this, the City of London declared its loyalty to the House of York, and Edward was conveyed to the Earl of Warwick's strong castle of Middleham in Wensleydale, where he was guarded by the Archbishop.

To Margaret and Louis in France these great events seemed to herald the restoration of the Lancastrians, but Warwick had apparently changed his mind, for he had no intention at this stage of putting Henry VI back on the throne. It is difficult to estimate what was in his mind, and for a time all was confusion. England had reached a unique point in her history. She now had two kings at the same time, and both were prisoners. If Warwick had decided to depose Edward, the only alternative was Clarence, for whom there was no support anywhere in the country, and Warwick certainly made no move to sponsor him. No doubt by now he had come to know the basic weaknesses in Clarence's character.

The watchers on the continent must have been even more mystified when they learned that a Lancastrian revolt raised by

Sir Humphrey Neville had been ruthlessly put down by Warwick. Sir Humphrey had been beheaded on 29 September 1469, and Edward, released from Middleham and taken to York, had ordered and witnessed the execution. From York, escorted by George Neville, the Archbishop, and John Neville, Lord Montague, Edward had returned to London where Burgundian ambassadors formally invested him with the insignia of the Order of the Golden Fleece, founded by Philip the Good. At a meeting of the Great Council in November, Edward accepted the explanations of Warwick and Clarence when he called on them to justify their resort to armed force, and he was genial and friendly. Apparently his royal authority had in no way been impaired and he obviously had no intention of renouncing his alliance with Burgundy.

No matter what Warwick's private intentions may have been, events had forced him along the course he had taken. His capture and imprisonment of Edward had in effect weakened his position, for his supporters made it clear to him that their objective was to overthrow the Woodvilles, not the king. No one wanted Clarence – or Henry VI for that matter – and Warwick found that by himself he could not exercise any control over the country. He was fortunate in that Edward seemed quite prepared to forgive and forget, and even published an amnesty which included all the insurgents in the north.

It must have been difficult for Margaret and Louis to believe the reports coming back to them, and it is not surprising that in one of his letters to Sforza, Camulio wrote, 'From England one never has one thing like another, but always more dissimilar than the day is to the night.'

Yet there was tension and distrust lying below the surface of mutual goodwill, and this is illustrated by the story that in February 1470, about twelve weeks after all the reconciliations, Archbishop Neville invited Edward and Clarence and Warwick to his manor of The Moor in Hertfordshire. While Edward was washing his hands before supper a servant whispered to him that an armed band had been seen lurking close by. Without pausing either for supper or to check the truth of what the servant had said Edward crept out of the house, mounted the horse brought to him at a side door, and rode all through the night to Windsor. His mother Cicely, who was a friend of Warwick, managed to bring about another reconciliation, but things could not go on like this for long.

In February 1470 another insurrection broke out, this time in Lincolnshire. It had been planned by Warwick and Clarence, but so successfully did they conceal from Edward their part in it that he authorized them to raise troops in his name to suppress it. Warwick based himself on Warwick Castle, where Clarence joined him early in March, and he instructed Sir Robert Welles, leader of the revolt, not to offer battle to Edward and his army who were moving up from London, but to join him at Leicester on 12 March. Welles, anxious about the safety of his father who was in Edward's hands, disobeyed these orders and on that day encountered Edward's force at Erpingham in Rutland. Unfortunately for Warwick, some of the rebels were wearing Clarence's livery and went into battle with confused shouts of 'A Warwick!' and 'A Clarence!'

This was all Edward needed to know. He ordered Warwick and Clarence to disband their force and wait upon him immediately. They marched their army to Burton-on-Trent. He moved to Grantham and then marched on a parallel route with them towards Yorkshire. At Newark, on 17 March, Edward received loyal addresses from both Warwick and Clarence, suggesting a meeting – with certain provisions for their safety – at Retford. Edward replied with another direct order to obey his summons. Ignoring it, they went on, but Edward, always able to inspire his troops to make an extra effort, moved faster and blocked their way. Warwick and Clarence decided that the time had come to exercise a little discretion. They abandoned their army, turned south and rode at full speed for Devonshire.

Edward's southern levies, made responsible for preventing the escape of the two newly-declared traitors, were unable to hinder them from embarking at Dartmouth with their wives, families and friends, and making for Calais. Again Edward moved too quickly. His messenger won the race to Calais and when Warwick arrived there he found the fortress held for the king and its guns trained upon him. A few days later he sailed into Honfleur and appealed to King Louis for help.

Thus began the last campaign for the restoration of Henry VI and Queen Margaret to the throne of England.

12   Tewkesbury (1470-1475)

When it had become clear to Margaret and Louis that Warwick's invasion had not been prompted by anything more than jealousy of the Woodvilles, and that he had no intention of rescuing Henry VI from the Tower, Margaret, bitterly disappointed, had returned to Saint Mihiel. Although Louis assured her of his support as soon as the right moment came, somewhat naturally after all these years of disappointment she was becoming disillusioned about the promises of princes. Yet she still believed that one day she and her son would return to England and ride in triumph through the streets of London to take her husband from his prison.

Warwick's arrival at Honfleur as a refugee signified to Louis that the right moment had at last come. He could now make effective use of the queen who, on the chessboard of international politics, had for so long been unable to make any move. Yet, though he felt reasonably sure that Warwick would agree to his plans, he was very far from certain about Margaret, and the first essential step was to persuade them to co-operate with one another. Another complication was that their aims were quite different. Warwick wanted revenge for what he regarded as the injuries and humiliation he had suffered at Edward's hands. Margaret was determined to secure the succession for her son. Warwick sought power; the power *behind* the throne. Margaret believed only in the autocratic, undisputed rule of the crown.

In May 1470 Louis sent Philippe Guérin and Louis Toustain to Saint Mihiel to ask Margaret and Prince Edward to come to the château of Amboise beside the Loire as soon as possible. On 8 June he received Warwick and Clarence there as honoured guests. But Margaret, who had hastened to Rouen in 1468, was not prepared to take the risk of making herself look ridiculous by hurrying a second time, and although Louis sent another messenger, Oudinet Pouilhay, to bid her make all possible speed, she and her son did not reach Amboise until 25 June.

Louis then put his proposal to her and was met with a flat refusal. Margaret told him it was out of the question for her to form any sort of association with the man who, more than anyone else, had been directly responsible for the fall of the House of Lancaster – who had even led her pinioned husband through London and thrown him in the Tower. Worse still, from a personal point of view, he had called her a bastard and publicly accused her of adultery by insisting that her son was a bastard too, and had no right to the throne. He had caused her endless distress and suffering, and all her hardships and misfortune were of his contriving. She told Louis that rather than come to terms with such an enemy she would forgo whatever opportunity Fate might be offering, and go back to Saint Mihiel.

But Louis's assessment of her character and ambition was exact, and his skill and patience in persuasion were unrivalled. Enlisting the support of Sir John Fortescue he applied himself to a task which must, at first, have seemed impossible. Slowly, gradually, he broke down her opposition, and at length she agreed to discuss possible plans provided she was first allowed to humble the fierce Neville pride by making Warwick kneel to her and beg forgiveness. This condition seemed reasonable enough in the circumstances, to everyone except Warwick. He denied vehemently that he had ever acted in such a way as to need pardon. He said he had fought against Henry and Margaret because they had tried to destroy him. He had done no more 'than that which a nobleman outraged and impaired ought to have done'. He accused them of corrupt and ineffective government, and claimed he had a perfect right to do all he could to bring their rule to an end. He had won and they had lost. The question of apology did not arise.

Louis called in his brother, Charles of France, and Margaret's father, King René, to help him in the discussions which went on for a week. Slowly the two principals began to move towards common ground. Supported by Charles and René, Louis urged Margaret to forgive her enemy and, by accepting him as an ally, seize what might be her only chance of defeating the Yorkists. He pleaded with Warwick to be patient with Margaret for she had endured a great deal and could not be expected to see at once all the advantages of a reconciliation. He tried to convince Margaret of his enduring support by asking Prince Edward to be godfather to his infant son, the future Charles VIII.

At length Margaret accepted the advice of her father and Sir John Fortescue and agreed to an alliance. The formal reconciliation took place on 22 July, in the castle at Angers, where René had been born. Warwick asked to be forgiven for all the injuries and wrongs he had committed against the House of Lancaster, and Margaret kept him on his knees for a quarter of an hour. Then she pardoned him, and taking her hand between his he did homage and swore fealty, swearing on a relic of the True Cross, kept in Angers Cathedral, that he would be a faithful subject to King Henry VI, Queen Margaret and Prince Edward – an oath which he kept to the letter, and the death. On the same surety Margaret promised to treat Warwick as a faithful subject, which she did, and Louis and his brother Charles undertook to give Warwick all the assistance in their power to restore the House of Lancaster.

There was still one more obstacle to be overcome. This was the proposal that the alliance should be confirmed by the marriage of Prince Edward to Warwick's daughter Lady Anne Neville. It is easy enough to see that Warwick wanted to keep one foot firmly in each camp. His daughter Isabella was his link with the House of York, he wanted to be sure of his continued influence if fortune favoured the Lancastrians. To Margaret, such a marriage offered no advantages whatsoever. It seemed to place her and her son on the level of conspirators planning a usurpation, whereas her whole campaign was being fought against the usurper Edward IV. From her point of view, she was planning to restore her husband and her son to their rightful inheritance, and Warwick, far from doing her a favour which justified a reward, was merely – albeit belatedly – doing his duty.

The years of exile had hardened her determination to win back the throne of England or die in the attempt. She wanted no strings attached to her son's future, and for the last seven years she and Fortescue had devoted most of their energy to schooling him for his role as King of England. Having a deep distrust of the whole Neville clan she had no wish to saddle him with a

Neville as a condition of his succession. Eventually she was compelled to give way, when it was made clear to her that without the marriage the alliance with Warwick would count for very little, and without Warwick there could be no Lancastrian revival. Even so, she insisted that Anne Neville should join her household – just as her sister had been made to join the de Vaudémont establishment – and that there would be no wedding until Warwick had been successful in England. Both Louis and Warwick wanted the ceremony to take place before Warwick's expedition sailed but, as Sir John Fortescue pointed out, unless Warwick did manage to restore Henry VI the marriage would have no significance.

By bringing together two such disparate personalities as Margaret and Warwick, Louis had achieved the apparently impossible, and of the marriage contract between Edward Prince of Wales and Anne Neville, Philippe de Commines wrote, 'An unaccountable match! To dethrone and imprison the father, and marry his only son to the daughter of him that did it!' He goes on, 'It was no less surprising that the Earl of Warwick should delude the Duke of Clarence, brother to the king whom he opposed, who ought in reason to have been afraid of the restoration of the House of Lancaster; but affairs of so nice a nature are not to be managed without great cunning and artifice.'

In any case, Clarence was never remarkable for his intelligence.

As usual, there were other motives underlying all these arrangements. Margaret regarded Anne Neville as a hostage for her father's loyalty, and Louis looked on Margaret and her son and future daughter-in-law as guarantees for the Anglo-French alliance as soon as Henry VI was back on the throne.

In planning his invasion, Warwick made no attempt to conceal his intentions, and he and Clarence even went so far as to write jointly to the Commons, saying they were bringing over a force 'to subdue and put under all falsehood and oppression, chastise and punish covetous persons in perpetual example to all other'. Edward refused to be alarmed. He had no great opinion of Warwick's abilities as a military commander, and the ease with which the Lancastrian insurgency in Yorkshire and Lincolnshire had been quelled had convinced him that his kingdom was now predominantly Yorkist and he had nothing to fear.

In September 1470 he was away in the north, dealing with a Lancastrian revolt specially arranged by Lord Fitzhugh, when Warwick put out from Honfleur on 9 September, escorted by a French fleet, and landed his invasion force four days later at Dartmouth and Plymouth. For some months Charles the Bold had been warning Edward that this was going to happen, only to be told by his agents that Edward refused to take even the most elementary precautions. No doubt Commines was right when he wrote: 'King Edward had indulged himself in ease and pleasures for twelve or thirteen years together, and enjoyed a larger share in them that any prince in his time. His thoughts were wholly employed upon the ladies (and far more than was reasonable), hunting and adorning his person.'

Another of Edward's failings was that despite all the advice given by Charles of Burgundy he had complete trust in Warwick's two brothers, the Archbishop and Lord Montague. Yet one of the main lessons of the civil war was that it was most unwise for the king to have absolute faith in anyone.

Thus, thanks to Lord Fitzhugh and Edward's over-confidence, when Warwick came ashore there was no Yorkist force in the south and no organized resistance, and for once Edward's acute military sense seems to have deserted him. Everything depended on beating Warwick in the race to London which, because of the trade with Burgundy, was firmly Yorkist, yet, unaccountably, he tarried on the way and was nearly taken prisoner when Montague went over to his brother's side. Warwick's advance from Devon became a triumphal march as deserters from Edward's forces rushed to join him. News of this, and of Montague's defection, convinced Edward that he was in no position to fight Warwick. The only alternative was flight. One of his own ships, carrying supplies for the army he had led against Lord Fitzhugh, lay at King's Lynn on the Wash, with two small Dutch vessels. Accompanied by a few lords and knights and about 300 men Edward just had time to embark on these vessels, 'without any clothes but what they were to have fought in, no money in their pockets, and not one of them knew whether they were going'. He landed at Alkmaar in the Netherlands, just at the time when the Seigneur de la Gruthuyse happened to be there on a tour of inspection, and was at once escorted to the court of his brother-in-law, the Duke of Burgundy. Thus it turned out that his sister's marriage had been a good investment, but Charles the Bold was not in the least glad to see him. Burgundy was now faced with the combination of Warwick in England and Louis in France.

When Warwick and his army reached London, the merchants offered some resistance until it was made clear to them that they could not hold out against the Lancastrian landslide throughout the country. Warwick's troops marched in on 6 October and the garrison of the Tower surrendered a week later. Henry VI was taken from his cell by the same man who, five years before, had thrust him into it.

Henry, now fifty, was found to be weak and thin, poorly clad and 'not so cleanly kept as should seem such a prince'. He was taken to the bishop's palace, bathed and tidied up, and a week later went in a state procession to Westminster Abbey accompanied by Warwick, Archbishop Neville, the Earl of Shrewsbury and Lord Stanley, where thanks were offered to God for his return to power.

In France, Margaret and Louis saw Warwick off on his mission and then had to wait for nearly a month in almost unbearable suspense for news of what had happened to him. When it came, they could hardly believe it, for nothing in recent intelligence reports from Louis's agents in England had led them to anticipate so spectacular a success. The moment for which Margaret had prayed, all through the long years of exile, had come at last. The Yorkist usurper, attainted at once as a matter of form, had been overthrown and was a destitute wanderer – as she and her husband had been. The House of Lancaster had come into its own again, and Warwick, the most powerful man in England, would see to it that her son Edward succeeded to the throne. Her joy and relief were unbounded.

Louis's immediate reaction was to order the nobles, clergy and good people of Paris to make processions to the honour and glory of God and the Virgin Mary and to continue them for three days as a thanksgiving for the defeat of the 'foul usurper, the Earl of March'. All France was ordered to rejoice, and Louis made his military preparations to deal with Burgundy. Charles the Bold made his plans too. He intended to support his brother-in-law in an invasion of England.

It was now of absolutely vital importance for Margaret to cross the Channel and take with her the heir to the throne – who had just had his seventeenth birthday – because any delay weakened the Lancastrian cause. Warwick, at first welcomed as a better alternative to the corrupt and nepotic rule of Edward IV, had never been particularly popular, and within a short time those who had supported him began to complain that he was just as selfish and unconstitutional as Edward. The restoration of Henry VI had brought no real change. No doubt Warwick's critics would have said this in any case, but the appearance of Margaret and her son, as the queen and the rightful heir returning from exile, would have been acclaimed, and in providing an excuse for holidays and festivities, would have given Warwick's government a badly-needed period of popularity which to settle down and get established.

There is no doubt that Margaret wanted to leave France, Louis would have been only too happy to see her go – the maintenance of her court was costing him a lot of money – and Warwick was insistent that she should come. In the first week of February 1471 a fleet of eight French vessels lay off Honfleur waiting for her to embark, but when she reached the coast she hesitated. She heard of the Burgundian preparations and she was told that Charles's warships were active in the narrow seas. She felt it was too great a responsibility to risk the capture of the heir to the throne in these dangerous waters and decided to wait until the Burgundian attack had been launched, the landing area was known, and she could be sure there was no hostile shipping within reach.

Once again she failed to seize the fleeting opportunity to exploit an advantage, but she had to make her decision on the basis of the information available to her at the time, and after all the years of anxiety and discomfort, hope and frustration, she was not prepared to hazard her life's work and ambition on what must have seemed to her a blind throw.

And so she waited. And Warwick, who at the end of February 1471 came down to the coast of Kent to greet her and escort her back to London with an army of loyal people of Kent, had to go back alone, disappointed and now apprehensive. He was having some difficulty with the irresponsible Clarence who, incapable of holding high authority, resented his father-in-law's power, while Warwick, having apparently won the great gamble of his life, was not prepared to share his influence with anyone. All he could do now was to wait with all the patience he could muster for Margaret to change her mind and bring across the Channel the son and heir everyone wanted to see.

Unfortunately, Edward, the 'foul usurper, the Earl of March', arrived before them.

For all his excessive fondness for the ladies and his passion for hunting, Edward was essentially a man of action when events provided a sharp spur. In a matter of days he had lost his kingdom and he was now determined to recover it equally swiftly. He was lucky in that his brother-in-law, threatened by Louis, really had no option but to assist him, and in less time than anyone in England believed possible, he and Charles of Burgundy had completed their plans.

On 11 March 1471 Edward sailed from Flushing with a small fleet of four ships, 900 Englishmen and 300 Burgundians. He tried to land on the Norfolk coast but the activities of Thomas de Vere, brother of that staunch Lancastrian the Earl of Oxford, compelled him to sail on, northwards. On 14 March he landed at Ravenspur in the estuary of the Humber, the little port (long since disappeared) where that other usurper Henry of Bolingbroke had landed in 1399.

To his surprise, no one was pleased to see him. The country had had its fill of civil war and the people of Kingston-upon-Hull, who closed their gates to him, had good reason to believe he had not come in peace. At York, away to the north-west, he had a similar reception until he gave solemn and sworn assurances to the city's representatives, who must have been unusually naïve, that he had come only to recover his duchy of York and had no designs whatever on the crown. Reluctantly, they allowed him to feed his troops.

Oddly enough, the news of his landing and progress through Yorkshire was greeted with a strange inertia. No one except Warwick seemed to be prepared to do anything, either to stop him or to join him. Even Warwick's brother Montague, commanding the Lancastrian forces in the north and in a position to crush Edward's little band at this stage without much difficulty, did nothing. Warwick rode rapidly to his estates in the Midlands and called his supporters to arms. Edward, apparently undismayed by the lack of response to the raising of the Yorkist standard, moved first to Wakefield and then set out for London.

It was a typical gesture of boldness and decision, and it reaped its rewards. 'False, fleeting, perjured Clarence' deserted the Lancastrians and joined his brother at Banbury. Warwick, taken by surprise and thrown off balance by the swiftness of Edward's movements and the perfidy of Clarence, took his stand at Coventry and prepared to hold out against a Yorkist siege. He was even more nonplussed when Edward ignored him and marched on, towards London. Warwick could hardly believe that any commander would deliberately place bimself between a city known to be in arms against him and a hostile army, but Edward knew exactly what he was doing. He was a splendid exponent of the dictum, later expressed by Napoleon as 'the moral is to the physical as three is to one'. He knew how much depended on swift action which carried with it a show of confidence in ultimate victory. If he himself appeared to be absolutely confident, others would believe in him, for confidence backed by decision is infectious. He was sure that if he advanced with boldness at the head of a disciplined force, the City of London would open its gates to him. And he was right. He succeeded where Margaret, with her large, victorious but undisciplined army in 1461, had failed.

On 11 April, exactly a month after sailing from Flushing, Edward marched into London. But, with his soldier's instinct working properly again, he knew there was nothing to be gained by cowering within the walls, waiting to be attacked by Warwick, now on his way south from Coventry.

On Saturday, 13 April, Easter Eve, Edward collected his army – now greatly increased – from its camp in St John's Wood and marched north to Barnet, where he spent the night. Warwick and his army bivouacked a little to the north, and that evening Clarence sent a messenger with an offer to act as mediator between his father-in-law and his brother.

'Go tell your master,' said the Kingmaker, 'that Warwick, true to his oath, is a better man than false perjured Clarence and will settle this quarrel by the sword to which he has appealed.'

The Lancastrian cannonade started before it was light, and the battle began in the half-light before the sun rose on the morning of Easter Day. The contestants were much hindered by thick fog.

In Warwick's army the Duke of Exeter led the left wing, the Earl of Oxford the right, and Montague commanded the centre, astride the road to St Albans. Warwick himself had the artillery and the reserve under his command, but the gunners could not see to fire. Edward's brother Richard Duke of Gloucester commanded his right wing which managed to turn Exeter's flank in the grey mist, while Oxford outflanked Edward's left wing led by William Earl of Hastings. In the confusion of the battle Oxford's troops lost contact with their own centre, where Edward was attacking Montague, but for a time it seemed that Warwick's decision to fight at Barnet was going to be justified. Edward's centre was on the point of breaking under Montague's pressure when Oxford's men, rallied with difficulty and brought back into the battle, fell upon their own centre in the fog, mistaking Montague's division for the enemy. The cry of treachery was raised – an all-too-familiar sound in these civil wars – Montague's centre broke, he was killed, and Warwick's reserve could not prevent the line from giving way. The Yorkists stormed through the breach with Edward, as usual, well up in front, and, borne down by the weight of numbers, Warwick was cut down and killed by some nameless Yorkist. The tide of battle flowed over him.

Later, when it was all over and Edward's army marched back to their camp outside London, Edward gave orders for the corpses of Warwick and his brother Montague, naked in case anyone had any doubts about who they were, to be laid in open coffins in St Paul's, at the foot of the statue of Our Lady of Grace.

On that very day, Easter Sunday, as Edward marched back to London, Margaret and her son landed at Weymouth.

When Louis and Margaret heard that Edward had landed unopposed at Ravenspur they could not imagine what had gone wrong, but Margaret realized she must join Warwick immediately. On 24 March she and the prince and her followers embarked on the ships waiting at Honfleur, but not until Saturday, 13 April, as Edward was marching from St John's Wood to the battle at Barnet, did the wind shift into a favourable quarter.

She did not know that by this time her husband, whom Warwick had left in the bishop's palace beside St Paul's, was back in his cell in the Tower. Archbishop Neville who, with an eye to the main chance, had turned traitor on his brother Warwick, brought the frail king out to meet his usurper and Edward, cold and distant, took his hand perfunctorily. Henry, unfailingly courteous, greeted him warmly.

'My cousin of York! You are very welcome. I know that in your hands my life will not be in danger.'

Not entirely unfeeling, Edward seemed a little embarrassed and assured him he had nothing to fear. Nor had he, while Prince Edward remained alive. There was no point in killing him and thus setting up his son as the Lancastrian champion.

Margaret and the Prince of Wales spent the night of 14 April at Cerne Abbey in Dorset, knowing nothing of the events of that dreadful day, but on Monday the news was brought to them by Somerset, Oxford and others who had escaped the slaughter. This Somerset was Edmund Beaufort whose elder brother Henry had been beheaded after the battle of Hexham. Their father had been killed at the first battle of St Albans.

Somerset's story was very nearly too much for Margaret to bear. Just at the moment when she was stretching out her hand to take all that she had planned and longed for ever since the birth of her only child it crumbled away into dust and, for the first time, convinced that like Sisera, even the stars in their courses fought against her, she gave way to despair. Her main battle force had been defeated and her general killed. Her husband was again a prisoner and his capital was in the hands of the enemy. With no heart left in her for the struggle against such hopeless odds she thought only of returning with her son to the safety of France. Somerset and Oxford gave her a little time to absorb the first shock and then began to work hard to persuade her that all was not lost. Barnet had been a defeat; no one could deny that, but it had been a very close-run thing and was only a temporary setback. Even now, Jasper Tudor was in command of a large Lancastrian army in South Wales. The south-western counties were all on the side of Lancaster, and many who would not fight for Warwick, the overmighty subject, would take up arms for the Prince of Wales.

Margaret listened to their arguments and was heartened by them. Summoning up her apparently limitless reserves of courage she agreed to fight on, and began with fresh enthusiasm the task of recruiting an army to defeat the hated 'Earl of March'. But Barnet had taken its toll in terms of trained soldiers and war material. There was now a serious shortage of weapons and horses and, as the Lancastrian leaders knew only too well, mere numbers could not make up for the lack of equipment and training. Margaret desperately needed time; time to re-organize, equip and train a force capable of standing against Edward's troops who, well armed and confident in their commander would not be easy to defeat.

Edward knew this, and time was the one thing he was not prepared to let Margaret have.

On Friday, 19 April, having heard on the 16th of Margaret's arrival at Weymouth, he moved his army out to Windsor where, four days later, he kept the feast of St George. Meanwhile his spies were busy in the West Country and his army was ready to move at short notice to intercept Margaret before she could muster all her forces. He calculated that there were two principal courses open to her. She could either march on London through Salisbury and join forces with the formidable Fauconberg who was raising an army in Kent in her name, or she could go north, link up with Jasper Tudor on the way, and then go on to collect the reinforcements now being assembled in her former recruiting areas of Cheshire and Lancashire. If she went north he could take her in the flank either at Gloucester, Tewkesbury or Worcester, before she could collect all her forces.

Margaret, who had moved from Cerne Abbey to Exeter to wait while Somerset summoned the West Country contingents, had in fact been advised by her council of war to go north but, to deceive Edward, she sent quartermasters along the route to Salisbury to requisition supplies and billets and give the impression the army was close behind them. Edward's scouts were not deceived. On Wednesday, 24 April, Edward left Windsor for Cirencester, a distance of some seventy miles, and arrived there on Monday, 29 April. His scouts reported that Margaret's army was on the move and would reach Bath, twenty-seven miles to the south-west of him, on the following day, Tuesday, 30 April. He also heard that the Lancastrian army proposed to fight at the earliest opportunity.

Edward at once took up a defensive position three miles from the town of Cirencester, down the road towards Malmesbury. Here he remained throughout the whole of Tuesday, 30 April, and when Margaret's force did not appear he went to meet her, marching twelve miles down the road towards Bath on 1 May

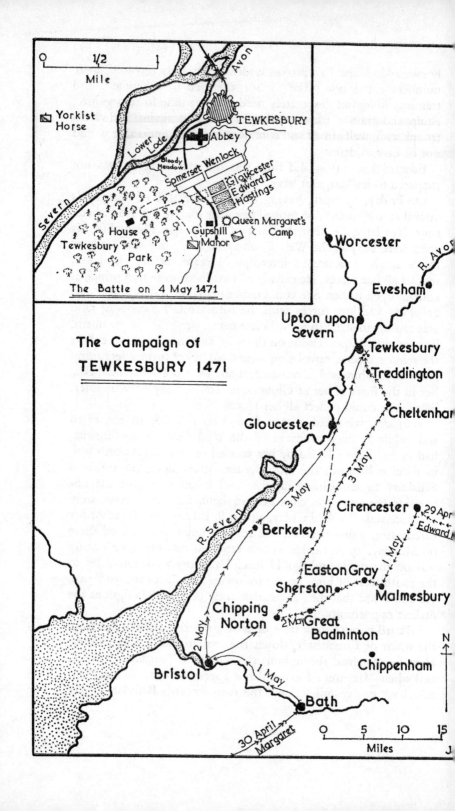

½ Mile

Yorkist Horse

Avon

TEWKESBURY

Abbey

Lower Lode

Bloody Meadow

Somerset Wenlock

Gloucester
Edward IV
Hastings

Severn

House
Tewkesbury Park

Gupshill Manor

Queen Margaret's Camp

The Battle on 4 May 1471

The Campaign of
TEWKESBURY 1471

Worcester

R. Avon

Evesham

Upton upon Severn

Tewkesbury

Treddington

Cheltenham

Gloucester

3 May

3 May

Cirencester   ● 29 Apr

R. Severn

Berkeley

1 May

Edward

Easton Gray

Sherston

Malmesbury

2 May

Chipping Norton

2 May Great Badminton

Chippenham

Bristol

1 May

N

Bath

30 April
Margaret

0   5   10   15
Miles

J.

and spending the night at Malmesbury. Margaret had in fact turned due west at Bath, away from him, and she went to Bristol to try to collect guns, ammunition, rations and money which she badly needed. She was there for a few hours only and, with the object of keeping Edward at bay until she could join forces with Jasper Tudor from Wales, she sent out a skirmishing force towards Chipping Sodbury, to give her time to get up to Gloucester and cross the bridge across the Severn.

She marched out of Bristol in the direction of Chipping Sodbury, to give any watchers on the walls the impression she intended to meet Edward's army there, but as soon as the lie of the ground took her out of sight she turned north. That evening (Thursday, 2 May) she rested for a while at Berkeley Castle, twenty miles north of Bristol, and then went on, marching all night in a desperate attempt to gain the bridge at Gloucester.

Edward, learning of her move towards Chipping Sodbury, took the route through the villages of Easton Gray, Sherston and Great Badminton, advancing in order of battle by 'Battalia' (battalions). He reached Sudbury Hill in the afternoon and his leading elements came in contact with the standing patrols Margaret had sent out to delay him. Since there was no sign of any main body coming up behind these skirmishers Edward sent out reconnaissance parties to find out where Margaret was. He spent that night (Thursday) on the site of the Roman Camp at Chipping Sodbury while Margaret's troops plodded northwards, widening the gap between the armies, and it was not until the early hours of the morning (Friday) that he learned what was happening. He at once ordered a small patrol of light cavalry to ride at top speed across country to Gloucester, carrying a message to Richard, son of Lord Beauchamp, captain of the city garrison, ordering him to hold the city and the bridge for the king, at all costs.

Edward broke camp next morning at first light and his army was on the move when the sun came up over the Marlborough Downs away to his right. At about the same time, Margaret's army reached Gloucester where Richard Beauchamp, despite 'great menaces' made to him, refused to open the gates. Kept well informed of Edward's movements by her mounted scouts, Margaret knew she had no time to negotiate, let alone lay siege to the place, and if she was to avoid battle until Jasper and his army from Wales joined her, she had no option but to press on with all speed northwards to the next bridge at Upton-upon-Severn, sixteen miles away.

By four o'clock that afternoon, Friday, 3 May, her exhausted troops staggered into Tewkesbury. With only short rests at Bristol, Berkeley and Gloucester, they had been marching almost continuously since leaving Bath and had covered a distance of fifty-seven miles in a little over forty-eight hours, a considerable achievement for the infantry levies of those days who had no training or proper equipment for long marches, no 'march discipline' and very little administrative support. Margaret's men had to eat, drink and sleep before they could move on, and meanwhile Edward's troops were coming up from the south as fast as their commander could drive them.

They marched all through that long dusty day under the hot May sun, and in the evening, with thirty miles behind them, came to the little village of Cheltenham, nine miles from Tewkesbury. Edward's scouts came back to report on the position of Margaret's force, and he, knowing she was only six miles from the bridge at Upton, felt she might easily escape him by moving before dawn and crossing the river. Therefore, as soon as his men had fed and rested, he marched on, and at length halted for the night at Treddington, only three miles from the Lancastrians.

He was now in a position to force Margaret to give battle on the following day, because it would be impossible for her to try to take her army across the narrow defile of either the Lower Lode ford at Tewkesbury or the bridge at Upton with an active and determined enemy immediately behind her.

Margaret's scouts, who had been keeping Edward under surveillance, reported his arrival at Treddington, and, at a council of war held in the midst of her sleeping army, Somerset, Margaret's Commander-in-Chief, gave out his orders for the fighting of a defensive battle on ground he had reconnoitred that evening. It was well chosen, and by morning the Lancastrians had strengthened it with ditches and earthworks bristling with sharp-pointed stakes.

The Yorkist chronicler Rosewood described Somerset's position: 'They pitched themselves in a field, in a close even at the town's end; the town and the abbey at their backs; before them and upon every hand of them, foul lanes and deep dykes, and many hedges, with hills and valleys – a right evil place to approach as could well have been devised.'

Somerset and his military commanders were reasonably confident of being able to defeat Edward, whose army was smaller and whose troops even more tired than the Lancastrians, and much of Somerset's confidence stemmed from the unusual tactical plan he had evolved during his evening reconnaissance. Margaret listened to his assurances, but she would have been much happier if she had been able to achieve the object of her forced marches and join Jasper Tudor.

Very early in the morning of Saturday, 4 May, Edward rode out from Treddington, against the advice of some of his officers who wanted him to wait for reinforcements, and having seen all he could of Somerset's position he drew up his army about 800 yards to the south of it, in three battalions, one behind the other. Somerset's force was in two divisions. One he commanded himself and the other was led by Lord Wenlock* and the seventeen-year-old Prince of Wales. In Edward's army, his brother Richard Duke of Gloucester commanded the leading battalion, Edward led the one in the centre and Lord Hastings the rearmost, which contained a cavalry element. When making his approach, Edward saw that the broken ground and the thick woods of Tewkesbury Park offered plenty of opportunities for ambush parties. To meet this threat to his left wing he detached a squadron of 200 Horse to conceal themselves in a copse over to the left of his line of advance, with orders to use their initiative and intervene in the battle whenever they felt they could be most effective.

Somerset's tactical plan was to meet Edward's initial attack with the usual artillery bombardment and storm of arrows and then, under cover of the gunsmoke and confusion, to lead his own division off to the right, its movement also being screened by the hedges and trees. He then proposed to wheel round and charge into Edward's left flank and roll up his battle line. He told Lord Wenlock that as soon as the forward troops of this

---

* The career of Sir John (Lord) Wenlock is not always easy to follow since he changed sides on several occasions. He had been a member of Margaret's household; he had fought for her at the second battle of St Albans and for Edward at Towton; he had prevented Warwick from landing at Calais in March 1470. He was now back on the Lancastrian side and, as events were to prove, regarded with justifiable suspicion.

flanking party appeared through the trees of Tewkesbury Park he was to charge forward with the main 'battle' or battalion in a straight frontal assault on Edward's centre and right. It was a sound idea. The combination of the two movements could be decisive, and Somerset had gone over the route for this right-hook attack with some care on the previous evening.

As Edward's army came up, Margaret rode through the ranks of her troops exhorting them to fight bravely and promising to reward them when they won the day. Then, after one last word of encouragement to her son, no doubt a little nervous before his first battle, she rode away, taking with her the Countess of Devonshire, Lady Catherine Vaux and Anne Neville. Crossing the Severn by the Lower Lode ford, she went to a house known as Payne's Place on the road running west out of Tewkesbury, where she waited in a state of tense anxiety for the result of the battle.

Aligned in close order on either side of the great red and white banner of St George, Richard of Gloucester led his battalion into the attack. It was met by the few guns of the Lancastrians and their accurate archery, but because of the difficult country there was some delay before the battle developed into the normal hand-to-hand encounter between the men armed with swords, axes and staff weapons (cutting or stabbing heads mounted on a stick or staff). The Yorkists also opened fire with light field pieces, brought well forward for the close support of their infantry, and while all this was going on, Somerset drew off his force, formed up in a clearing and charged Edward's left flank, on foot, with great vigour. Lord Wenlock stayed where he was, possibly because in the fog of battle he did not see Somerset's men coming out of the clearing.

In bitter close-quarter fighting Edward held this flank attack and drove it back, and at just the right moment the concealed squadron of Yorkist cavalry came down on Somerset's infantry with levelled lances and caught many of them in the open. Most of them fled. Somerset's flank attack had failed completely. In a towering rage he mounted a horse and rode back to the main battle position where Wenlock stood defending the entrenchment. Somerset was convinced that Wenlock had turned traitor yet again and had deliberately failed to support him. There is in fact no evidence of this but Somerset was in no mood to discuss it.

Riding up to Wenlock, who was a much older man, he denounced him as a traitor and without waiting for any reply struck him a mighty and fatal blow with his battleaxe. This display of bad temper had an unfortunate effect on the Lancastrian troops, who believed that so drastic a way of dealing with an unsatisfactory divisional commander must indicate that the battle was going against them.

Thus, unsettled and apprehensive, they were in no state to stand firm against the resolute assault, a few minutes later, by Richard of Gloucester as he led his battalion across the ditch and into the main battle position of the Lancastrian army. After only a brief show of resistance, Margaret's men broke. Many hoped to escape through the woods of Tewkesbury Park, others forced their way through the hedges behind them, making for the abbey half a mile away, and sanctuary, but the battle had become a rout and many were cut down in what became known as Bloody Meadow – like the field at Towton – near their defensive position, or were drowned trying to cross the Avon and the Severn.

Margaret's son was killed in action, probably during this general stampede; but there are many accounts giving a wealth of detail about his capture – how Edward struck him in the mouth with his steel gauntlet and how he finally died on the daggers of Richard of Gloucester and other Yorkist nobles. Shakespeare, who based what he wrote mainly on Hall's *Chronicle of Lancaster and York,* tells this story at length, but there is no support at all for it in any contemporary account. For example, Philippe de Commines, who could never resist an anecdote, is strictly factual:

> ... for though the Prince of Wales's army was more numerous than the king's, yet King Edward got the victory; and the Prince of Wales, several other great lords, and a great number of common soldiers, were killed upon the spot, and the Duke of Somerset, being taken, was beheaded the next day.

One can be reasonably sure he would not have been so succinct if there had been a tale to tell.

Also killed in the battle were John Beaufort, brother of Edmund Duke of Somerset, and Margaret's faithful servants Sir Robert Whitingham and Sir Edmund Hampden. Yorkist soldiers entered the abbey with drawn swords – so defiling it that it had to be re-consecrated – and dragged from the altar several leading Lancastrians, among them, the Duke of Somerset, Sir Humphrey Audley, Sir Hugh Courtenay, Sir Gervase Clifton, Sir Thomas Tresham and Sir John Langstrother. They were all brought before Richard of Gloucester and the Duke of Norfolk who, as the Constable and Marshal of England respectively, constituted themselves as a court martial. The inevitable sentence was carried out on Monday, 6 May, by an executioner on a block placed in the market square of Tewkesbury.

No doubt for some family reason Edward spared the life of Exeter, his brother-in-law who had married his sister Anne, and sent him to the Tower. When Exeter was released a few months later, his marriage was dissolved, and in the following year (1472) the duke's body was found floating in the Channel between Calais and Dover. His death remains a mystery. No mercy was shown to any of the other Lancastrian nobles, but the soldiers of the defeated army were allowed to return home, and what might be described as the less important gentry such as Sir John Fortescue, who was not a warrior, and Dr Morton the chaplain, who had both been members of Margaret's household, were released and pardoned after a brief imprisonment. Edward, delighted with his victory, knighted forty-three of his followers immediately after the battle.

Before noon on that Saturday morning Margaret heard the terrible news, and the loss of the battle counted for little against the death of her adored son. Utterly heartbroken, her ladies hurried her away in a carriage to find asylum in 'a poor religious place' traditionally believed to have been Little Malvern Priory, but the Yorkists were out, searching the countryside for her. On Tuesday, 7 May, Edward was told she had been captured, and a few days later she was brought by Lord Stanley to his court at Coventry.

Then, on 21 May, she rode into London, not in triumph and with her son by her side, as she had for so long prayed and dreamed, but as a captive in Edward's victory march. But no humiliation, no further disaster, could touch her now. Military defeat and the slaughter of her adherents were nothing new. In the past she had accepted these and similar blows of Fate philo-sophically, even drawing from them an increase of strength to continue the struggle, but this time the death of her son had destroyed her. Inconsolable in the bitterness of her grief she could fight no more, and Edward realized that in her sorrow she was no longer a threat, no longer even an opponent. Though she had fought for the House of Lancaster, her real battle had been for her son's inheritance, and the sword or battleaxe that struck him down killed at the same time her will to resist the House of York. Since her motives had been so personal, there was no likelihood that she would give any thought to any other Lancastrian heir.

It may well be that during her journey from Coventry to London she found some consolation in the thought that after eight years of separation she would be able to see Henry again, and he, amidst all these enemies, might lighten the burden of her grief a little by sharing her sorrow and her tears. But even this was to be denied her. Though taken to the Tower and lodged at no great distance from him they were not allowed to meet, and on the same night as her arrival he was murdered.

The Yorkist Fleetwood says Henry died of 'pure displeasure and melancholy', but there is no doubt what happened. *How* it happened is another matter. When his bones were examined in their coffin at Windsor in 1911 it was found that the back of his skull was crushed, presumably by some heavy blow, and there were traces of blood in his hair. Commines says he was assassinated either by or on the direct orders of Richard of Gloucester, who certainly came to the Tower that night, but the story of Gloucester has been so twisted, often deliberately, by Tudor and other historians that it is now almost impossible to separate fact from fiction.

Though Edward was determined to ensure that no Lancastrian capable of challenging his claim to be King of England would remain alive, it is possible that Henry might have been allowed to live out his days in the Tower had it not been for the resolute attack on London launched by Fauconberg while Edward was away at Tewkesbury. This assault, carried out in the name of Henry VI, had been beaten off only with great difficulty, and on the morning after the murder Gloucester rode on into Kent to deal with Fauconberg. He failed to catch the experienced old warrior, and Fauconberg became a pirate in the Channel.

Edward tried to make out that he had not wanted Henry's

death, though politically it was the obvious step after what had happened at Tewkesbury. There was an element of risk in disposing of him for he had long been an object of pity and sympathy, and his popularity as an individual remained unaffected by his misfortunes. Edward could be completely ruthless when he felt that circumstances warranted strong measures but he did not want to appear unnecessarily cruel. He made sure that Henry's corpse was treated with respect but he also took steps to see that everyone knew he was dead. The body lay in state in an open coffin in St Paul's for twenty-four hours after the murder and then was borne up the river for burial in the Benedictine Abbey at Chertsey.*

Confined in a cell, Margaret remained in the Tower for only a few weeks after the killing of her husband, and then was taken to Windsor. She was kept there as a prisoner for the first few months after Edward's restoration, but at the end of 1471, when he felt confident there was no real danger of another Lancastrian rising – and even if there was, Margaret would take no interest in it – he allowed her to be taken into the custody of her old friend the Duchess of Suffolk who had escorted her across France from the proxy wedding at Nancy, so long ago. The duchess had a large and comfortable house on the Thames at Wallingford, twelve miles to the south-east of Oxford, and Margaret lived there for the next four years. She was to a large extent dependent on the generosity and hospitality of the duchess since Edward had granted her a pension of only five marks a week.

At Wallingford she did her best to shut out the world around her. She made no attempt to get in touch with any survivors of the Lancastrian cause or even with members of her former household. Having lost her husband and her son, like so many other women in this blood-soaked era of English history, she had ceased to be of any importance in international politics, although her cousin Louis never lost sight of her potential value in his plan to strengthen the sovereignty of the French crown. Of her energy, her resilience and her indomitable courage, little remained,

---

* Thirteen years later, hearing that there had been a number of 'miraculous healings' at the tomb, Richard III arranged for the body to be taken to Windsor, where the public could not visit, and reburied. Thus Margaret's unfortunate husband was twice crowned, in London and Paris, and twice buried, in Chertsey and Windsor.

she seemed now to be afflicted by what Wordsworth described as 'thoughts that do often lie too deep for tears', and there was no heart left in her.

Being isolated from the political scene, and indifferent to what was happening in Europe, she found some solace for her distress in the quiet house beside the river, and in the gardens and surrounding woods and meadows where she could enjoy the companionship of a friend who had suffered almost as much as she. It therefore came as a brutal shock to her when, in July 1475, a party of horsemen arrived suddenly at the house, led by the Earl of Dudley. He brought a paper, signed by Edward, ordering 'Margaret lately called Queen' into close captivity in the fortress of Calais.

She was made to ride first to London and then, in the custody of Richard Haute esquire, who was paid £20 for the duty, to Sandwich. Then there was a long delay while negotiations, of which she probably knew very little, went on between Edward IV and her cousin Louis XI.

Since the victory at Tewkesbury had secured him in his kingdom, Edward had once more entered the field of international diplomacy by making plans with his brother-in-law Charles of Burgundy for a joint attack on Louis. But Charles refused to be tied down to exact dates, and meanwhile became involved in a long and costly siege of Neuss, on the west bank of the Rhine. Angered by what he regarded as prevarication, Edward resolved to put pressure on Charles, and took a large army across the Channel to Calais. To make sure there was no trouble while he was away, he gave orders for all potential rebels to be rounded up and imprisoned in Calais until his campaign was over. Margaret was on the list.

Edward arrived in France and, much to everyone's surprise, abandoned his Burgundian alliance and made peace with Louis after a long conference with him on the bridge over the Somme at Picquigny. 'During this,' says Commines, 'a very heavy fall of rain came on, to the great vexation of the French lords, who had dressed themselves and their horses in their richest habiliments in honour to King Edward.' The rain at Picquigny finally extinguished for ever the ashes of the Hundred Years' War, and the Treaty was signed on 29 August 1475.

One side issue in the main agreement was that Louis offered

to ransom his cousin Margaret of Anjou for the sum of 50,000 crowns, paying 10,000 when she was handed over and the remainder by instalments of 10,000 on successive Michaelmas Days. In return, Edward was to transfer to Louis all rights over the woman now described as the daughter of the King of Sicily, and Margaret herself was to make a formal renunciation of all her property in England, granted to her in her marriage contract.

The wording of this renunciation raised one or two problems because Edward would not give the title of queen to Margaret, or that of king to Henry VI. In official correspondence Margaret was called 'the Lady Margaret', and in October 1475 she finally signed a document which read, 'I, Margaret, formerly married in the Kingdom of England, hereby assign all that I could pretend to [claim] in England by the articles of my marriage, with all other things thereto, to Edward, now King of England.'

On 13 November 1475, still at Sandwich, she was committed to the care of Thomas Thwaytes who later handed her over to Sir Thomas Montgomery for the voyage across the Channel in a small fishing boat. So, for the last time, at the age of forty-five, she returned to her own country, and one cannot help wondering what thoughts were in her mind as the cliffs of the South Foreland faded into the winter mist. She may have been too seasick to think of anything; she may perhaps have looked back across the gap of thirty years to the time when the Duke of Suffolk carried her ashore as Queen of England. A whole new world had lain in front of her then. Now, she was returning as a ransomed prisoner, leaving behind her, in his grave in Tewkesbury Abbey, the boy for whom she had lived and endured all things.

The little vessel took her down the Seine to Rouen, the city where she had twice been fêted by welcoming citizens. She landed on 14 January 1476, and on 29 January Louis's two commissioners, Jean d'Hangest, the Captain of Rouen, and Jean Raguier the Receiver-General of Normandy, handed Sir Thomas Montgomery the first payment of her ransom. She was then free to go wherever she wished. Her part in history had been played.

Epilogue

Louis XI invariably had a sound motive for all his actions, and he was neither chivalrous nor generous. If he had to spend money he expected to get something for it, and he would have been perfectly content to allow Margaret to die in sorrow and misery in some English prison had she not possessed something he wanted. Although his cousin was no longer able to exercise any influence on public affairs, she was still the inheritor of large estates in Lorraine through her mother Isabelle, and it was probable that on the death of her father she would succeed to the territories of Provence, Anjou and Bar. It was Louis's intention to purchase all these with the 50,000 crowns paid for her ransom; a bargain, even by his standards.

Through his mother, Marie of Anjou, Margaret's aunt, he felt he had some claim to the Angevin estates, and by adding Margaret's rights to his claim he was confident of being able to take over, in due course, all King René's titles and territories without argument. The acquisition of all these lands would be a great advance towards 'La France arrondie'. Therefore, on 7 March 1476, Margaret was required to sign another document, prepared by two of his legal clerks and two papal notaries, in which she made over to him the last of her worldly possessions.

That she did so, meekly, obediently, and with no trace of her former regal independence, is some measure of the effect upon her of the death of her son and the murder of her husband. Even now, nearly five years after that dreadful moment when she heard that her boy Edward had been killed, she could find little reason for holding on to life. She did what she was told, not because there was no alternative but because she no longer cared what happened. Since there was no one now to inherit her possessions she was prepared to let them go, and if Louis wanted them, he could have them; nothing mattered any more. Much had changed since John Paston wrote in one of his letters, 'the

212 THE ARDENT QUEEN

Queen is a great and strong laboured woman, for she spareth no pain to save her things'.

She gratefully accepted Louis's offer of a pension of 6,000 crowns, and wrote to her father asking his permission to live at his court at Aix, in the sunshine of Provence. There was little comfort in his reply:

Ma fille, que Dieu vous assiste dans vos conseils, car c'est rarement des Hommes qu'il faut en attendre dans les revers de fortune, Lorsque vous desirierez moins ressentir vos peines, pensez aux miennes: elles sont grandes.*

Nevertheless she travelled down to Aix and found that her father, preferring the company of his second wife, Jehanne de Laval, less than half his age, had little time to spare for her. In his conversation he spoke almost exclusively of his financial difficulties and of the way Fate seemed to have singled him out for ill-luck and suffering. He was of no help to Margaret in her anguish, and she withdrew, as much as she could, from court life. He died on 10 July 1480, at the age of seventy-two, and was buried in the ornate tomb he had designed for himself in the choir of the cathedral at Angers. Margaret saw the great estates of Anjou and Bar pass into the hands of Louis, as he had planned. Provence was inherited by her cousin Jean Count of Maine and son of René's brother Charles, but he died without an heir in the following year, and so this county reverted to the crown.

Margaret's brother-in-law Ferri de Vaudémont, Duke of Lorraine, had died in 1470 and she might have been able to go and live with her widowed sister Yolande had they not quarrelled over the deed of renunciation, prepared by Louis's lawyers, which involved them both in lawsuits over the inheritance of Lorraine. So Margaret went back to Anjou, where François de la Vignolles, Sieur de Morains, who for forty years had been one of her father's faithful servants, allowed her to live in his little Château de Souzay, on the south bank of the Loire on the road that runs from Saumur to Chinon. This was the country in which she had spent the happiest years of her life, living with her grandmother Yolande of Aragon, and from the tower of the château she could see the castle of Saumur, away to the north-west,

* 'My child, may God guide you in your counsels, for men seldom give help in time of ill-fortune. When you are inclined to lament your misfortunes, think of mine: they are great.'

guarding the bridges of the Loire and the town she knew so well.

In the spring of 1482, soon after her fifty-second birthday, her health began to fail, and, growing worse, on 2 August she drew up her brief, pathetic testament in which she left what little she had to her cousin Louis.

I, Margaret of Anjou, sane of understanding but weak and infirm of body, make and declare this my last Will and Testament in the manner following. First I give and recommend my soul to God, my body also I give to God and it is my will and desire that it be buried in holy ground according to the good will and pleasure of the King, and, if it pleases him, I elect and choose to be buried in the Cathedral Church of Saint Maurice d'Angers with Monseigneur, my late father, and Madame, my mother. Moreover my wish is, if it please the said Lord King, that the small amount of property which God and he have given to me be employed in burying me and in paying my debts, and in case my goods are not sufficient for this, as I believe will be the case, I beg the said Lord King of his favour to pay them for me, for in him is my sole hope and trust, and he is the sole heir of the wealth which I inherited through my father and mother and my other relatives and ancestors.

The will was witnessed by Jehan Lespinay, Mace de Lespinay, Madame Catherine de Vaux, Blanche Alorrete, Perreete de la Riviére and others.

A few days later, perhaps feeling a need to get away from the damp air beside the river, she went up to the Château de Morains, even smaller than Souzay, on the top of the hill about a mile away, on the road to the château where Pierre de Brézé had once lived. According to local tradition she had built the house herself, though no one quite knows when, and she certainly had very little money to pay for such things when she came back from England. It seems probable that it also belonged to François de la Vignolles who was the Sieur de Morains.

It was at Morains that she died, probably of cancer, on 20 August 1482.

Nevertheless, the traveller today will find on the outer walls of both Souzay and Morains an identically-worded plaque which, beneath the name of the respective château in each case reads:

où mourut le 20 Août 1482
Marguerite d'Anjou
Reine d'Angleterre, fille du Roi René
Heroine de la Guerre des Deux Roses
La plus malheureuse des Reines, des Epouses et des Mères*

Her last wish was granted, and she was buried in her father's splendid tomb. Like so many other things, it was destroyed during the French Revolution and panelling now covers the site of it on the wall of the Cathedral choir. A marble tablet with a detailed inscription, let into the grey flagstones in the centre of the choir, commemorates the deaths of Margaret and her father and mother.

Few of the other principals in her tragic story outlived her for very long, and one at least came to a violent end before she died.

Charles the Bold, trying to join the provinces of Alsace and Lorraine to his possessions in Burgundy, was soundly beaten by the Swiss in the battles of Granson and Morat in 1476 and, still believing himself to be a great soldier, was then killed in a badly planned attack on Nancy on 5 January 1477. Since he had no heir, the former appanages of Burgundy and Picardy automatically reverted to the French crown, and all Louis's troubles with Burgundy were over.

Edward IV, who had never denied himself the pleasures of bed and board, died either of a stroke or a heart attack at the age of forty, on 9 April 1483 – not quite eight months after Margaret. His small son, Edward V, who had been born in the sanctuary of Westminster in 1470, at the time when his father was fleeing from the Earl of Warwick to Flanders, did not long survive the ambition of his uncle Richard of Gloucester, and he and his brother were murdered in the Tower.

Almost exactly a year after Margaret's funeral, on 30 August 1483, death came to her cousin Louis in his castle at Plessis-les-Tours, despite the fact that for some time he had been paying his doctor, Jacques Coitier, about £1,000 a month so that he

---

* Where died on 20 August 1482, Margaret of Anjou, Queen of England, daughter of King René, heroine of the Wars of the Roses, the most unfortunate of Queens, wives and Mothers. (The use of the term Wars of the Roses indicates that the plaques must have been put up comparatively recently.)

would have a genuine interest in keeping him alive. He was succeeded by his son, Charles VIII, who was thirteen – the same age as the unfortunate Edward V.

Though so many of Margaret's household and supporters had been killed in battle or executed for their loyalty, some managed to survive. Dr Morton, for example, rose to be a Cardinal and Bishop of Ely. Sir John Fortescue turned his pen as well as his coat and, at Edward's request, wrote his famous *The Governance of England* setting out all the evils of Lancastrian rule. As a result he was allowed to die peacefully in his bed at a great age. The gallant Earl of Oxford escaped from the disaster at Tewkesbury and went on fighting against the House of York. He raided the coast of Essex, not very successfully, in May 1473, and in the winter of that year took and held St Michael's Mount off the Cornish coast for several months. He was caught at last and spent ten years in the gloomy castle of Hammes near Calais, but his loyalty to the Lancastrian cause was amply rewarded when Henry Tudor came to the throne. All his honours and estates were restored to him and he was appointed to the posts of Admiral, Great Chamberlain and Constable of the Tower of London. He lived to the age of eighty-four.

The greatest escaper of them all, Jasper Tudor, was never caught. Having heard what had happened at Tewkesbury he fell back on his castle at Chepstow and without argument or delay executed the representative Edward IV sent to arrest him. When Edward came to take his revenge personally Jasper retired to Pembroke, and when that fortress was besieged he slipped across the Channel with his young nephew Henry – to whom he had virtually devoted his life ever since the death of his brother Edmund in 1456. They found refuge with François Duke of Brittany. François refused all Edward's demands for extradition, but since he promised to see that they made no more trouble, the two fugitives were virtually his prisoners. Henry Earl of Richmond told Commines some years later that he had spent twenty-five years of his life as a captive.

It is said that Jasper and his nephew Henry went to see Margaret at Souzay, not long before she died, and she begged Henry to continue the struggle against the House of York. It is possible that Henry did make some sort of promise, if only to try and bring some cheer to this forsaken queen, ending her days in sorrow, poverty and loneliness beside the Loire in a house that was not even her own. If he did, he fulfilled it most nobly; destroying the House of York for ever on the battlefield of Bosworth and marching into London in the way that Margaret had dreamed her own son would one day enter it – triumphant and acclaimed, to restore the House of Lancaster.

But Henry Tudor, with Welsh, Valois and Beaufort blood in his veins, was no partisan of either House. Founding his own dynasty, he united the White and the Red in the Tudor Rose, symbol of the undisputed, powerful and autocratic government that Margaret, for so much of her life, had tried, against hopeless odds, to establish.

Bibliography

BAGLEY, J. J. *Life in Mediaeval England* (London 1960)
—*Margaret of Anjou, Queen of England* (London 1948)
BARANTE, G. P. DE. *Histoire de Ducs de Bourgogne de la Maison de Valois, 1364–1477* (Paris 1824–6, 7 Vols)
BAUDIER, MICHAEL. *An History of the Memorable and Extra-ordinary Calamities of Margaret of Anjou, Queen of England* (London 1737)
BODIN, J. F. *Recherches Historique sur la ville de Saumur* (Saumur 1845, 2 Vols)
CHASTELLAIN, G. *Chronique des Ducs de Bourgogne* (Paris 1825)
COMMINES, PHILIP DE. Memoirs, ed Andrew R. Scoble (London 1900, 2 Vols)
DICTIONARY OF NATIONAL BIOGRAPHY
EGGENBERGER, DAVID. *A Dictionary of Battles* (London 1968)
ESCOUCHY, MATHIEU D'. *Chronique*, ed par G. du Fresne de Beaucourt (Paris 1863, 2 Vols)
FOWLER, KENNETH. *The Age of Plantagenet and Valois* (London 1967)
GAIRDNER, J. (Ed). *The Paston Letters 1422–1509* (London 1895, 3 Vols)
GREGORY, W. *The Historical Collections of a Citizen of London in the 15th Century*, ed J. Gairdner, Camden Society (London 1880)
GUIGNAND, JACQUES. *Chateaux en Anjou* (Paris 1966)
HALL, E. *Chronicle of Lancaster and York*, ed H. Ellis (London 1809)
HARVEY, JOHN. *The Plantagenets* (London 1948)
HINDS, A. B. (Ed). *Calendar of State Papers and MSS existing in the archives and collection of Milan*, Vol I (London 1912)
HOOKHAM, MRS MARY ANN. *The Life and Times of Margaret of Anjou* (London 1872, 2 Vols)
HUME, DAVID. *The History of England* (Edinburgh 1818, 8 Vols)
JAMES, M. R. Translation of J. Blacman's *Collectarium mansuetudinum et bonorum morum Regis Henrici VI* (Cambridge 1919)

LEVRON, JACQUES. *Le Bon Roi René* (Paris 1972)

MONROE, CECIL (Ed). *Letters of Margaret of Anjou*, Camden Society (London 1863)

MONSTRELET, ENGUERRAND DE, *Chronicles*, Tr Thomas Johnes (London 1810, 12 Vols)

ROWSE, A. L. *Bosworth Field and the Wars of the Roses* (London 1966)

STALEY, EDGCUMBE. *King René d'Anjou and his Seven Queens* (London 1912)

STOREY, R. L. *The End of the House of Lancaster* (London 1966)

STOW, J. *Survey of London*, ed L. Kingsford (London 1908)

STRICKLAND, A. *Lives of the Queens of England*, Vol II (London 1885)

THOMSON, REV. THOMAS. *The Comprehensive History of England* (London 1860, 12 Vols)

WAURIN, J. DE. *Anchiennes Cronicques d'Engleterre*, ed Mille Dupont (Paris 1858, 3 Vols)

YOUNG, BRIGADIER PETER & JOHN ADAIR. *Hastings to Culloden, Battlefields in Britain* (London 1964)

Index

Agincourt, battle of, 19, 21
Alençon, Duke of, 23, 47, 112
Alfonso of Aragon, 29–30
Alorette, Blanche, 213
Andrews, Richard, 39
Angers, 18, 21, 28, 31, 212
Angus, Earl of, 162
Annabelle, d. of James II, 116
Anne of Geierstein, 110
Antoine, Count of Vaudémont, 24, 25, 32
Armagnac, Count and faction of, 19, 19n, 21, 93
Arras, peace conference at, 37; Treaty of, 163
Arundel, John, 105
Arundel, Lord, 125
Audley, Lord, 75; killed at Blore Heath, 123
Audley, Sir Humphrey, 206
Ayscough, William, Bishop of Salisbury, 54; murdered, 79–80, 102

Barnet, battle of, 196–197
Basin, Thomas, 71
bastard feudalism, 16–17
Baudier, comment on Margaret, 56
Beauchamp, Anne, 60
Beauchamp, Eleanor, 99
Beauchamp, Henry, Earl of Warwick – see Warwick
Beauchamp, Richard, 201
Beaufort, Cardinal Bishop of Winchester; meets Margaret at Chinon, 34; opposition to Gloucester, 36, 37; legacy to Henry VI, 43; gives Henry ring, 44; opinion of Margaret, 53; in retirement, 61; death of, 70, 73, 111, 159
Beaufort, John, 205
Beaufort, Margaret, 51, 77
Beaugé, battle of, 18, 22, 28
Beaumont, Lord, 133
Bedford, John, Duke of, 20, 21, 32, 36, 37, 44, 154
Belisarius, 30
Blacman, 51, 173
Blore Heath, battle of, 123
Boccaccio, 28
Bolingbroke, Henry of, 195
Bona of Savoy, 175
Bonham, Edith, Abbess, 71
Bonville, Lord, 125, 142, 146
Booth, Henry, 71
Booth, Laurence, 115
Booth, William (Margaret's Chancellor), brother of Laurence, 80, 89, 115
Bosworth, battle of, 110, 216
Bourchier, Henry, Viscount, 112, 114, 115, 142
Bourchier, Thomas – see Ely
Bourges, little king of, 21
Buchan, John Stuart, Earl of, 18n, 21

Buckingham, Humphrey Stafford, Duke of, 66, 75, 81, 92; at 1st St Albans, 108–109; killed at Northampton, 132–133
Bulgnéville, battle of, 24–25, 32
Burgundy, Duke of – see Charles the Bold
Burgundy, Duke of – see Philip the Good
Burgundy, faction of, 19, 19n
Burneby, Thomas, 70
Butler, James – see Wiltshire
Bydon, Dr, 173

Cade, Jack, rebellion led by, 81–83; death of, 84, 84n, 90
Calais, Somerset's operations against, 126–127; Margaret's offer to sell, 128
Camulio, Prospero, 176, 179, 186
Carbonnel, Clemence, 39
Carbonnel, Jean, 135
Carew, Jane, 71
Carew, Sir Nicholas, 71
Castillon, battle of, 94–95
casualties, at St Albans, 109; at Northampton, 133; at Wakefield, 146; at Towton, 151; at Tewkesbury, 205–206
Catherine, Princess, of France, 20, 35; 2nd marriage of, 51, 99, 143
Cecily, Duchess of York – see Neville
Chamberlayne, Margaret (tire-maker), 54
Champchevrier, Guy de, 34–35
Charles II of Lorraine, 19
Charles V of France, 42
Charles VI of France, 19, 20; lunacy of, 50, 97, 97n
Charles VII of France, as disinherited Dauphin, 20; meets Jeanne d'Arc, 21; crowned, 24; meets Agnes Sorel, 27; at Saumur, 30, 32–33; Champchevrier incident, 34–35; terms for peace, 36, 38; his part in Margaret's marriage, 40–41; at Metz, 45; at Margaret's wedding, 46–47; system of government, 58–59; terms for peace, 61; ends truce, 76; successes against English, 79–80; final campaign in Guienne, 93–95, 112, 116; foreign policy problems, 122, 128; caution after Northampton, 135; actions after Wakefield, 140, 142; death of, 156
Charles, Count of Nevers, 32
Charles d'Anjou, Count of Maine, 31, 36, 39, 160, 212
Charles, Duke of Orleans – see Orleans
Charles of France (brother of Louis XI), 189
Charles the Bold, Count of Charolais (Duke of Burgundy), 32; tries to help Margaret, 135, 156, 158; still loyal to Margaret, 163; welcomes, Margaret, 167, 168; assures Henry VI of support, 170, 171; wins battle of Montlhéry, 174; reconciled with father, 178; his proposed marriage, 179; becomes Duke of Burgundy, 180; makes treaty

with Edward IV, 180; changes policy, 180–181; marries Margaret of York, 182, 183, 192; plans to restore Edward IV, 193; at Neuss, 209; death of, 214

Charolais, Count of – see Charles the Bold

Chichele, Archbishop, 73

Chicken pox, 49–50

Chinon, 21; Cardinal Beaufort at, 34; treaty signed at 160

Christopher Columbus, 175

Civil War, causes of, 107; summary of, 110

Clarence, George, Duke of, 155, 176, 179; marries Isabella Neville, 184; joins Warwick in revolt, 184–187; flees to France, 187; deserts Warwick, 196

Clarence, Lionel, Duke of, 84

Cleger, John, 134

Clere, Edmund, 105

Clere, Elizabeth, 69

Clermont, Comte de, 80

Clifford, Lord John, 47, 75; killed at St Albans, 109

Clifford, Lord (son of Lord John), 118; story of killing of Rutland, 139, 146; killed at Ferrybridge, 148–149

Clifton, Sir Gervase, 127, 206

Clinton, Lord, 124

Cobham, Lord, 90, 97

Cokke John, 49

Coitier, Jacques (doctor), 214

Combe, John, 134

Commines, Philippe de, on animosity between English and French, 15; on civil war, 106–107; on dispute between Somerset and York, 110; on Edward IV, 152; on Duke of Exeter, 177, 182; on Edward IV, 192; on death of Edward Prince of Wales, 205; on murder of Henry VI, 207; on Picquigny, 209, 215

Coppini, Francesco, 131–133, 141, 156

Cosenza, 30

Council of Regency, 36

Courtenay, Sir Hugh, 206

Cousinot, Guillaume, 60, 61, 170, 171

Crespin, Jeanne, 161

Cromer, William, Sheriff, 83

Cromwell, Lord, 97

Dacre, Lord, killed at Towton, 150

de Brézé, Jacques, 161, 162, 165

de Brézé, Pierre, 39, 39n, 113, 115; raids Sandwich, 116–117, 122, 128–129, 134–135; fits out fleet, 140, 142, 156; banished, 157; visited by Margaret, 159

de Croy, Antoine, 164, 168

de Janlis, Sieur, 135

de Lambarde, Sieur, 156, 159

De la Pole, William – see Suffolk

De Laudibus Legum Angliae, 170

de Laval, Jehanne, 159, 212

de Rupibus, Peter, 50

de Scales, Lady Emma, 47

d'Escouchy, Mathieu, 78

des Ursins, Juvenal, 60

de Vere, Thomas, 195

Devonshire, Earl of, 87, 88, 89, 106, 125, 140; beheaded after Towton, 151

d'Hangest, Jean, 210

di Monti, Peter, 42

Docket, Andrew, 73–74

Dorset, Earl of, 109

Doucereau, agent, 128, 129

Drayton, Michael, poet, 55

Dudley, Lord, 109 209

Dunois, Jean, Bastard of Orleans, 23, 38; takes Rouen, 76, 93

Duras, Sieur de, 94

Dynham, Sir John, 124; attacks Sandwich, 127; raids Sandwich again, 130; at Towton, 149

Edgecote, battle of, 185

Edmund Tudor, Earl of Richmond, born, 51; elevated to peerage, 99, 114; death, 215

Edward II, 66

Edward III, 19, 117, 137

Edward IV (Earl of March), 73, 96, 112; flees from Ludlow, 124; attainted, 125; lands at Sandwich, 130; goes to Northampton, 132, 136; disapproves of father's activities, 137, 141; raises army in Wales, 142; wins battle of Mortimer's Cross, 143; advances to London, 146; acclaimed king, 148; marches north to Towton, 148; wins battle of Towton, 149–151; his character, 152; demands surrender of Henry and Margaret, 154; meets Elizabeth Woodville, 154; crowned, 155; relations with Warwick, 156; delighted by death of Charles VII, 157; propaganda against Margaret, 160; reaction to Treaty of Tours, 161, 163; witnesses executions, 172; marries Elizabeth Woodville, 174; upsets Warwick, 175–176; builds up own party, 177; foreign policy, 178–179; makes treaty with Burgundy, 180; taken prisoner, 185; released, 186; flees from The Moor, 186; action against Warwick and Clarence, 187; flees to France, 192–193; returns, 195–196; wins battle of Barnet, 197; meets Henry VI, 197–198; his moves before Tewkesbury, 199–202; at battle of Tewkesbury, 202–206; goes to Picquigny, 209–210; death of, 214

Edward V, 214

Edward, Prince of Wales, 16; born, 99; christened, 99–100, 125; growing up, 128; deprived of inheritance, 137; insignia of, 144; knights warriors after 2nd St Albans, 146; taken to Scotland after Towton, 151; betrothed, 153; goes to France, 165; at St Mihiel, 169–170, 180, 183; becomes godfather to Charles VIII, 190, 193; lands at Weymouth, 197, 198; killed at Tewkesbury, 203–205

Edward the Confessor (St Edward), 15, 99, 148

Egremont, Lord, 104, 118; killed at Northampton, 133

Eleanor, Duchess of Gloucester, 109

Eleanor, Duchess of Somerset, 114

Eleanor of Aquitaine, 50, 93

Ely, Thomas Bourchier, Bishop of, 90; promoted to Archbishop of Canterbury, 104; made lord Chancellor, 107, 114; as peacemaker, 119, 130, 132; crowns Edward IV, 155

Erpingham, skirmish at, 187

Eton College, founding of, 72–73

Exeter, Henry Holland, Duke of, 75, 81, 104, 106; failure as a sailor, 121, 125; avoids naval action, 129; raises an army, 134, 138, 140; escapes from Towton, 151, 165, 169, 176–177, 196; mysterious death of, 206

Exodus, quotation from Book of, 16

Eytone, Foulkes, 63

Faceby, John, 105

Fastolf, Sir John, 34–35

Fauconberg, Thomas, Bastard of, 132, 148, 150, 207

Ferdinand of Aragon, 175n
Ferri de Vaudémont, 27, 32, 45–46, 159, 180, 212
Ferrybridge, skirmish at, 148
Fitzhugh, Lord, 192
Fleetwood, chronicler, 207
Foix, Count Gaston de, 93
Formigny, 76; battle of, 80
Fortescue, Sir John, 160, 169, 171, 183, 189–191, 206, 215
Fougères, sacking of, 76
Fountaine, Thomas, 71
Fox, Richard, 66
Francisco, Master (doctor), 50
François, Duke of Brittany, 159, 170, 171, 215
Freon, Collin, 49
Fulford, Sir Baldwin, 129, 154

Gascarick, Elizabeth, 71
Gascarick, William, 71
Gloucester, Duke of – see Humphrey
Gloucester, Richard, Duke of (Richard III), 155; at Barnet, 197; at Tewkesbury, 203–205; involved in murder of Henry VI, 207, 214
God's House Hospital, 49–50
Golden Fleece, Order of the, 186
Gough, Matthew, 63
Grace Dieu, 127
Gresham, James, 115
Grey, Lord, of Ruthyn, 133
Grey, Sir John, 154
Grey, Sir Ralph, 172
Grey, Thomas, 176
Greystocks, Lord, 47
Gruthuyse, Seigneur de la, 135, 192
Guérin, Philippe, 188

Hall, chronicler, 205
Hampden, Sir Edmund, 205
Harington, Sir James, 173
Hastings, William, Earl of, 197, 203
Hatclyff, William, 105
Haute, Richard, 209
Havart, Jean, 61
Hedgeley Moor, battle of, 172, 175
Henry II, 50
Henry IV, 17
Henry V, 17, 19, 20, 35–36
Henry VI, 17; birth of, 20; proclaimed King of France, 20, 34; disadvantages of minority, 37; appoints Suffolk to negotiate marriage, 38–39; prepares for wedding, 43–44; childhood and character, 50–53; question of sanity, 50–51; sees Margaret, 53; marriage and progress to London, 54–56; attitude to France, 59; negotiations over Maine, 60–64; founds Eton and King's College, 72; tries to save Suffolk, 78; religious faith, 81; attitude to York, 88; courage in crisis, 89–90; his first breakdown, 97–107; loyalty to family, 99; recovery from breakdown, 105; at St Albans, 108–109; attitude to York, 111; his 2nd breakdown, 113; his impartiality, 114; efforts for peace, 118–120; his magnanimity, 125; distrusts Coppini, 131; at Northampton, 132–133; ordered by York to leave palace, 136; reunited with Margaret, 146; penniless refugee, 153; remains in Bamborough, 165; visited by Cousinot, 170; appeals to France for help, 171; on the run after Hexham, 172–173; imprisoned in the Tower, 173–174; released, 193; restoration

brings no change, 194; murdered in the Tower 207, 208, 208n
Henry VII, Henry Tudor, Earl of Richmond, 51, 110, 215–216
Henry of Castile, 180
Herbert, Sir William (Lord), 115; made Earl of Pembroke, 163; killed at Edgecote, 185
Hexham, battle of, 166, 172, 175
Hill, Sir William, 151
Holinshed, 42
Holland, Sir William, 154
Hoo, Sir Thomas, 39, 44
Humphrey, Duke of Gloucester (Good Duke Humphrey), 34, 36–38; meets Margaret, 55; attacks Suffolk, 63; death of, 65–67, 74, 111, 184
Hungerford, Lord, 132, 156–158, 162; beheaded, 172, 174

Iden, Alexander, 83
information, difficulty of obtaining, 141
insanity, of Henry VI, 50–51; of Charles VI, 50–51
Isabeau of Bavaria, 19, 21
Isabella Neville, 179, 184; marries Clarence, 184; flees to France, 187, 190
Isabella of Castile, 175, 175n
Isabella of Portugal, 34
Isabelle of Lorraine, 17, 19, 25–27, 30, 42, 45, 78, 159, 211

Jacquetta of Luxembourg, 154
James II of England, 15
James II of Scotland, 56, 112, 114, 134; killed at Roxburgh, 135
James III of Scotland, 135, 153
Jargeau, battle of, 38
Jasper Tudor, Earl of Pembroke, born, 51; elevated to peerage, 99, 114, 125, 134, 138, collects army 142; goes to France, 160; loses titles and estates, 163, 170; returns from Brittany, 171; raises army in Wales, 198; escapes, 215
Jean, Count of Maine, 212
Jeanne d'Arc, 21–24, 35
Jeanne, d. of James II of Scotland, 116
John II of France (The Good), 42
John of Calabria, 25, 30, 39, 47, 158
Jourdemayne, Margery, the Witch of Eye, 109
Justinian, Emperor, 30

Kemp, Archbishop, 75, 77, 100, 102–103, 104
Kent, Earl of, 161
Kent, Robert, 69–70
King's College Cambridge, 72–73
Kipling, Rudyard, 103
Knoghton, Frutes and Agnes, 70
Kyme, Lord, 151
Kyriel, Sir Thomas, 80, 142; executed, 146

La France arrondie, 156, 181, 211
l'Anglade, Sieur of, 94
Langstrother, Sir John, 206
La Pallice, raid on, 117
Lehard, Bishop, 80
l'Esparre, Sieur of, 94
Lespinay, Jehan, 213
Lespinay, Mace de, 213
Levron, Jacques, 45
Loches, 27, 159
Lory, cordwainer, 71

Louis I of Anjou, 42

Louis II of Anjou, titles of, 18

Louis III of Anjou, 28–29

Louis XI of France, birth of, 20–21, 27, 128, 132, 142; becomes king, 156; his aims and policy, 158; meets Margaret at Chinon, 159; signs treaty, 160, 163; plans to acquire Somme fortresses, 163, 167–168, 171, 174; comments on Margaret's letter, 176; character and description, 179; foreign policy, 179–180; plans against England and Burgundy, 181–182; attacks Brittany, 182; destroys Anglo-Burgundian alliance, 182–183; announces aid to Margaret, 183, 185; summons Margaret to Amboise, 188; brings Margaret and Warwick together, 189–191; orders Te Deum for Warwick's success, 193; plans to acquire Margaret's inheritance, 208; meets Edward IV at Picquigny, 209–210; acquires Margaret's inheritance, 211; death of, 214–215

Louis XII, 159

Louis, Cardinal Duke of Bar, 18

Louis d'Anjou (Margaret's brother), 25

Lovelace, Captain, of Kent, 145

Lovell, Lady, 128

Ludford, Rout of, 123–124

Lumley, Bishop, 77

Lunéville, 44

Magdalene of France, 112

Maine, County of, problems over surrendering, 36, 39, 59–63, 76–77, 86

Manning, Dean, 173

Mansfield, Robert, 54

Margaret of Anjou, suffered at hands of chroniclers, 15; reputation and purpose, 15–16; natural leader, 17; birth of, 23; taken to Vienne, 25; goes to live with grandmother, 28; becomes princess, 29; at Saumur, 30–31, 1st marriage contract, 32; meets Cardinal Beaufort, 34; not responsible for faction in England, 36; her engagement, 40–41; betrothal, 42; wedding ring, 44; proxy marriage, 45; departure for England, 46–47; journey to England, 47–50; meets Henry, 53; married at Titchfield, 54; progress to London, 54–56; coronation, 56; character, 57–58; dowry, 59; lack of influence, 62–63; agent for Charles VII, 64; accused of Gloucester's murder, 67; her love for Henry, 67–68; private letters of, 69–72; unpopularity of, 71; founds Queen's College Cambridge, 72–74; tries to save Suffolk, 77–78; slandered, 78; distress at death of Suffolk, 79; growing political awareness, 81; her attitude to York, 84; her association with Somerset, 85–86; disillusioned, 91–92; copes with Henry's 1st breakdown, 98–106; gives birth, 99; churched, 100; claims regency, 102; love for husband and son, 103; takes family to Coventry, 104; husband recovers, 105–106; hatred of York, 106–107; mobilizes strength of Lancaster, 107; her situation after 1st St Albans, 111–112; becomes political leader, 113; seeks help from France, 116–117; at peace service, 120; international aspect of her quarrel with York, 122; success at Ludford, 123–124; activities after Ludford, 125–127; offers to sell Calais, 128; escapes after Northampton, 133–134; mobilizes resources, 134–135; goes to Scotland, 135–136; not at Wakefield, 139; signs treaty with Scots, 140; leads army from Scotland, 142; her march south, 143–145; wins 2nd St Albans, 145–147; fails to exploit success, 146–147; flees to Scotland after Towton,

151; negotiates surrender of Berwick, 153; effect on her of death of Charles VII, 157; returns to France, 159; invasion fails, 161–163; takes Alnwick, 164; sees Henry for last time, 165; arrives in France, 165–166; offered asylum in Bar, 168; at St Mihiel, 169–170; unable to help Henry, 171–172; burdens and sorrows, 174; writes to Louis, 176; invited to French court, 180; shattered by disloyalty of Charles the Bold, 180–181; moves to Rouen, 183; returns to St Mihiel, 188; reconciliation with Warwick, 189–191; joy at Warwick's success, 193; fails to seize opportunity, 193–194; lands at Weymouth, 197; learns of Warwick's death, 198; fights on, 198–199; her moves before Tewkesbury, 199–202; at Tewkesbury, 203; heartbroken, 206–207; taken to Tower, 207; at Wallingford, 208–209; taken to Sandwich, 209; ransomed, 209; makes her property over to Louis, 211; accepts pension, 212; at Aix and Souzay, 212; her Will, 213; dies of cancer, 213; buried at Angers, 214

Margaret of Lorraine (Margaret's grandmother), 25, 27, 28

Margaret of York (sister of Edward IV), 179; marries Charles the Bold, 182

Marguerite of Savoy, 29

Marie d'Anjou (Margaret's aunt, wife of Charles VII), 20, 21, 27, 30, 42, 45, 211

Marie of Bourbon, 30

Marshall, John, 105

Mary of Gueldres, 135, 139, 140, 153, 157, 163–164

Mary of Hampton, 49

Meaux, siege of, 20

Metz, siege of, 44–45

Moleyns, Dr Adam, of Chichester, 39, 61, 68; murdered, 77, 102

money, value of, 48

Monstrelet, his version of robber story, 166–167

Montague, John, Marquess of, 172, 185, 186, 192 195, killed at Barnet, 196–197

Montelar, Baron de, 29

Montferand, Sieur de, 94

Montgomery, Sir Thomas, 210

Montlhéry, battle of, 174

Morains, château de, 213

Mortimer, Anne, 81

Mortimer, John – see Cade

Mortimer's Cross, battle of, 143

Morton, Dr, 146, 162, 206, 215

Mountford, Sir Osbert, 130

Nancy, ducal palace at, 23–25

Naples, René and Isabelle at, 30

Napoleon, 196

Neville, Cecily, Duchess of York, 87, 125, 155, 184, 186

Neville, George (brother of the Kingmaker), made bishop of Exeter, 144; appointed Lord Chancellor, 136; made Archbishop of York, 176, 184; takes Edward IV prisoner, 185–186, 192–193; turns traitor, 197

Neville, Isabella – see Isabella Neville

Neville, Lady Anne, 190, 191, 204

Neville, Richard – see Warwick (the Kingmaker)

Neville, Sir Humphrey, 171, 186

Neville, Sir John, 142

Nicholas of the Tower, 79

Norfolk, Dowager Duchess of, 176

Norfolk, Duke of, 81, 87, 97, 99, 100, 125, 142, 149–150, 206

Northampton, battle of, 132–133
Northumberland, Henry Percy, 2nd Earl of, 75, 104, 109
Northumberland, Henry Lord Poynings. 3rd Earl of, 112, 118, 125, 140, 149, 151

Oldhall, Sir William, 125
Orleans, Charles, Duke of, 34, 39, 48, 159
Orleans, siege of, 22
Ormonde, Earl of, 169
Oxford, Earl of, 195, 196–197, 198, 215

Paris, Peace of, 20
Pasquier, Etienne, 25
Paston, John, 105, 115, 211–212
pay, rates of, for Margaret's escort, 47–48
Peasant's Revolt, 52
Pembroke, Earl of – see Jasper Tudor
Penthièvre, Count of, 93, 95
Percy, Sir Ralph, 162, 164, 172
Philip, Matthew, jeweller, 44
Philip the Good, Duke of Burgundy, 24–25; negotiations with René d'Anjou, 27; releases René, 30; abandons alliance with England, 37, 101, 122 127, 135; sends 'handgunners' to England, 142, 156–157; becomes ill, 158, 163–165; sympathetic to Margaret, 167–168, 175, 177; death of, 180, 186
Picquigny, Treaty of, 209
plague, 16
Pleshey, castle of, 59
Pole, John, valet, 54
Pont à Mousson, 23, 28, 169
Porchester Castle, 49
Pot, Philippe, 165–166
Pouilhay, Oudinet, 189
Prévost d'Exiles, 34

Queen's College, Cambridge, founding of, 72–74

Raguier, Jean, 210
Rauzan, Sieur of, 94
Ravenspur, 195
René d'Anjou, born, 18; education of, 18–19; marriage, 19; joins Armagnacs, 24; defeated at Bulgnéville, 24–25; released, 27; inherits titles, 28–29, 35; endows daughter with worthless property, 40; at siege of Metz, 44–45, 56; his paintings at Cambridge, 74; visited by Margaret, 159, 171, 189–190; his letter to Margaret, 212
Richard II, 52
Richard III – see Gloucester
Richard Duke of York – see York
Rivers, Lord, captured at Sandwich, 127, 154; pardoned, 155; promoted, 177, 183; beheaded, 185
Rivière, Perreete de la, 213
robber, incident of the, 166–167
Robin of Redesdale, 184–185
Roos, Sir Robert (Lord de), 39, 44, 162; beheaded, 172, 174
Rosewood, chronicler, 202
Roxburgh, attack on, 135
Rutland, Earl of, 124–125; killed at Wakefield, 139

St Albans, 1st Battle of, 108–109; 2nd Battle of, 144–146
St Andrews, bishop of, 164
St George, chapel of, 45
St Mihiel, 169

St Omer, meeting at, 164
St Paul's, special peace service at, 120
Salisbury, Richard, Earl of (father of Warwick the Kingmaker), 66, 90, 99; made Lord Chancellor, 104; forced to resign, 107, 118; joins York at Ludlow, 123–124; attainted, 125; lands at Sandwich, 130, 136–137; beheaded, 139, 141
Sandwich, de Brézé s raid on, 116–117; Yorkist raids on, 127, 130, Margaret taken to, 209
Saumur, 28
Say, Lord, 81
seasickness, Margaret's, 49–50
Scales, Lord, 75, 83, 132; murdered, 133
Scott, Sir Walter, 110
Sforza, Francesco, 131, 142, 158, 179, 186
Shakespeare, quotations from, 16, 38; makes out Margaret and Suffolk were lovers, 67; describes death of Edward Prince of Wales, 205
Shelford, Thomas, 69
Shrewsbury, John Talbot, 1st Earl of, 47–48, 76–77; death of at Castillon, 94–95
Shrewsbury, John Talbot, 2nd Earl of, 107, 115, 125; killed at Northampton, 133
Shrewsbury, 3rd Earl of, killed at Towton, 151
Shrewsbury, 4th Earl of, 193
Sigismund, Emperor, 27, 50
Sisera, 198
Somerset, John, 1st Duke of, 86
Somerset, Edmund Beaufort, 2nd Duke of, 68, 73, 75; failure in France, 76–77; loses Normandy, 80; association with Margaret, 85–86; attacked, 88; courts unpopularity, 92, 98; rumoured to be father of Margaret's child, 100; arrested, 101, 104, 106, released, 107; killed at St Albans, 108–109
Somerset, Henry Beaufort, 3rd Duke of, 116; sent to Calais, 126; abandons siege of Calais, 138, 140; wastes time after Wakefield, 142; commands Lancastrians at Towton, 149–150; escapes, 151; sent to Burgundy, 156; arrested, 157; returns to Scotland, 159; surrenders, 162; quarrels with Edward, 171; defeated and beheaded, 172, 174
Somerset, Edmund Beaufort, 4th Duke of, 116; persuades Margaret to fight on, 198; his tactical plan for Tewkesbury, 202–203; at Tewkesbury, 203–205; executed, 206
Sorel, Agnes, 25–27, 45, 161
Souzay, Château de, 212–213
Stafford, Lord, 75; killed at St Albans, 109
Stafford, John, Archbishop, 53, 56, 75
Stafford, Sir Humphrey, 81
staple towns, 183n
Stourton, Sir John, 66
Suffolk, Marchioness of, 47, 208
Suffolk, William de la Pole, Earl of, opposed to Henry VI's marriage, 38; leads delegation to France, 39–41; created Marquis, 43; acts as Henry VI's proxy, 44–45; escorts Margaret to England, 47–50, 53; foreign policy, 59–60; negotiations over Maine, 63–64; involvement in death of Gloucester, 65–67; unpopularity, 68; arrest and death, 77–79, 109, 210

Tailboys, Sir William, 172
Tarascon, 32
Tewkesbury, Battle of, 202–206
Thomas, Duke of Clarence, 18n
Thomson, the Rev., 184
Thwaytes, Thomas, 210

Tiphaine la Magine, 28
Titchfield Abbey, 54, 54n
Toulongeon, Marshal de, 25, 28
Tours, Treaty of, 160
Toustain, Louis, 188
Towton, Battle of, 149–151
Tregory, Michael, 71
Tresham, Sir Thomas, 206
Trinity, 127
Trollope, Sir Andrew, at Ludford, 124–127; at 2nd
    St Albans, 145; knighted, 146; killed at Towton,
    149–150
Troubadours, 18, 28
Troyes, Treaty of, 19–20, 36
Tudor, Edmund – see Edmund Tudor
Tudor, Henry – see Henry VII
Tudor, Jasper – see Jasper Tudor
Tudor, Owen, 51, 99; beheaded at Hereford, 143
Tunstall, Richard, 162

Upholme, Robert, 71
universities in France, 73

Valois, physiognomy, 21; character, 50
Van Eyck, Hubert and Jehan, 18
Vaudémont, Antoine de – see Antoine
Vaudémont, Ferri de – see Ferri
Vaux, Lady Catherine, 204, 213
Vere, Sir Robert, 71
Verneuil, Battle of, 21, 23, 37, 80
Vienne, 26
Vignolles, François de la, 212, 213
Vincennes, 20, 35
Visconti, Filippo Maria, 29

Wakefield, Battle of, 138–139, 141
Wareyn, Robert, 105
warfare, attitude of nobility and gentry to, 118–119
Wars of the Roses, Margaret's part in, 15; misnamed
    by Sir Walter Scott, 110
Warwick, Henry Beauchamp, Earl of, 44, 50
Warwick, Richard Neville, Earl of (the Kingmaker),
    60, 90, 99; made Governor of Calais, 101; helps
    York raise army, 107; at St Albans, 109, 112;
    dominates Channel, 116–117, 118; pirate, 121;
    attack on, 121–122; approaches Burgundians, 122;
    joins York at Ludlow, 123–124; executes deserters,
    127; joins York in Ireland, 129–130; lands at
    Sandwich, 130; enters London, 131; makes use of
    Coppini, 132–133; at Northampton, 133; surprised
    by York's actions, 137; accuses Margaret of
    illegitimacy and adultery, 138; advantageous
    position after Wakefield, 141; Londoners give him
    support, 142; at St Albans, 144–146; links up with
    Edward IV, 147; marches to Towton, 148; at
    Towton, 149–150, 155; sent to Scotland, 157; takes
    the northern castles, 162; drives Margaret back to
    Scotland, 164; throws Henry VI in the Tower, 173;
    plans upset by Edward's marriage, 174–175; con-
ceals his anger, 176; takes delegation to France,
    179; returns, 180; reconciled with Edward, 183;
    his campaign against Edward, 184–187; flees to
    France, 187; reconciled with Margaret, 189–191;
    invades England, 191–194; summons resistance to
    Edward, 195; killed at Barnet, 196–197
Waurin, chronicler, false story of Margaret at
    Wakefield, 139; 146
Waynfleet, William, bishop of Winchester, 90, 100,
    105, 115, 119, 136
wedding ring, Margaret's, 44
Welles, Sir Robert, 187
Wellington, Lord, 141
Wenlock, Sir John (Lord), 39, 73, 109, 122, 124, 125,
    127, 130, 149, 157, 159; killed at Tewkesbury, 203,
    203n, 204–205
Wentworth, Sir Philip, 162; executed, 172
Westminster, peace conference at, 118
Westmorland, Ralph, 1st Earl of, 87
Westmorland, Ralph, 2nd Earl of, 140
Whethamstead, Abbot of St Albans, 66
Whitingham, Sir Robert, 162; killed at Tewkesbury,
    205
wildfire, 142n; effect of, 145
William of Worcester, 66
Wiltshire, James Butler, Earl of, 47, 125, 142;
    beheaded after Towton, 151
Woodville, Elizabeth, 73; meets Edward IV, 154–
    155; marries him, 174; crowned, 176; promotes
    interests of her family, 176–177
Woodville, Sir Anthony, 127
Woodville, Sir John, 185
wool, importance of, 175, 175n
women, role of in mediaeval France, 17
Worcester, Earl of, 107
Wordsworth, William, 209

Yolande of Anjou (Margaret's sister), 25; betrothal,
    27, 32; wedding, 45, 159, 212
Yolande of Aragon, 17–18, 18n; 19–20; investigates
    Jeanne d'Arc, 21; clanks in to see Dauphin at
    Chinon, 22; death of, 30; claims to Minorca and
    Majorca, 40, 101
York, Richard, Duke of, 37, 48–49; joins Gloucester
    against Suffolk, 64; takes Gloucester's place, 68, 81;
    leaves Ireland, 83; his claim to throne, 84–85;
    hatred of Somerset, 86; reasons for return to
    London, 87; lacks support, 88; attempts *coup*,
    90–91; loses more support, 96–97; power increases,
    99–102; becomes King's Lieutenant, 102; ap-
    pointed Protector, 103; raises army, 107; at St
    Albans, 108–109; his situation after St Albans, 111–
    112; again appointed Protector, 113; accused, 115;
    deals with James II of Scotland, 116; moves to
    London, 118; his failure at Ludford, 123–124;
    attainted, 125; leaves Ireland, 136; strange scene in
    House of Lords, 137; goes north to stamp out
    Lancastrian resistance, 138; killed at Wakefield,
    139, 140–141, 147
Young, Thomas (MP), 89

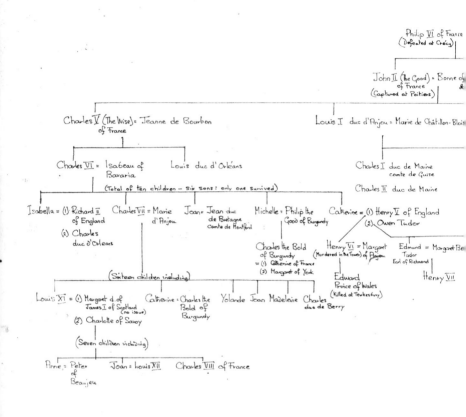

Philip VI of France
(Defeated at Crécy)

John II (the Good) = Bonne of
of France   &
(Captured at Poitiers)

Charles V (The Wise) = Jeanne de Bourbon
         of France

Louis I duc d'Anjou = Marie de Châtillon-Blois

Charles VI = Isabeau of
             Bavaria

Louis duc d'Orléans

Charles I duc de Maine
comte de Guise

(Total of ten children – six sons: only one survived)

Charles II duc de Maine

Isabella = (1) Richard II
             of England

         (2) Charles
             duc d'Orléans

Charles VII = Marie
              d'Anjou

Joan = Jean duc
       de Bretagne
       Comte de Montfort

Michelle = Philip the
           Good of Burgundy

Catherine = (1) Henry V of England

            (2) Owen Tudor

Charles the Bold
of Burgundy
= (1) Catherine of France
  (2) Margaret of York

Henry VI = Margaret
(Murdered in the Tower) of Anjou

Edmund = Margaret Be
Tudor
Earl of Richmond

(Sixteen children including)

Edward
Prince of Wales
(Killed at Tewkesbury)

Henry VII

Louis XI = (1) Margaret d. of
               James I of Scotland
               (no issue)

           (2) Charlotte of Savoy

Catherine = Charles the
            Bold of
            Burgundy

Yolande Joan Madeleine

Charles
duc de Berry

(Seven children including)

Anne = Peter
       of
       Beaujeu

Joan = Louis XII

Charles VIII of France